KNUCKLEBALL

THE HISTORY OF THE UNHITTABLE PITCH

LEW FREEDMAN

SPORTS
PUBLISHING

Sports Publishing books may be purchased in bulk at special discounts for sales promotion, corporate gifts, fund-raising, or educational purposes. Special editions can also be created to specifications. For details, contact the Special Sales Department, Sports Publishing, 307 West 36th Street, 11th Floor, New York, NY 10018 or sportspubbooks@skyhorsepublishing.com.

Sports Publishing® is a registered trademark of Skyhorse Publishing, Inc.®, a Delaware corporation.

Visit our website at www.sportspubbooks.com.

10 9 8 7 6 5 4 3 2 1

Library of Congress Cataloging-in-Publication Data is available on file.

Cover design by Rain Saukas
Cover photo courtesy of Phil Niekro's knuckleball grip by Lew Freedman.

Print ISBN: 978-1-61321-766-5
Ebook ISBN: 978-1-61321-794-8

Printed in the United States of America

To all the pitchers who made a career out of throwing the knuckleball, the most difficult pitch to rely on.

CONTENTS

PREFACE

I LOVE THE knuckleball. I love watching that slow-motion pitch float to home plate, twisting and turning in so many directions. I love watching behemoth sluggers contort themselves into pretzels with their mighty swings at thin air.

Every knuckleball thrown that tantalizes and fools a hitter seems like a victory for the underdog. Conditioned to swat 95 mph fastballs long distances, it is somehow satisfying and amusing to see the best hitters in baseball find themselves incapable of coping with such a tantalizing, innocuous weapon.

It is one thing to be overpowered by a pitch you can barely see. Everyone can identify with the difficulty of connecting safely with a fastball that travels faster than you will ever drive your car. But the knuckleball is a tease; a pitch that looks easy to hit. It is a pitch that everyone in the stands who ever played Little League baseball feels they can hit. And why wouldn't they, since the radar gun might tell them the pitch sailed into range at something like 62 mph?

Of course if it were that easy, everyone would do it. Not everyone can hit the knuckleball. Not everyone can throw the knuckleball, although half of the people in the sport think they can because it looks so easy to throw. Maybe it is easy to throw, but not to control. That's the trick to the infamous pitch.

A fundamental tenet of baseball is the balance between the offense in the persona of the hitter standing in the batter's box and the pitcher standing on the mound. This duet has been the hallmark of baseball since before the National League was founded as the first professional league in 1876.

The pitcher has an arsenal of flavorful choices to throw, although many heavily rely on just a couple of selections. The fastball is predominant. The curveball and the changeup are generally necessities. Always looking for an edge over the course of baseball history, pitchers have tinkered and invented new pitches, experimenting with new ways to get batters out. We have seen the slider, the splitter, the fork ball, the cutter, the spitter, the screwball, and the slurve. Some have been outlawed, while others have fallen out of fashion.

The hitter, preferably with 20-20 vision, studies the pitcher's motion, tendencies, habits, and grips, and tries to figure out what the hurler will throw to him. If all goes well he guesses accurately and lays lumber against the horsehide and it travels a great distance where no fielders stand to seize it.

If ever there were a wild card in the mix to confuse both batter and pitcher, however, it is the knuckleball. The knuckleball answers to no master. It can be a deadly weapon or the death of its practitioner. It is safe to say that thousands of players know how to throw a knuckler, but only a tiny number have ever understood how to make it work. The knuckleball is shrouded in mystery. On the same pitch, the batter may wonder how he did not smash it into the center field bleachers and the pitcher may wonder how the heck he registered a strike.

The knuckleball has been around as part of baseball for more than a century. Historians suspect, but cannot agree with certainty, who invented it. The knuckleball is so baffling that it handicaps not only hitters, but pitchers who set out to employ it. The knuckler drives both hitters and pitchers crazy. Often a pitch of last resort to save a career, there is no guarantee even a blind-faith commitment to the knuckler will bring salvation.

Those who succeed by throwing the knuckleball share a special bond and camaraderie because their brotherhood is so small. Periodically, it seems possible that the knuckleball will die out and disappear altogether, but it always experiences a revival. Perhaps most amazingly, at least four devotees of the knuckleball have ridden its quirky nature into the Hall of Fame.

Appropriately, the story of the knuckleball—much like the flight path it follows between the mound and the plate—is not a straight line.

Lew Freedman

INTRODUCTION

NOT ONLY IS the knuckleball the all-time oddball baseball pitch, it isn't even thrown with the knuckles. To throw a worthwhile knuckler the pitcher must dig in with his fingertips for control.

Go figure.

Phil Niekro stood in a wide open room inside Coolray Field on an off-day for the Gwinnett Braves, the AAA affiliate of the Atlanta Braves in suburban Lawrenceville, Georgia. In his right hand nestled a baseball. Niekro, who had just turned seventy-five, manipulated the ball into position and showed off the knuckleball grip that carried him to most of his 318 career victories and a place in baseball's Hall of Fame.

Not a single knuckle came into contact with the borrowed baseball that displayed the writing "Official Ball International League." If Niekro had rested his knuckles on the ball, his manicurist would have been surprised.

A short while earlier, Niekro, the most prominent living supporter, endorser, teacher, and practitioner of the knuckleball, was asked a simple question that has no simple answer: "What is a knuckleball?" It was suggested that might be a provocative question.

"It ain't all that provocative an answer," he said. "I've been trying to figure that out. I'm still trying to figure it out."

Since Niekro was first tutored on the nuances of the knuckler roughly sixty-five years ago, he is the most successful starting pitcher to employ it in baseball history and is on speed dial as "Dr. Phil" for knuckleball throwers in need of emergency lessons—if he can't define it, the rest of the world might as well give up.

It is not as though Niekro is a magician like David Copperfield, Doug Henning, or Ricky Jay, who refuse to unveil the secrets of the trade to spoil the illusion for the audience. Indeed, Niekro is generous with thoughts, ideas, and instruction about the knuckleball for anyone who asks, especially professionals in serious need of insights and coaching.

Yet for all of his openness—and that of other knuckleball artists who have preceded and followed him as exemplars of the knuckler—the pitch defies the cleverest minds attuned to trying it. Unlike the professional magicians, knuckleball illusionists will happily tell you how to throw the pitch, what it is supposed to do, and explain its effects, but they cannot ensure that the novice will be capable of putting it to good use.

There are basically two categories of baseball pitches. One is the fastball, the absolute pure, heat-seeking missile that might buzz past a batter's head so swiftly he can only see a blur and most definitely can't get his bat around fast enough to make good contact. The other is just about everything else, a curve, splitter, or whatever. Those pitches spin either away from or in towards a batter. Then there is the knuckleball, which neither arrives from the mound 60 feet, 6 inches away at the speed of a rocket, or with the spin of a top. A knuckleball is characterized by its lack of spin. To the hitter's practiced eye it just kind of meanders to the plate like a butterfly on a vague mission; a big, fat, juicy meatball of a pitch waiting to be slugged out of the park.

When a knuckleball pitcher is on, however, that ball without spin might suddenly take off in a fresh direction to the right and then turn back to the left. The batter keeps his eye on the ball, but cannot believe what it is doing, seeming of its own volition. It becomes some spicy meatball.

In 2013, some folks who combined their ability to make documentaries with their fascination with the bizarre pitch, turned out a video called "Knuckleball!"

Those who make or made their living in Major League Baseball by counting on the knuckleball are few. One of those pitchers was Charlie Hough, who was quoted in the documentary noting, "The wind currents make the ball bob around like a Wiffle Ball and it might break two or three different times on the way to the plate." So before stepping into the batter's box, the hitter should not talk things over with his team's batting coach. He should call the National Weather Service.

That may sound absurd, but the fact is a meteorologist may have has much value to figuring out the vagaries of the knuckleball as anyone else. The more knuckleball pitchers are consulted about their specialty, the more they sound like voodoo practitioners or adherents to a cult religion, as if a lot of praying for something good to happen goes into their routine. Throwing a knuckler may be a dark art, one characterized by uncertainty, but it also can be laden with humorous side effects.

Pitchers admit that when they release their knuckler they don't really have confidence where it will go. Catchers are on the receiving end of knucklers that are not smacked fair or batted foul and they only have a rough idea where the ball is going to land. It might be in their mitt or it might bounce two feet in front of the plate. Any time a knuckler is unleashed in their direction they hope they are not embarrassed while being forced to run all of the way to the backstop to retrieve the pitch. The best result of a play like that is the pitch only counts as a ball. If a man is on base then it is either a wild pitch charged against the pitcher or a passed ball charged against the catcher.

Bob Uecker, equal parts former Major League catcher, long-time Major League broadcaster, and renowned humorist, was famous for giving knuckleball receiving advice. "The way to catch a knuckleball is to wait until it stops rolling and then pick it up," Uecker said of the most logical defensive strategy.

Somehow it is appropriate how difficult it is to ascertain parenthood of a pitch so fraught with potential nerve-wracking results. Could it be that no one wanted to be known as the originator of the knuckler? Probably not. It's just that there is no smoking gun to pinpoint the precise moment of inception. That is something unusual for baseball, a sport that prides itself on virtually inventing the statistic—and still has a hunger for more of them, from WHIP to WAR to OPS—and also for slapping a date on the first anything that ever occurred between the lines.

Of course, for all of the supremely dedicated mad statistical scientists probing mountains of box score minutiae to find one more RBI for Hack Wilson, Major League Baseball got the most important of its historical stories wrong. For generations,

MLB announced as gospel that Abner Doubleday invented baseball in Cooperstown, New York. Later investigation made fans wonder if Doubleday ever saw a baseball in his life.

General belief credits the introduction of the knuckleball to Ed Cicotte, one of the primary guilty parties in the "Black Sox Scandal" of 1919. For one thing, Cicotte's nickname was "Knuckles." Phil Niekro, whose opinion is as valid as anyone's in baseball, says that he has heard that Cicotte is *the* guy, *the* originator. Others differ and consider Lew Moren, who made his debut in 1903, as perhaps the chicken who laid the egg. (The quote was said to have been in the New York Daily Press on April 17, 1908.) Others around at the time dabbled with the newfangled pitch.

One of the truly remarkable aspects of knuckleball pitching history is how few acknowledged knuckleball artists there have been since Cicotte's Major League debut in 1905. Barely more than two dozen are recognized by list makers (unofficially) as pitchers for whom the knuckleball played a prominent role in their careers.

A common theme of the small group of big winners amongst knuckleball pitchers is that they did not start out relying on the knuckler, but seemed to possess other tools to become big-league regulars. In some cases, their fastballs proved to be a few mph too slow. In many cases, adding a new pitch to the arsenal represented the only way to gain another shot at the bigs.

It should be noted that four pitchers whose careers were high-lighted by their relationship with the knuckleball are in the Hall of Fame. The St. Louis Cardinals' Jesse "Pop" Haines' Major League throwing dates to 1918. Ted Lyons was the mainstay of the Chicago White Sox staff from 1923 to 1946. Hoyt Wilhelm, who made a living with the New York Giants, White Sox, and Baltimore Orioles starting in 1952, was the first great knuckleball reliever. And then along came Phil Niekro, starting in 1964 (with a younger brother, Joe, who started in 1967 and won more than his share of games, too).

Another common theme amongst the best of the best knuckleball pitchers is that they enjoyed long careers, several sticking with big-league teams well into their forties. The pleasant common denominator was that although they had to cope with the aggravating offshoots of the knuckleball, it produced the pleasing side effect of limited stress on the arm. While those young fireballers were heaving arms out of their sockets and tearing rotator cuffs with the frequency of football running backs ripping ACLs in their knees, the knuckleball gang just went on and on, threatening to earn AARP cards while still holding spots on Major League rosters.

Those same accomplished hurlers did have to put up with the mocking Average Joe believing that he too could throw a knuckler with ease, make it dance the way he wished, and catch it with no problems. Mark Howe, the Hall of Fame hockey star who is the son of legendary hockey player Gordie Howe, mentioned in his autobiography his own fascination with the knuckleball. Mark fancied himself a pretty good ballplayer, until the day dad Gordie flung two knuckleballs to him while playing catch. The first ball hit him in the nose, drawing blood. The second hit him in the forehead. And that was the end of that.

Johnny Sain, who may have been the greatest pitching coach of all time, could not teach the knuckleball. The best he could do was work with a knuckleball pitcher on his mechanics and hope that made a difference. If Sain couldn't teach it, nobody could—except for another knuckleball specialist—and even then there was no guarantee what the education would produce.

Dr. Phil can be hired and will come to your house and display the rudiments of throwing the knuckleball, but there are no money-back guarantees if you don't follow his footsteps to the majors or even strike out the next round of batters in your high school or college game. Around the world there are more ex-leaders of nations, Your Excellencies, still living than there are excellent former knuckleball pitchers.

"I know a lot of people say that you master it," Phil Niekro said, "but I don't think you ever master the knuckleball."

Everyone loves a good mystery.

1

WHERE DID THE KNUCKLER
COME FROM?

TUCKED INTO A player file in the National Baseball Hall of Fame's research library is an ancient, undated, unbylined newspaper clipping that does not identify the newspaper it was clipped from. The headline reads: "Cicotte Inventor Of Knuckle Ball: Pitcher Of No-Hit Game Against Browns Uses It With Much Success."

The game in question took place on April 14, 1917, when the Chicago White Sox clobbered the St. Louis Browns, 11–0. In the story, the author of the no-hitter was referred to as Edward V. Cicotte. More commonly during his Major League career (1905–1920) he was called Ed. In later years, the same Mr. Cicotte was called by other names, most of them none too flattering.

That was because he was singled out as a ringleader of the 1919 "Black Sox Scandal," where selected players on the White Sox roster fixed games and lost the World Series to the Cincinnati Reds. Until this ill-advised crooked involvement that disgraced his name, it might well be argued that Cicotte was on his way to a Hall of Fame career. His final numbers were quite favorable, with a 209–148 record, a lifetime 2.38 earned run average, and a high-victory season of 29.

Plus, he no doubt would have gained additional stature if more widespread credit were offered and repeated of Cicotte being labeled the creator of the knuckleball pitch. As it was, his besmirched name overshadowed any accomplishments for the rest of his life and beyond his journey to the grave.

Cicotte was using his knuckleball and counting on it as his premier tool to get batters out by 1908, dating back to the time he played for the Boston Red Sox. He spent the better part of two years working on the knuckler and the first indications he was ready to use it regularly emerged from spring training in Little Rock, Arkansas, that year.

In 1917, though, when Cicotte twirled his no-hitter, the 5-foot-9, 170-pound right-hander, it was a rarity for him to be prominently associated with the baffling pitch. It just wasn't talked about all that much. However, his nickname, as further proof of his creative achievement, was "Knuckles." And it was not applied because he was the light-heavyweight champion.

The Hall of Fame newspaper clipping included a few passages that went beyond description of Cicotte's mound gem versus the Browns. It read in part, "Cicotte is credited with being the inventor of the knuckle ball in pitching. He is certainly its most successful and persistent proponent. In an interview in the current issue of *Baseball Magazine* he says that he uses the knuckle ball in about 75 percent of his throws to the plate."

The article also veers off in such a manner that it begins to sound more like *Scientific American* in efforts to explain just what the knuckleball pitch is. "The knuckle ball," the story reads, "is essentially different from all other deliveries in that it works on a directly different principle from that used in curved and fast pitching. It is thrown with considerable speed, but the object is to send it to the batter in such a manner that it does not revolve at all. It looks as big as a balloon, but just as it nears the plate it almost invariably shoots to one side or the other due to the seams hanging in the varying resistances of such an unstable medium as the air.

"This might not seem possible to a person not familiar with baseball, but hundreds of ballplayers can sorrowfully testify to the fact. How the ball will break neither the pitcher nor the catcher can foresee. Sometimes it fails to break and then it is not infrequently hit into the next county."

From the vantage point of nearly one hundred years in the future, it is difficult to best the summation of the erratic nature of the knuckleball. Let's just say that the pitch has not changed its stripes . . . or seams.

On the matter of paternity, Phil Niekro, the 318-game winner, who is the most overall successful knuckleball pitcher in history, figured to be a man who knew just where the knuckleball got its start. However, it turns out that he had not made a true study of the pitch's origins. Still, he said, "I have always heard it was Ed Cicotte."

The anonymous newspaper clip about Cicotte as the inventor of the knuckleball did give passing mention to a pitcher named George "Nap" Rucker, who played for the Brooklyn Dodgers from 1907 to 1916.

"Nap Rucker, when his arm began to go bad and he had to rely upon his head, took up the knuckleball with highly gratifying results," the story read.

One interesting aspect of this switch by Rucker to the knuckleball is that it foreshadowed the future, when certain devotees to the pitch only took it up when all else had failed, either because of injury or losing speed on their fastball. Rucker, who was born in 1884 in Crabapple, Georgia, may well have been the first such pitcher to adopt the knuckleball out of desperation to keep his career going.

Rucker was a southpaw who completed his 10-year Major League career with a 134–134 mark and a 2.42 earned run average. His best season was in 1911, when he finished 22–18. During an era when players were not routinely interviewed after their performances in games, sportswriters commented on efforts without the benefit of talking to them. Rucker appeared to have a great deal of respect amongst the newspapermen, though. A 1914 story, featuring a picture of Rucker, carried the headline "Nap Rucker Voted Best Southpaw; Brooklyn Pitcher's Great Record; Majority of Base Ball Writers Favor Him."

Several writers backed Rucker over Philadelphia Athletics star Eddie Plank as the finest left-hander in the game. That was either a supreme compliment or a basic error in judgment, given that Plank would go on to win 326 games and was inducted into the Hall of Fame in 1946.

One writer, William Peet, representing the *Washington Herald*, summed up these findings with the words, "Nap Rucker of the Brooklyn National League club is easily the best southpaw in the game today." Peet specifically claimed Rucker was Plank's superior. As Rucker and Plank played in different leagues (Rucker in the NL for the Dodgers and Plank in the AL for the A's), the only chance of them facing each other would have been in the World Series, but the teams never faced each other during their playing days. A few hundred words of analysis of Rucker's career and accomplishments followed without a mention of the word "knuckleball." However, a stretch of copy refers to a peculiar occasion early in Rucker's career when he was throwing for Augusta in the South Atlantic League.

The tale continues in this manner: "Speed always had been the boast of his village admirers and his spit-fire control, which is considered one of the Seven Wonders of the World for a southpaw [and] had gained for him quite a bit of popularity." Suddenly, when Rucker attempted a somewhat different motion, he found the ball behaving quite differently when it left his hand. "Much to Rucker's surprise the ball turned turtle, dipped at the plate, and the batter swung like a rusty gate. Most pitchers would have given little or no attention to this unexpected incident, but Rucker realized on the spur of the moment that the twist he had given the sphere before sending it down the line had netted a new delivery. He studied the matter carefully and in a few days he learned how the high drop was thrown, but it was three months before he had the control and confidence to spring this puzzle in a regular conflict. Having assured himself that he was the master of the trick he resorted to its continued use and to this day it is, perfected by his major league experience, the most remarkable and deceptive delivery in base ball when the break splits right."

Rucker turned to the knuckleball as his primary pitch over the last three years of his career when a sore arm limited him to pitching once every two weeks.

Is William Peet writing the true story of the invention and development of the knuckleball, sans name? That would indicate Rucker came upon the knuckler as a weapon when he was a minor league player, but did not employ it until the latter stages of his big-league career.

Some adherents advance the name of Lew Moren as inventor of the knuckleball. Moren was born in 1883 in Pittsburgh, and made his Major League debut in 1903 with the hometown Pirates. His big-league career was relatively brief and hardly sensational. Spanning 1903 to 1910, parts of six seasons with the Pirates and Philadelphia Phillies, Moren finished with a record of 48–57. The key element in his background suggests that Moren won a June 1907 game for the Phillies against his old team by relying on the knuckleball. At least the *Pittsburgh Post-Gazette* said so.

Moren said that when he was just a boy he experimented with a new pitch that he called the knuckleball, but could not control it and abandoned attempts to fashion it into a useful weapon for years. Over the last few years of his Major League career, between 1907 and 1910, Moren said he employed the pitch regularly. "To my amazement," he said, "The ball on being thrown that way took queer shoots. I continued to experiment with it until now I have very fair control of it."

Moren's nickname was "Hicks" and he lived to be eighty-three, though rather than passing away from old age, he ended up committing suicide by slitting his own throat.

Ed Summers, who broke into the majors with the Detroit Tigers in dramatic fashion in 1908, is a claimant to knuckleball evolution. Summers, born in 1884 in Ladoga, Indiana, was a hot-stuff rookie for the Tigers, going 24–12 with a 1.64 earned run average spread over 301 innings of hurling in '08. Certainly it seemed as if he had a secret weapon the way he dominated much of the American League.

The pitch that Summers threw has been classified as a modified knuckleball. Summers' toss was labeled a "dry spitter," and he did not say that he invented the knuckler but rather that he studied Cicotte and changed the delivery somewhat. Summers said that back in the day, Cicotte and others were actually resting their knuckles on the ball, unlike later practitioners such as Niekro, who relied on their fingernails. Summers said that's what he did. "I watched Eddie Cicotte, who first used it," Summers told *Baseball Magazine* in 1908. "He rested the ball on his knuckles, but I couldn't see the value of that because I couldn't control it and one can put little speed on it. I found that by holding the ball with my fingertips and steadying it with my thumb alone I could get a peculiar break to it and send it to the batters with considerable speed and good control."

Summers stood six foot two, tall for the time, and weighed 180 pounds. He threw righty and seemed on his way to a special career. But he was forced to retire after four seasons because of rheumatism when he was only twenty-seven. Summers' rookie ERA is still the best in Tigers history. Summers did not call his pitch either a knuckler or a spitter. He said, "It's just this." Just this? Well, someone had to call the pitch something.

As if the knuckleball itself didn't tend to drive people crazy by going in circles, the story of the early days of the knuckleball may also be a circle.

"Shoeless" Joe Jackson, the phenomenal hitter with a lifetime batting average of .356, was a teammate of Cicotte's with the ill-fated 1919 Chicago White Sox, and, like Cicotte, was banned for life from baseball because of the "Black Sox Scandal."

Jackson told a sportswriter for the *Detroit Free Press* in 1908 that the actual inventor of the knuckleball was a fellow named Forrest

"Frosty" Thomas. Thomas played just two Major League games in 1905 for the Tigers. Jackson believed that Thomas invented the knuckleball in the minors and taught it to Summers in Augusta, Georgia, and that Summers taught the pitch to Cicotte. And then Cicotte took it from there. Of course, Summers admits he copied Cicotte, the reversal of Jackson's comment.

In an issue of *The Sporting News* from October 30, 1919, ironically published at the conclusion of the tainted 1919 World Series, a headline appeared referring to Cicotte's knuckleball. It read: "Cicotte Bares Pitching Secrets—As Far As He Has Any." It was later revealed that Cicotte had one gigantic, dastardly pitching secret: He threw the pitch as a signal to gamblers that the fix was in on the 1919 Series.

Accompanying the story was a slew of graphic illustrations demonstrating how Cicotte threw his knuckleball. Despite all previous discussion from Summers and others, as well as the application of the nickname "Knuckles," a photograph showing Cicotte's right hand and fingers in the manner he gripped the ball for the pitch clearly showed that his knuckles were *not* flush against the ball. However, neither were his fingernails digging into the seams. Cicotte's fingers were bent at the knuckles, but the tips of his fingers gripped the ball.

The anecdote introducing Cicotte's delivery was itself fascinating. It referred to the recently played fifth game of the World Series against Cincinnati and noted that White Sox catcher Ray Schalk picked up a ball thrown by Reds pitcher Hod Eller and called it a "shine ball," as he showed it to the umpire. The umpire replied, "Just the same as Eddie Cicotte's pitching."

Not exactly. The shine ball was actually another description for the spitter, which was outlawed a year later in 1920. Cicotte called his knuckler a shine ball in an attempt to fool batters into believing it was the same as a spitter.

Cicotte's knuckler was so baffling to hitters and so confusing to the baseball establishment that people thought he must have been doctoring the ball in some manner. Balls he used in games were turned into the American League president's office, but President Ban Johnson could find no evidence they were tampered with. Even then the knuckleball was little understood. The secret of knuckleball magic was to get it to do tricks *without* altering the surface.

"I don't do anything to the ball that anyone can discover," Cicotte said in *The Sporting News* piece. "The umpires have taken enough balls out of the games I have pitched to put ball bearings under a courthouse, but Ban Johnson has never found any of them tampered with. Of course when a ball breaks so a batter can't hit it, he naturally will squawk to the umpire. But my ball has stood up under fire and nothing illegal has ever been found on it."

It should be noticed how carefully Cicotte tap-danced around the description. He sounded very much like Gaylord Perry decades later when indicating he did not throw a then-illegal spitter. Cicotte did admit in other forums that he sometimes dirtied up half of the ball, again in an effort to mess with batters' minds, but the big change in baseball banning the spitter, Vaseline ball, and mud ball occurred a year after Cicotte's interview with *The Sporting News*.

Even though the best knuckleball pitchers have trouble controlling or defining it, about the same number of people have taken stabs at doing both. First and foremost the knuckler is characterized by the lack of spin on the ball, hence the usual observation that it seems to float up to the plate. It is also not thrown with a powerful motion, so typically a knuckleball pitch travels much slower than a fastball or another pitch. Even big-league knuckleball pitchers may have their throws clocked in the 60-mph-plus range, while their partners on the team might well be throwing 98 mph.

Another key element of the knuckleball is that it changes direction, shifting either right or left, on a given pitch. The unpredictable nature of a knuckleball in flight is something that flummoxes hitters. But it also makes great demands on catchers. If anyone should doubt that Cicotte threw the modern-day equivalent of a knuckleball, they should study the comments he made about his poor catchers—Ray Schalk most prominent among them with the White Sox.

Cicotte said catchers should be pitied while trying to catch the knuckler if the wind is blowing and that even the best catchers were likely to suffer wrist or finger injuries as they tried to grab the ball with their mitt as it swerved.

"The knuckleball is the best, I have found," Cicotte said. "It does not give the batter any tip as to what is coming and that is an important point for pitchers to watch. The ball is delivered with an overhand or sidearm delivery, that is, with the pitcher's natural sweep. The object is to have the ball leave the upper and lower grips simultaneously so no rotary movement will be given to the ball. It will take a long time to perfect this pitch, but when perfected it is an invaluable asset."

Not so long after giving the incisive interview about his pitching and employment of the knuckleball, Cicotte was on the outs as a player. Grumblings during the 1919 World Series provided suspicions that the games between the White Sox and

Reds were not on the up-and-up. Chicago was felt to have a much better team and was heavily favored. The Reds won the Series five games to three in what was a best-of-nine games format that year, but the high-pitched buzz of rumors was so loud that eventually a number of White Sox players were indicted and charged with taking money from gamblers to intentionally lose games.

It took months for a grand jury to be convened and all White Sox players were allowed to compete during the 1920 season. The matter heated up with indictments by the next season and a trial commenced in late June of 1921.

Eight players were charged and went to trial in Chicago, where they were all acquitted. However, baseball owners, incited by the stench of scandal, appointed an all-powerful commissioner for the first time to oversee the game. They hired federal judge Kenesaw Mountain Landis and gave him carte blanche control of the sport.

Landis wielded his enormous power and banned the eight White Sox players from baseball for life with the allegation that at the least they had all colluded and had knowledge of the scandal. That ended several distinguished careers, including those of Cicotte, "Shoeless Joe" (who said that he played to win), and Buck Weaver (who said that the only thing he did wrong was not squeal on his teammates).

In 1920, the year after the corrupted World Series, Cicotte recorded a 21–10 mark. He was thirty-six. Chances were that he had a few more good years in his arm and that if he performed at a similar level he would have retired with a Hall of Fame-style record. He would also likely have received far more attention for his role in introducing the knuckleball to the sport.

At the time of his interview, Cicotte was eighty-one years old and still growing strawberries on a farm. He died about three and a half years later in Detroit at eighty-four. Eddie Cicotte is still banned from baseball. His name is not much happily connected to the invention of the knuckleball as it is associated with the infamy of baseball's worst scandal.

2

WHO'S WHO IN THE KNUCKLEBALL WORLD

YOU CAN'T TELL a pitcher without a scorecard. There is
no definitive list of knuckleball pitchers throughout baseball history. Some pitchers were true knuckleball specialists,
while some just dabbled with the pitch and failed with it. The
earliest days of the knuckleball's origins were the murkiest.

Going back to history, before the Ed Cicotte, Lew Moren,
Ed Summers debate formed, others were sometimes credited
with inventing the knuckleball. A fellow by the name of Toad
Ramsey was occasionally mentioned in this vein. Ramsey was
born in 1864 in Indianapolis, Indiana, and played Major League
ball for the Louisville Colonels and St. Louis Browns from 1885
to 1890.

Ramsey, who had a lifetime record of 113–124, comes under
the Mordecai "Three Finger" Brown category. Brown suffered
the mangling of his pitching hand and loss of fingers in a farm

accident, and the Hall of Famer became an expert at firing a curveball as a result of the way he held the ball.

Ramsey incurred his own accident with a trowel, severing the tendon in his left index finger. Because he could not straighten the finger, it is said that gave him a natural knuckleball form. But analysts say his pitch more resembled a knuckle curve.

For a time, until research proved otherwise and anointed Cicotte as the most likely first true proponent of the knuckler (with whatever credit Moren and Summers are due), it was believed that a pitcher named Ed Rommel was the first knuckleball hurler. However, since Rommel did not make his big-league debut until 1920, the timeline does not hold up. Rommel pitched his entire career, from 1920 to 1932, for the Philadelphia A's, and then became a Major League umpire. He would ump in the American League for over twenty years.

Rommel won 171 games and is the rare figure who has participated in the World Series as both a player and umpire. By the time Rommel switched assignments in the game, others had come along and showed how lethal a weapon the knuckleball could be.

Right-hander Jesse Haines broke into the majors with the Cincinnati Reds in 1918 (appearing in only one game), but spent the rest of his 19-year big-league career with the St. Louis Cardinals. Haines retired in 1937, and was elected to the Baseball Hall of Fame in 1970.

A Haines contemporary who made his mark with the knuckler was Chicago White Sox star Ted Lyons. Lyons broke in during the 1923 season and was active until 1946, just after World War II. (Though he was not drafted, Lyons enlisted in the Marines and served his country from 1943–45.) He also became a Hall of Famer.

Despite the obvious success of Haines and Lyons while counting on the knuckler, there was no line of youthful twirlers seeking coaching advice from them on how to throw one. The knuckleball, as it always had, seemed to scare off pitchers trying to throw it as much as it did batters trying to hit it.

During this era, before velocity of pitches was routinely measured on a radar gun, baseball officials really could only approximate how fast a pitcher threw. Concurrently, they could not measure how slowly a knuckleball cruised. To the naked eye, all-time great pitchers like Walter Johnson ("The Big Train") and Cy Young threw fastballs that made batters' knees shake. The same batters would stare at a Haines or Lyons knuckler and try to time it with a sun dial.

The hitters' eyes told them the floating round object headed their way should be easy to power over the fence, but their reflexes transmitting information from the eye to the hands lost something in the translation. To all appearances, the knuckleball looked easy to hit and easy to throw. The reality was quite different. The knuckler did its own little freelance dance in the air on the way to the plate so the batter frequently swung and missed. And because the knuckler was doing its own boogying involving little consultation with the pitcher, even the best of them could not 100 percent trust it.

The question was raised early on and has been raised with regularity for decades: If the knuckleball is such a tough pitch to hit, why don't more pitchers use it?

The answer is multifaceted, but the bottom-line simple answer is that it is equally as tough to throw with control and effect.

No modern-era knuckleball pitcher has been interviewed about the pitch, consulted on how to throw it, or even coached it more than Hall of Famer Phil Niekro, but he is far from a know-it-all. If Niekro by nature was a man pretending to know and understand all about the pitch, he would be viewed as someone smug and stingy. Instead, he shares all of his wisdom, but at the same time confesses that the word "wisdom" when applied to the knuckler is an iffy term.

"The ideal knuckleball is the one that doesn't turn at all when it leaves your hand," Niekro said once. "That's the one that's unhittable. That's the one that goes up and explodes in the batter's face. I get the ball back and say I'm going to throw another one just like that and I can't."

Niekro won 318 games during his career and was elected to the Baseball Hall of Fame in 1997. The knuckleball defined his career, and he couldn't count on throwing two knuckleballs in a row the way he would want them to go? That essentially is why so few pitchers are willing to stake their careers on the knuckler.

Niekro is many years past the point of being surprised about that minor issue involving the knuckler. The late Hoyt Wilhelm, one of Niekro's knuckleball predecessors and also a fellow Hall of Famer (elected in 1985), said that the only way a knuckleball pitch could be replicated was if the pitcher held it and released it exactly the same way. "It does different things every time because nobody holds it so those seams are exactly the same way every time," Wilhelm said.

Charlie Hough, another of the living (but retired) knuckleball pitchers, added a little flavor to the maddening aspect of being unable to match knuckleball form and results time after time. "Nobody knows what a given knuckleball's going to do, the pitcher least of all. It's a sick way to make a living."

It just may be that every knuckleball devotee knew what he *didn't* know, shrugged, and learned to live with the uncertainty. Entirely possible. Ron Luciano was a Major League umpire who was known for his wit, and wrote several laugh-provoking books on baseball, highlighted by his observations on the sport and anecdotes about it. This is what he had to say about the knuckleball: "Like some cult religion that barely survives, there has always been at least one, but rarely more than five or six devotees throwing the knuckleball in the big leagues. Not only can't pitchers control it, hitters can't hit it, catchers can't catch it, coaches can't coach it, and most pitchers can't learn it. The perfect pitch." And he had to call it for balls or strikes.

While Lyons and Haines pitched very well for their teams during long stints in the majors, there was no rush of players following in their footsteps. Then, as now, it was a fastball game, with a dollop of off-speed pitches and balls that curved one way or another. If a pitcher could live without the pressure of including the knuckler in his repertoire, he did so.

Historically, there have been no more than a handful of knuckleball artists in the majors at one time—and often fewer than that—although it has never been in danger of becoming extinct . . . at least not yet. Given the rarity of its use, the single most startling and unusual phenomenon surrounding knuckleball history was how an entire World War II-era rotation featured knuckleball pitchers.

In 1945, when pitching rotations consisted of four men (not five as we see in today's game), pitching every fourth day, the Washington Senators had four—count 'em, four—pitchers who used the knuckleball either almost all of the time or liberally. Since knuckleballers are almost worthy of endangered species status and have been for decades, the odds against four landing on the same team at the same time and being part of the same starting rotation were monumental. This quartet consisted of Roger Wolff, Mickey Haefner, Johnny Niggling, and Dutch Leonard.

Emil "Dutch" Leonard was a right-hander who broke into the majors in 1933 and won 191 games during his 20-year career. He was the foremost practitioner of knuckleball artistry on the staff and was not to be confused with a prior Major League pitcher who also went by Dutch Leonard. The earlier Dutch was Hubert Benjamin Leonard, and his rookie year predated the second Dutch's by twenty years. That other Dutch Leonard won 139 games and most notably compiled an earned run average of 0.96 in 1914, the lowest for a single season in history.

If anything, after that peculiar upsurge of knuckleball throwers concentrated on the Senators, knuckleball specialists became even scarcer. They also were not necessarily headliners who made big news with their throws. Al Papai broke into the majors in 1948, and his lifetime record spread over parts of four seasons amounted to 9–14. He did have the distinction of pitching for both the St. Louis Cardinals and St. Louis Browns.

In 1948, the Cleveland Indians won the American League pennant and the World Series (a feat not yet replicated in that town) and one of the key reasons was an unheralded rookie pitching star named Gene Bearden. Bearden seemed to be an unlikely asset to make the roster coming out of spring training, yet became the most important player on the team. He never duplicated his success, but his knuckler carried the Indians to their first World Series win in almost thirty years (their previous win being in 1920).

The '50s brought to the majors Hoyt Wilhelm, an eventual Hall of Famer (1952), Bob Purkey (1954), Barney Schultz (1955), Wally Burnette (1956), and Eddie Fisher (1959), who earned whatever notoriety they gained (a mixed bag) with the knuckler.

Wilhelm may be the best knuckleball thrower of all time, most certainly up on a pedestal with Phil Niekro for results and accomplishments. Purkey helped bring the Cincinnati Reds a pennant in 1961. Schultz found the limelight in the 1964 World Series. Burnette's career was limited, but Fisher's was solid. For some reason, like Cicotte, Lyons, Wilhelm, and others, Fisher recorded a good chunk of his baseball success with the White Sox.

Wilbur Wood, another White Sox knuckleball user, broke into the majors with his hometown Boston Red Sox in 1961, but never injected himself into the club's rotation. Phil Niekro made his big-league debut in 1964, and his younger brother Joe joined him in 1967. Although he was known for other things beyond being thought of as a knuckleball specialist, Jim Bouton is a member of the fraternity, who broke in with the New York Yankees in 1962. Charlie Hough joined the Major League knuckleball club with his attainment of the Los Angeles Dodgers' roster in 1970.

Dan Boone had a brief fling in the majors in the '80s and '90s because of his knuckleball. Tom Candiotti settled in for a long run in 1983. Tim Wakefield, closely identified with his long years as a versatile Red Sox pitcher, initially played for the Pittsburgh Pirates, starting in 1992. Steve Sparks, now a Houston Astros broadcaster, made the jump to the majors in 1995. Dennis Springer showed up with the Phillies in 1995.

The 2000s introduced to the scene a handful of wannabes hoping for the best and believing they could extend careers because of the knuckleball. Things did not work out so well for Jared Fernandez (2001), Charlie Haeger (2006), or Charlie Zink (2008). But R. A. Dickey's career was saved because of the knuckler. He broke into the majors in 2001, and in 2012 he won a Cy Young Award as the best pitcher in the National League.

Dickey is currently one of the best-known knuckleball throwers, and for a couple of years was the only active knuckleballer in the majors.

Although almost no one gets scouted because he possesses a good knuckleball, not everyone can adapt to reliance on the knuckler either, so there is a perpetual shortage of experts. Returning to pitching coach Johnny Sain, the supreme teacher of mechanics and conveyor of information to rescue pitching careers, admitted that his talents did not generally extend to aiding knuckleballers in distress.

"You don't help them much with a knuckleball," Sain said once. "Either they develop it, or they don't. I don't really understand the pitch." The latter comment merely puts Sain on a very crowded bus.

But Sain's admission spells difficulty for a knuckleballer in need of tutoring. If his pitching coach cannot provide it, then who can? The answer seems limited to the other members of this brotherhood. The older, retired knuckleballers have long made themselves available to help younger pitchers. There is an axiom amongst knuckleball pitchers that they are pretty much on their own to succeed or fail with little to no help. But retired knuckleball pitchers have been there and can offer a sympathetic ear, some general advice, or a quick look at a struggling pitcher's delivery.

It can be lonely being a knuckleballer whose stuff has gone south. Help is usually a thousand miles away and it is easy to feel like you're imposing on a former knuckleball man when you urgently call for assistance. The 911 number for Dickey would be the phone of Phil Niekro or Charlie Hough. It's pretty much all he's got.

The challenges of being a knuckleball specialist are great, and only a small number of knuckleball pitchers achieve greatness as defined by selection to the Hall of Fame. But what a surprising number of them do attain is longevity. Long after the typical pitcher—who has won his games with a standard fastball and curve—is retired, the knuckleballer toils on.

Only a limited amount of torque and stress is placed on the arm when throwing the knuckleball, so the pitcher can throw forever. Knuckleball pitchers don't need Tommy John surgery or months of rehab. They throw and they throw and they throw.

Wilhelm was forty-nine when he retired, almost Satchel Paige-like. Phil Niekro was forty-eight when he quit. Hough was forty-six. Lyons was forty-five, as was Wakefield. Joe Niekro was forty-three. If you've got the goods with the knuckleball, you can make it work for you for a long time.

Any pitcher who lasts more than twenty years in the majors and keeps pitching well into his forties has something going for him. On the list for most wins including and after age forty, there are three knuckleballers in the top ten: 1. Phil Niekro, 121 wins; 8. Charlie Hough, 67 wins; 10. (tied) Hoyt Wilhelm, 54. For a select few that is the dancing knuckleball. If anyone had the right to chuckle on the mound after watching the most feared hitters in the sport create a breeze with their bats, it was Wilhelm. And he admitted that he did laugh sometimes, although he tried to be discreet about it, turning his head aside or putting his glove up to his mouth. "I couldn't help myself," Wilhelm said, "because on those days I had a good knuckleball—almost no rotation and throwing it at three-quarters speed—putting a little on and taking a little off, I could really make it look easy."

Those knuckleballers knew, though, that they had to laugh when they could because just as easily as the weather changing their knuckleball could cause them pain and humiliation by not behaving.

Steven Wright, a knuckleballer who tried to fight his way to the majors through the Cleveland Indians chain, only to be traded to the Red Sox in 2012, went 2–0 for Boston in brief appearances during the 2013 season. He may be tossing an old-fashioned pitch, but Wright is a modern guy with a Twitter account listing of @Knucklepuck23. "I don't know where it's going to go," Wright said. "But on a good day, I know where it's going to start."

Wright's admission did not serve as sufficient warning to Boston catcher Ryan Lavarnway on August 6, 2013, the occasion of Wright's first big-league start. Lavarnway was charged with a record-equaling four passed balls that day. Lavarnway may have complained of a pulled hamstring or of running a high fever if he had read up on knuckleball pitchers before his date with

Wright. If so, he might have come across a comment by former big-league star and Hall of Fame manager Joe Torre. "Use a big glove and a pair of rosary beads," was Torre's advice to catchers drawing the assignment of catching a knuckleball.

Wright began 2014 by undergoing surgery that put him on the 60-day disabled list. The operation was not on his right throwing arm, however, but rather for a sports hernia. When he became healthy, Wright was optioned to AAA Pawtucket. He still realistically holds out hope of joining Dickey in the majors as another knuckleball regular at the top level of the game. But Wright did make it to the show, and that put him in the exclusive club of Major League knuckleball hurlers.

3

A PITCHER COULD MAKE THE HALL OF FAME WITHOUT KNUCKLING UNDER

NO TEAM HAS had more success with knuckleball pitchers than the Chicago White Sox. It must be a coincidence and not related to drinking the water in Lake Michigan. There is no logical reason why one team should feature more knuckleball specialists than another over a period of decades, but that is the way it has worked out for the American League club in ChiTown.

For starters, especially if one subscribes to the theory that Ed Cicotte started it all, the White Sox connection goes back to the beginning. Although Ted Lyons came along a couple of years after Cicotte was sent into exile because of his ties to the "Black Sox Scandal," the right-hander's career was deeply affected by the remnants of the scandal.

When Commissioner Kenesaw Mountain Landis banned eight White Sox players from baseball, he essentially ruined the team. The White Sox had been one of the best clubs in the game for several years. But without Cicotte, "Shoeless Joe" Jackson, and the other conspirators, the White Sox nose-dived in the standings. They were plunged into a tailspin which in terms of postseason play lasted forty years, or as long as Moses wandered through the desert.

Lyons joined the White Sox in 1923, and remained with the team through the 1946 season. Rarely has such a good pitcher labored for so long with such a lousy team. Lyons managed to win 260 games in his career, but it was always a struggle because he never had any run support.

Nor did Lyons win his way onto the White Sox roster by impressing anyone with a knuckler. At the beginning of his Major League career, when he signed with Chicago out of Baylor University in Waco, Texas, Lyons' pitching repertoire was similar to most other hurlers.

Along with his studies of textbooks at Baylor, the five-foot-eleven, 200-pound Lyons regularly examined *The Sporting News*. While he was still attending classes he came across a story that talked about Ed Rommel's use of the knuckler. Intrigued, Lyons applied himself to this new subject: inspecting the diagrams of Rommel's grip.

"I started working on that sort of freak delivery that very day," Lyons said.

For Lyons, knowledge of the knuckler was pretty much a rainy day insurance policy. He remained a fastball pitcher and his regular stuff was good enough to make him a star. His first 20-win season occurred in 1925 when he was twenty-four, and he pitched a no-hitter soon after. (Lyons pitched a no-hitter on August 21, 1926, against the Boston Red Sox, winning 6–0.)

Lyons, who was from Vinton, Louisiana, did learn other subjects in college and when he entered Baylor his parents were sure that he was going to become a lawyer, not a big-league pitcher. Determined to graduate from college, as well as keep up his involvement with the college band as a trombone player, Lyons twice turned down entreaties from Philadelphia A's owner Connie Mack to sign with his club. Part of Mack's offer included covering the expenses of Lyons' final years in college, but Lyons did not believe he was ready for the pros.

Later, as he neared the end of his college career, his coach contacted White Sox catcher Ray Schalk and asked him to watch Lyons throw. The White Sox were training in Texas at the time, and Schalk did one better by grabbing a mitt and sampling Lyons' wares firsthand. Schalk loved what he saw and recommended Lyons highly to Chicago. At twenty-two, Lyons made his first starts and seemed ready for the majors.

In his prime during the '20s, Lyons was considered one of the best pitchers in the American League and at least once was touted as the best, ranked ahead of the Senators' Walter Johnson during a fallow stretch for "The Big Train." "If I had a choice of any pitcher for a clutch game, the guy I would pick would be Ted Lyons," said Hall of Fame outfielder Tris Speaker.

One of Lyons' hallmarks was longevity. He won more than 20 games in a season three times, but he hung tough in the sport after a fluke injury in 1931 could have finished his career. Lyons was horsing around with teammate Willie Kamm on a spring training trip. Kamm threw his arm around Lyons' shoulders in a gesture of goofiness, but wrenched Lyons' neck and right shoulder.

"That was just like taking 30,000 volts," Lyons said. "My, it hurt."

Worse than that, when Lyons tried to throw as usual, his right arm had no power. It was dead.

"I could hardly hold the ball, let alone get it up to the plate," he said. The incident could have spelled the end of Lyons' pitching career, but that is when he turned to throwing the less stressful knuckleball and successfully prolonged his pitching career.

The bad break could have easily finished him, and Lyons stubbornly and ineffectively stuck to most of what had brought him through a frustrating 1931 campaign, during which he went 4–6 in just 101 innings. He knew he had to adapt, and when he returned to the White Sox for the 1932 season, he was coming off a long off-season of hard work. He had mastered—to whatever degree it is possible—the knuckler that had lain rusty in his arsenal.

The ease with which Lyons won early in his career was replaced by a constant struggle to hang on, win games, and prove his value to the White Sox. Although he never posted a record quite as gaudy as his pre-injury stats, Lyons recorded ten additional seasons in which he won at least 10 games (and in true knuckleball spirit, he also had six seasons in which he lost 10 or more games, with a high of 21 in 1933). His original high-speed fastball was a thing of the past, and Lyons had to become a pitcher who got hitters out more with guile and guts than hot stuff.

Lyons never did become the true knuckleball pitcher akin to those of the modern era because he never gave himself over completely and unreservedly to its use. At the time, sportswriters and Lyons seemed to alternate in descriptions of his pitch between a knuckleball and a slow curve.

In 1940, when he finished 12–8, Lyons said, "I use a knuckler occasionally. Threw about five of them last Sunday. There is no secret about the art of pitching—just keep the ball where you know the batter doesn't want it and try to outguess him."

As he approached the end of his career, Lyons could muster up enough juice in his still-sagging arm to pitch just once a week for the White Sox. Typically, the White Sox would give him a start on Sunday and Lyons' nickname became "Sunday Teddy." At one point he joked, "I'm a Sunday pitcher. Every time I hear the church bells ring I know it's my day to pitch."

It wasn't only that Lyons' arm still ailed him if he tested it too harshly. By the closing days of his career, much as in the tradition of knuckleballers to follow, Lyons was in his mid-forties. He joined the Marines at forty-one, missed three years of baseball play, and finished up his career in 1946, with a 1–4 mark. Though already forty-five years old, his earned run average was still very good at 2.32.

Lyons well understood that if he had not polished his knuckleball, his retirement would have kicked in long before he hung up his spikes. "If it hadn't been for the knuckleball," he said in 1939, "I would have been through eight years ago."

Lyons—who after finally retiring as a pitcher, coached for the Detroit Tigers, Brooklyn Dodgers, and White Sox—was elected to the Hall of Fame in 1955. He died at age eighty-five in 1986.

Over the first forty years or so of the twentieth century, knuckleball pitchers were very scarce—somewhat like they are today. Although sportswriters would sometimes mention if a pitcher of the '20s or '30s used a knuckler, they never seemed to make much of a big deal out of it. And unlike later generations of hitters and catchers, nobody seemed to have much of a sense of humor about the knuckler, either.

That might simply stem from the fact in that era the sportswriters for large newspapers where the eight American League and National League teams were based did not traipse down to the locker room to obtain quotes from the participants after the games. There was no television and radio broadcasts were limited. It was the job of the sportswriter to stay in the press box and faithfully report the play-by-play, not to dash down to the clubhouse and ask players what they thought about the result or what their take was on a critical turning point. It was up to the sportswriter to tell the audience what happened and what it meant.

Presumably the catcher who caught Ted Lyons or the hitters whom he fooled with the knuckler might have had something colorful to say, but no one asked them. Not everybody in the sport could have been boring.

Joe Garagiola broke into the majors with the St. Louis Cardinals in 1946, the same year that Ted Lyons retired. The weak-hitting catcher was known for his clever wit and became even more popular after a so-so Major League career as a banquet speaker and television announcer. Garagiola compiled a lifetime .257 batting average in nine seasons and made himself the butt of many jokes, but he batted way above .300 as a comedian.

Garagiola, also the author of humorous baseball books, naturally had something to say about the difficulties the knuckler presented. Another umpire even sounded quite a bit like Ron Luciano evaluating the knuckler.

"I once asked umpire Augie Donatelli why he had called a knuckleball pitch a strike," Garagiola said. "He gave me an answer I'll never forget. 'The pitcher doesn't know where it's going. The hitter can't hit it. The catcher can't catch it. And it's all over the ballpark before it gets here. It's been enough places that I figure sometime on the trip it must have crossed home plate for a strike.'"

After that explanation, Garagiola the catcher conceded that there was no way to argue the call.

When Garagiola became a broadcaster he had to call pitches for the audience and it wasn't difficult for him to identify the arrival of a knuckleball even if he hated them as a hitter and a catcher.

"I can't explain it, just like I couldn't hit and I couldn't catch it," he said. "Some pitchers use their knuckles, but the good ones throw it by gripping the ball with their fingertips. So even though it sounds strange, a hangnail to a knuckleball pitcher is a serious injury. You don't know how many times I rooted for the hangnail. The pitch is ugly. Even the name is ugly.

"I never seemed to feel as hostile toward the knuckleball when I listened to the French-speaking broadcasters in Montreal, who call it 'le papillon,' the butterfly. You can't feel as bad about a passed ball knowing it was caused by le papillon. But the word "knuckleball" should have a health warning attached to it."

Luciano, the former ump who wrote more funny books than Garagiola, soaked in knuckleball behavior—and player reaction to it—from both pitchers and hitters when he manned home plate.

"Not every trick pitch is illegal," Luciano said. "The knuckleball, for example, is not illegal—most batters, catchers and umpires consider it immoral. A batter once claimed that Phil Niekro's knuckleball 'actually giggles at you as it goes by.'"

Somehow Jesse Haines amassed a Hall of Fame career and relied on a knuckleball to do it without emblazoning his exploits in many memories. He wrote history, but didn't stamp it very hard into consciousness.

Haines was a six-foot, 180-pound right-hander from Ohio who spent his entire career with the St. Louis Cardinals from 1918 to 1937. He overlapped with Lyons, though he spent all of his time in the National League instead of the American League where the Sox twirler worked. Like Lyons and so many future knuckleballers, Haines managed to stick it out on the mound until he was forty-three.

In some ways, Haines was fortunate that he had a big-league career. His auctioneer-farmer father was not in favor of him wasting his time throwing pitches when he could have been doing chores, and his dad especially was against him playing ball on Sundays. Haines used to hide his uniform in the corn crib and then sneak out to play in games when his father was looking the other way.

Haines' heyday was at the outset of the lively ball era, perhaps explaining his lifetime 3.64 earned run average. He won 20 or more games three times, pitched a no-hitter, and retired with 210 victories. He was elected to the Hall of Fame in 1970.

A high point for Haines was defeating Lefty Grove and the Philadelphia A's in the fourth game of the 1930 World Series, although the Athletics won the big prize. At the time, Haines, whose nickname was "Pop," was thirty-seven and admitted that he needed five days between starts to be effective. One personal highlight in the 3–1 triumph was getting the powerful Jimmie Foxx to bash a knuckler into the ground for a double play, while later striking him out with a man in scoring position (on second base) in the eighth.

Like many of those in the knuckleball fraternity, Haines began his baseball career with more conventional pitches. Only when he realized that he must develop another pitch to survive, did he work hard on learning and "mastering" the knuckler. His grip actually did rely on the knuckles lying flat against the ball rather than using the fingertip style. His index and middle fingers rested on the top of the ball and his pinkie and second finger from the outside rested against the side.

"When I came to the Cards," he said, "I had a fastball and a curve. But it was not much of a curve. I soon found I would have to have something else if I stuck around long, so began at once to work on a knuckleball. I worked on that ball for years. Thought I had it in 1923 (when he finished 20–13), but it eluded me the next year. Not until midsummer of 1926 did the mystery of it come back to stay. And then I started to throw a slow ball. That helped almost as much as the knuckler. The longer a man lives, the more he learns."

That may or may not be true in the case of the knuckleball, but if it works for him it would be easy for a man to believe that was so.

"I had very good control of it," Haines said, "and threw it from different positions. I'd say that some years it added eight to ten victories to my total. Mine acted like a spitball."

The funny thing about a pitcher who threw a ball that floated and confused hitters because it moved so slowly was that he worked very quickly on the mound. The Haines win over Grove lasted just one hour and forty-one minutes, and that was equal to the time of another Series game Haines pitched. At the time he was speaking in 1969, Haines still owned more Cardinals victories than Bob Gibson, although he would eventually be surpassed.

"I pitched a lot like Bob," Haines said. "He doesn't fool around out there. I didn't either."

From a personality standpoint, Haines was regarded as a nice guy by his contemporaries and those who knew him later in retirement. He was quite capable of brushing back hitters, however, and was really famous for giving them nothing good to swing at; whether it was the knuckler dancing or some other pitch.

"That guy wouldn't give his mother a good ball to hit at," said Dizzy Dean, a Haines teammate with the Cardinals. "Never saw anybody like old Pop. He can work those corners like nobody's business. Them mugs break their back[s] trying to hit that knuckler of his. And then he crosses 'em with a fastball that's plenty good."

Haines was born in 1893, and Hall of Fame recognition came to him in 1970. He shared induction honors with players such as Earle Combs and Lou Boudreau, but was the first one presented with his plaque that summer day in Cooperstown.

"Friends of this great old game," Haines said, "they called on me first today and maybe there's a reason. I just got out of the hospital and maybe they thought I wouldn't last. But I am here for what has to be the greatest of all my thrills."

Haines was able to enjoy his stature as a Hall of Famer for eight more years, until 1978, when he passed away at eighty-five—the same age as Lyons.

4

THOSE WILD AND CRAZY
WASHINGTON SENATORS

BEFORE THERE WERE the Washington Nationals, there were the Washington Senators. Before there were the Texas Rangers, there were the Washington Senators. Before there were the Minnesota Twins, there were the Washington Senators.

Given that there were two different Washington Senators, the original ones fleeing to Minneapolis-St. Paul for the 1961 season, and the second, expansion ones fleeing to Arlington, Texas, for the 1972 season, there were more Washington Senators than there were United States Senators in Washington.

The original Senators recorded just three winning seasons from 1945 to 1960, and that was typical of the American League club's history. The running joke for those born too late to appreciate it was: "Washington, first in war, first in peace, and last in the American League." And it was pretty much true, at least from a baseball standpoint.

In 1945, the last year of World War II, the Senators were actually pretty good. Under manager Ossie Bluege, they finished 87–67, just one-and-a-half games out of first place in the AL. The Detroit Tigers won the pennant, but baseball fans in the District of Columbia were plenty happy. The second-place finish was Washington's best since 1933, when the Senators claimed a rare pennant.

A year earlier, in 1944, the Senators, who had much less success, had four pitchers in the starting rotation who threw a knuckleball, plus a fifth spot starter. In 1945, the Senators employed five starting pitchers; four main ones in the rotation plus a fill-in. The four mainstay starters, carryovers from 1944, all wielded the knuckler as a key weapon. Never before or since has any big-league franchise counted on four starting pitchers that threw a knuckleball the way the 1944–45 Washington Senators did. Several franchises have not had four knuckleball throwers in the team's history, never mind all at once.

This is how those knuckleball guys—also sometimes referred to as Knuckleheads, much like the Three Stooges—fared in 1945:

	Wins	Losses	ERA
Roger Wolff	20	10	2.12
Dutch Leonard	17	7	2.13
Mickey Haefner	16	14	3.47
Johnny Niggeling	7	12	3.16

Besides Niggeling, who was 10–8 in '44, all four pitched much better in 1945. Leonard was 14–14 in 1944, Haefner 12–15, and Wolff a horrible 4–15.

The fifth 1945 starter, Marino Pieretti, started eight fewer games than the next busiest man in the rotation, but finished 14–13 with a 3.32 ERA. Pieretti was not a knuckleball specialist. He probably warmed up on the opposite side of the diamond, lest he catch the knuckleball disease from one of the others.

Pieretti, born in Luccia in the Tuscany section of Italy, pitched parts of six years in the majors and never had a better season. Maybe he should have given the knuckler a nod after all.

The 1945 season was an unusual one—even during the war years—with the Senators outdoing the dynastic New York Yankees. Years later, Joe DiMaggio remembered facing all of the Senators' knuckleball artists, though he was in the service and missed the 1943, 1944, and 1945 seasons. Still, he said, "All of them knuckleballers. We'd see knucklers on Friday nights, followed by Saturday afternoons and doubleheaders on Sundays."

DiMaggio could be forgiven for slightly out-of-step memory recall since Leonard, Wolff, and Haefner were still members of the Senators full-time when Joltin' Joe returned to the Yankees for the 1946 season. Niggeling was present with the Senators for only eight appearances that year, going 3–2 before joining the Boston Braves to wrap up his career at age forty-two.

In 1944, the Senators had Bill LeFevbre on the staff as well. He also threw a knuckler, just not very often, and went 2–4 in 24 appearances. Although a young pitcher at the time and later a 300-game winner enshrined at Cooperstown, Early Wynn was the inconsequential fifth starter in 1944, going 8–17. It was said—perhaps getting into the spirit of things—that Wynn sometimes tossed a knuckler that year. If so, there was no evidence to give him the confidence to continue using it.

The talented but unlucky player who won the right to catch all of those knuckleballers, day after day during both long seasons, was Rick Ferrell. Later elected to the Hall of Fame (who was going to say he didn't deserve it?), Ferrell never said it was an easy assignment. He said Wolff's knuckler broke more sharply and that all four of the pitchers relied on a different grip of the ball to throw their go-to pitch.

Ferrell said that he went to bed early that season, eschewing any late-night hours or partying, in order to be at his best for the challenge of snaring those twisting, swerving, and frequently bouncing knuckleballs.

"I know the knuckleball makes me look bad at times," Ferrell said. "But what the hell? As long as we get men out and win games, what's the difference? The ones I can't catch, I'll run down." Well, at least he had a good attitude.

Ferrell was a seven-time All-Star with a lifetime batting average of .281 and a brother, Wes, who was one of the best pitchers *not* to make the Hall of Fame. The pitching Ferrell posted six 20-plus-win seasons and won 193 games, but had his career cut short by injury. Catcher Rick was just about retired after handling that knuckleball quartet. He did not play in 1946 and returned for just 37 games in 1947, his 18th big-league season.

Rick Ferrell stayed in the sport as a coach, scout, and then general manager of the Detroit Tigers, and his fielding was always well respected. During spring training he would work with Tiger organization catchers. On occasion he served as a consultant to other Major League teams that had knuckleball pitchers. His job was to tutor the receivers and familiarize them with what they might face.

Long-time big-leaguer Hobie Landrith was one of those catchers who picked up pointers from Ferrell in the '50s when he was with the St. Louis Cardinals.

"He advised us not to crouch or squat as low when catching knuckleball pitchers as we would for others," Landrith said. "He told us that from a half-standing position, I'd guess you'd call it, we could move laterally better and also drop on a knuckler falling off the table."

Haefner, a southpaw, broke into the majors with the Senators in 1943 and spent the bulk of his career in Washington. He was a thirty-year-old rookie in 1943, but won at least 10 games a season for the Senators for five straight years and his career ERA was a solid 3.50. He'd finish his eight-year career with a 78–91 record. Amongst the 1945 knuckleball starters, Haefner was the only one who threw from the left side and tossed the knuckler with two fingers on the seams.

"Wolff especially could get the big break with his knuckleball," Ferrell said. "Leonard and Niggeling had better control, while Haefner used the knuckler as an off-pitch."

He must have meant as an off-off pitch, or an off-the-wall pitch.

Niggeling, originally from Iowa, was one of the all-time late bloomers. He did not pitch his first big-league game until 1938, when he was thirty-four years old. Niggeling's career surrounded the World War II years, and he pitched for the Cincinnati Reds and St. Louis Browns. His best season, in 1942 at age thirty-eight, came with the Browns when he finished 15–11 with a 2.66 earned run average. His lifetime mark spread across nine seasons was 64–69. Niggeling said he was the only pitcher in baseball who threw a knuckler with one finger, the middle finger on his right hand, to steady it.

As a young pitcher, Niggeling believed he was destined for an earlier arrival in the majors, but an illness suffered in 1932 sapped his strength and threw his form off. It took him about three years to regain his stuff. Niggling was not a one-note singer. Besides the knuckler, he owned a screwball, curve, and fastball. He was aware that no experts classified his fastball in the same class as Bob Feller.

"Now, don't laugh when I say I have a fastball," Niggeling said. "I know they all say I am a slow-ball pitcher. That is because I do work more slow stuff than fast, but I actually do have a faster ball than they give me credit for having."

Niggeling's best single season came with the Browns, and it just so happened that Ferrell was also the main catcher for St. Louis at the time. Niggeling said he very much enjoyed working with Ferrell because of the catcher's expertise with the glove and in calling a game.

"It's a pleasure to work with such a master," Niggeling said. "Rick has the faculty of snatching my difficult pitches. Few get away from him."

That was a serious compliment for a knuckleball pitcher, well aware of how the pitch can drive catchers nuts.

Ferrell was pretty candid himself in explaining how Niggeling's pitch behaved at its best. "Have you ever reached out and tried to catch a butterfly?" Ferrell said. "If you have, you'd understand why Niggeling's knuckler gets its peculiar name. It wavers in front of the plate, blinds the batter, and then the catcher tries to snatch it. I've only missed catching one of the 25 games Niggeling has pitched this year and I always marvel at his coolness and control."

One of Niggeling's trademarks, especially with the Browns, was defeating the Boston Red Sox. At one point he was 12–4 against Boston, almost single-handedly knocking them out of the pennant race in 1942. (Niggeling finished his career with an 18–8 record and 2.91 ERA against the Red Sox.)

"I don't pitch any differently against the Red Sox than I do against any other club," Niggeling said. "I just seem to have them on my hip. I suppose there may be a certain psychology about it."

For quite some time, Niggeling said, it didn't really matter what he threw to Boston slugger Ted Williams because Williams, perhaps the greatest hitter of all time, found a way to adapt.

"That guy is not human," Niggeling said. "I have thrown him knuckleballs, screwballs, curves, and fast ones and he hit a home run off each delivery. But I finally found a way to stop him. I walked him and that's how I beat the Red Sox four times in six starts."

Sportswriters marveled at Niggeling's 1942 success because he had spent years in the minors in obscurity, and even when he hit the bigs he did not make a major splash at first. Then he won 15 games in a season. Sure enough, he said the difference-maker was the knuckleball—another career saved.

"I guess my ace card in my success with the Browns, especially this season," Niggeling said, "has been my knuckleball. It is a hard ball to hit because the batter doesn't know whether it will break in or out. I don't know myself. Neither does my catcher, which makes it a difficult ball to catch."

Niggeling—no surprise there—admitted he didn't even understand the mechanics of his knuckler, but was just happy to get people out with it.

Nobody could have been more surprised by Roger Wolff's 20–10 season of 1945 than Roger Wolff. In a seven-year career with a final mark of 52–69, that was the only season the then-Senator notched a winning record. He was coming off an ugly 4–15 record, and in 1946, followed up his 20-win season with a 5–8 record. Wolff never won more than 12 games in any other season and was 12–15 in that 1942 campaign.

Apparently, for one brief, shining moment, Wolff lived in Camelot, his knuckleball working with style, grace, and a bit of magic for an entire season. That made little sense, of course, and neither did the right-hander's knuckler the rest of his career. It was umpire Cal Hubbard who observed in 1943 that Wolff's knuckleball was the only one he ever saw that "broke upward. Not always, you understand, but sometimes the knuckler of that Curly Wolff really does rise, which is peculiar even for that most peculiar and difficult delivery. I can't figure out why it is, but that is how it is, as I've seen it."

Wolff was another latecomer to the majors, turning thirty during his rookie season with the Philadelphia A's in 1941 after playing for fourteen teams in seven minor leagues. For most of his long journey below Major League radar, Wolff was throwing the knuckler and had been used as mostly a reliever until joining the Senators' rotation. After Wolff hung around the majors for a few years, a *Sporting News* story referred to his odyssey as "bouncing around the country like a rubber check."

Once the big league players and managers got a gander at Wolff's floater, they could not stop raving about it. Washington manager Joe Cronin told A's manager Connie Mack, "That guy has the best knuckler I ever saw." And Jimmy Dykes, who was managing the Chicago White Sox during the first half of the forties, called it "the best in the league. That fellow drives my team nuts. We never know when he's going to throw the ball, never mind which way it's going to break."

When Wolff's knuckler was on, he was on. *The Sporting News* noticed with this comment: "When Wolff got his knuckleball over the plate he was invincible, but when he had to depend on his fastball it was curtains and flowers (not nice ones)."

Wolff was out of baseball by 1947.

The best of the Senators' knuckleballers was Dutch Leonard. Leonard, whose 20-year career spanned from 1933 to 1953 (he retired when he was forty-four), may have sparked a knuckleball renaissance after Ted Lyons and Jesse Haines retired. He showed it was possible for a determined knuckleballer to have a long career and to actually win his share of games—191 of them in Leonard's case.

Leonard's nickname was Dutch, but he was not. His family heritage was Belgian. There had already been an accomplished pitcher called Dutch Leonard, predating him by a generation, but now there were two in baseball history.

The right-hander Leonard, who stood six feet tall and weighed 175 pounds, made his Major League debut with the Brooklyn Dodgers in 1933. In 1934, he showed promise with a 14–11 record. Still, his performances were all over the map for a little while (going 2–9 in 1935) and he was demoted to the minors again before settling into a long run in the majors.

At the time, the Dodgers had several young pitchers vying for starting slots. Leonard did not have command of his knuckler at first and only blamed himself for slipping to 2–9 in '35. He also began doubting the knuckler after some coaches in the Dodger system informed him throwing it might injure his arm. Historically, of course, the opposite is true.

"The Brooklyn club paid me well last year," Leonard said. "I jumped from the poverty level to the point where I had to pay an income tax. And still I failed. Gosh, it hurt me terribly. The more I tried the easier it was for the other club to beat me."

It took until 1938 for Leonard to win as many as 12 games again. By then Leonard was with the Senators. Leonard spent the 1937 season in the minors for the Atlanta Crackers (no Dodger catchers wanted to handle him), but Washington liked his potential.

"I'd like to have his future," said Washington manager Bucky Harris. "He pitched against us once when he was with Brooklyn and we didn't get a loud foul against him."

It did not hurt at all in Washington that Rick Ferrell minded the plate and Ferrell predicted correctly that Leonard would win more than 12 games the following season.

"All he needed right along was a catcher who wasn't afraid to call for his knuckleball," said Senators owner Clark Griffith.

The belief in Leonard seemed well placed when he finished 20–8 for the Senators in 1939.

Although Leonard was selected for four All-Star teams during a career that also took him to the Philadelphia Phillies and Chicago Cubs, his season-by-season marks were erratic. One year he was on target, the next he wasn't even close. Leonard did often top the American League's nemesis, the New York Yankees. After a 2–1 victory featuring Leonard, one sportswriter wrote of a 1939 game, "Bewildered by the insane antics of Dutch Leonard's knuckleball . . ." That was the knuckleball for you.

Leonard kept pitching well into his forties and even when he concluded his two-decade-long career in 1953, it was accompanied by reluctance. Not long before, when he passed forty-two, he said, "I have always said that you can't measure a ballplayer by birthdays, but by what he produces on the diamond. Sure, I'm forty-two, but I feel twenty years younger and I want to stay up here with the Cubs as long as I feel I can help them."

Dutch won 10 games in 1951, but when he turned forty-three in 1952, his win total dropped to two. He returned for one more try with the Cubs and won two more games. He kept up a good face, though, during that season, becoming the object of a lengthy story in the *Saturday Evening Post* topped by the headline, "Too Old To Pitch? Don't Make Me Laugh!"

The Cubs honored Leonard with a special day at Wrigley Field that season, and he told the magazine, "It's more of a surprise to me than to anyone else" that he was still playing Major League Baseball at forty-three. One of the points was that even as Leonard was still pitching he was facing batters who had not yet been born when he reached the majors. "No other ballplayer ever went as far—or as long—on limited ability."

Leonard estimated that 1,000 pitchers had come and gone since he broke in with the Dodgers and that they all threw harder than he did. The knuckleball, he said, was "my meal ticket for the last fifteen years."

Leonard figured that he could get his recalcitrant knuckler over the plate three times out of five. "And as everyone knows," he said, "I always come through in a situation where a hit can hurt me."

KNUCKLEBALL

Like all good things, Leonard's Major League knuckleball run came to an end. He lived to be seventy-four, passing away in 1983, and was the anchor of that wild Washington Senators staff of 1945, which owed more to the knuckleball than any other rotation ever.

5

THE ONE-YEAR WONDER

EVEN IN THE context of the weird career developments of knuckleball pitchers, Gene Bearden's story is off the charts. While it is not uncommon for a knuckleball pitcher to burst upon the Major League scene and turn in a great year, more often than not it means the knuckler specialist has made it and will be around for a while.

Knuckleball lore is jam-packed with stories of guys who were late bloomers but then almost universally stuck around for years and years—well into their forties—making up for time lost in their early twenties.

Not Bearden. Bearden was a southpaw from Lexa, a small town in Arkansas. The Philadelphia Phillies thought they saw something in him, and signed Bearden in 1939. It took until he was twenty-six in 1947 for Bearden to make his Major League debut. By then he was property of the Cleveland Indians and only appeared in one game. Lasting just one-third of an inning, Bearden was hit pretty hard and completed his showing with an earned run average of 81.00. That was also most likely the temperature in Cleveland that day.

Bearden went to spring training with the Indians in 1948, and it just so happened that a very good Cleveland club under the tutelage of manager Lou Boudreau was looking for one more solid starter. The odds of that pitcher being Bearden were about the same as the United States putting a man on the moon.

Well, both came to pass, though not on the same time schedule. Bearden beat the astronauts by a couple of decades and although Boudreau didn't trust him much at the start of the season, by the end of the Indians' glorious ride to the American League pennant and second World Series championship in team history, Bearden was the main man on the mound. During the course of the summer, Bearden and his knuckleball surpassed luminaries Bob Feller and Bob Lemon in reliability and as Cleveland's big-game pitcher.

Getting the opportunity in 1948 followed an epic adventure for Bearden. World War II derailed his progress and nearly took his life. At the very end of the war, Bearden was serving in the engine room as a machinist's mate aboard the US Navy cruiser *Helena* when it took two torpedoes from a Japanese destroyer. The ship sank and Bearden was seriously wounded. Doctors implanted a metal plate in his head and another in a knee.

It took more than one operation and lengthy hospital stays for Bearden to recover, but when he regained his pitching prowess, Bearden appeared to be a prospect for the New York Yankees, winning 15 games one season for their farm team in Binghamton, New York.

Another man working his way to the top in the Yankees' minor-league system was manager Casey Stengel, who took over the big club in 1948, but not before seeing Bearden's knuckleball in motion and giving his endorsement. The recommendation was ignored in-house, and when sharp Indians owner Bill Veeck was on the prowl for a pitcher, he obtained Bearden. Stengel had previously managed for Veeck in the minors, and the new Indians owner contacted him to ask for his opinion on Bearden. The funny thing was that Veeck originally coveted Frank Shea, but didn't think the Yankees would part with him. In fact, even Stengel told Veeck that Shea was the one ready-made for the majors. Veeck requested Shea in a trade, was turned down, and settled for Bearden. He won a pennant because of that move.

Bearden's father, Henry, later gave credit to Stengel for helping his son develop the knuckler with the Oakland Oaks. "I thought Gene had the stuff, and I knew he had the control," Bearden's dad said, "but it wasn't until he picked up his knuckleball under Casey Stengel at Oakland that he really arrived."

The Yankees didn't seem to notice their loss until Bearden began tearing up the AL in '48 as a key weapon for the Indians as they shoved New York aside in the pennant race. More people sought out Stengel for his views on Bearden after his name was being splashed across so many sports pages.

"Gene Bearden, an amazing success story," Stengel said. "He played two great years for me and I never knew he was almost crippled during the war until I read about it after he left me."

Initially, Bearden kept his war wounds quiet because he felt a team might discriminate against him and release him because it would not believe he could handle a professional sport workload. After being wounded, in fact, Bearden at first was not sure he would be able to pitch again, although he always had baseball on his mind. Bearden's bad leg remained stiff for a long time and he considered shifting to first base and trying the sport from that angle. But constant strengthening of his leg allowed him to give pitching a try.

Bearden truly became the sensation of the league in '48. From his nearly anonymous start in spring training, Bearden became the name on everyone's lips that followed baseball. In that singular season, Bearden went 20–7, led the league in earned run average at 2.43, and was chosen as the *Associated Press*' American League Rookie of the Year. First used out of the bullpen, Bearden did not notch his first victory of the 1948 season—or of his career—until May 8. He tossed a three-hitter in a 6–1 triumph over the Washington Senators, which helped earn him future starts.

One of the key elements of Bearden's sudden success in 1948 was the addition of the knuckler two years earlier to his repertoire. The scarcity of any steady diet of knuckleball pitchers over roughly the thirty-year period following the end of Ed Cicotte's career meant that Cleveland sportswriters still felt compelled to inform their reading audiences just what a knuckleball was. Well, it was not completely true that Bearden adopted the knuckler for the first time only two years before he employed it with such wisdom against big-league batters. He had fiddled with it in high school and semi-pro ball as a teenager, but a coach urged him to improve his curveball instead and to drop the knuckler. That was a brief flirtation, but he was serious about his new love affair with the pitch in 1946.

Bearden threw his knuckler with the left index finger's nail curled up on a seam, but *only* that finger. The *Cleveland News* ran a photograph of the grip and when that paper's baseball writer quizzed Bearden on what exactly a knuckleball was, he said, "It's just another pitch. Some fellows throw it with their knuckles. That's how it got its name. I throw mine with my fingertips. You might call it a 'fingertip ball.' I file my fingernails way down."

With his career stagnant, Bearden began teaching himself the knuckleball in '46. He said that there was no mentor to demonstrate the pitch's "proper" technique. In those days there was not an open phone line to past knuckleball pitchers.

"Nobody showed me," Bearden said. "I was just fooling around to see if I could add another pitch to my fastball and slider. I found the batters didn't like it, so I kept on using it. Now it's my main pitch. The fastball and slider are just mixed in, now and then, for variety. I use it so much my fingertips developed calluses."

A Cleveland paper offered a virtual treatise on the knuckleball, literally consulting with scientists to determine an explanation for why the ball does so many unusual things on its way to the plate. Appropriately, there were mixed comments from these alleged experts on what a knuckleball could and could not do. For those who followed knuckleball lore back then, in recent decades, and still do so today, the scientists seem like Ghostbusters of a sort.

Thurman Tucker, an outfield teammate of Bearden's, testified that he had batted against Dutch Leonard's knuckler when it was fluttering at its best and one pitch simply rose up and smacked him on the chin. Bearden said his knuckler sometimes "wiggles, waves, or jumps. When I throw it slow, it jumps."

The article couldn't resist a line reading, "It's a mystery to science, too," when trying to provide empirical evidence for why it moves the way it moves. While one scientist proclaimed enough interest to conduct tests, another sounded like a pure skeptic. This scientist said, "I bet it can't wave. I'd question seriously that it can even dip. Furthermore, I'm morally certain that the ball never rose and hit anybody on the chin."

It was explained that this particular scientist had even experimented throwing a knuckler, but from his comments it seems he may not have thrown an effective one and it definitely didn't sound as if he had batted against one.

"Now I'd hate to contradict any sharp-eyed batters," the doctor said, "but there's such an awful lot to this optical illusion business. I'll admit that when I tried to throw a knuckler it almost floated and there was no appreciable spin. I swore it looked as though it were going to dip. But physicists agree that a ball can't dip unless it spins. I've never seen or heard the knuckleball explained scientifically."

Listening to that fellow talk, one might have deduced that Bearden was a sleight-of-hand trickster who also had an ability to hypnotize batters. When the same writer approached Dr. Bearden for his own analysis, the pitcher didn't waste much time trying to explain why the knuckler had dance moves equal to Fred Astaire's. "I don't have to explain it," Bearden said. "I just have to pitch it."

The more Bearden pitched it in 1948, the more success he and the Indians had. It was a hectic pennant race, and for the first time in history, the American League chase ended in a tie. The Indians faced the Boston Red Sox in a one-game playoff to decide who advanced to play the Boston Braves. Bearden won whenever he was tested, and when Boudreau had to pick a starter for the bonus game, he turned to the knuckleball man.

Boudreau did not confer with the National Academy of Scientists when inserting Bearden into his rotation. He just liked the way his knuckleball acted.

"His knuckler is effective," the player-manager said, "because he throws it hard and the hitter is meeting it out in front too far." No hitter actually relishes meeting a knuckleball—in a social or professional setting—and often the occasion is more embarrassing than only getting partial wood on it.

In spring training when Bearden was making his case for a roster spot, he was such an unknown quantity to foes they didn't know what kind of pitches he was tossing. Once, when Bearden took a turn hitting against the Red Sox, Boston catcher Birdie Tebbetts quizzed him from behind the mask. "Say, what kind of a pitch do you throw anyway?" Tebbetts asked. "Oh, just everything," Bearden said.

Even Bearden's teammates were studying his repertoire with interest. First baseman Eddie Robinson said watching Bearden pitch was "like watching a show, to see the way the ball acts when he throws it." It was ever thus with the knuckleball.

At that point in the season just about everything Bearden was doing worked, so why wouldn't he get the playoff game call? The Indians beat Boston, 8–3, behind Bearden's arm and moved on to their first World Series in twenty-eight years.

Since there was no gap in the schedule between the Red Sox win and the start of the World Series, Bearden could not throw the opener, or no doubt Boudreau would have called on him for that, too. By the time Bearden's turn came around following Feller and Lemon, it was Game 3. The game was played on October 8 and the leaves were starting to fall from the trees in Cleveland.

In those days the Indians played in cavernous Municipal Stadium (also called Cleveland Stadium), which was better suited for football than baseball. But on special occasions like this, it could hold more than 70,000 fans—and that's how many showed up to watch Bearden pitch a five-hit shutout. One of the things that impressed the Braves in the 2–0 game was how Bearden did not hesitate to throw his knuckler on a 3–2 pitch.

Since the knuckler brings with it a certain amount of unpredictability, even in the best of times—and these were the best of times for Bearden—there was a feeling that any pitcher would retreat to his bread-and-butter pitch in the clutch. For most that would be the fastball. What the Braves were slow to recognize was that at that moment in time, the knuckler was more caviar on crackers than even Bearden's bread-and-butter pitch. He threw it with such supreme confidence, that why not on 3-and-2? He was so slick and he had the knuckler under such control he didn't even worry about walks.

One of the many thousands in attendance for Bearden's slick performance was the doctor who operated on him during the war. Somehow a newspaper reporter found Dr. A. H. Weiland in the crowd and asked about Bearden overcoming his medical woes.

"He got what we call a 'T' fracture of the knee," Weiland said. "He was knocked from pillar to post until he finally reached the Navy hospital at Jacksonville where we had some real personnel. Any bone fracture is serious, but one around the knee is the worst because the knee carries so much weight. I hear from Gene every once in a while and while his leg is mechanically sound, he tells me that on cold days he has to be careful when he starts warming up. Unprofessionally, I would say he is a guy with a lot of guts."

The Indians won the Series in six games, and Bearden was on the mound when it ended, in relief of starter Bob Lemon.

Cleveland beat the Braves, 4–3, and Bearden picked up the save. The Indians led in the game, 4–1, but the lead shrank to 4–3 when Bearden came in during an eighth-inning rally. The original plan was for Bearden to start a seventh game, so when Boudreau summoned Bearden, it was a win-it-now strategy that paid off.

At a press conference a few days earlier, Boudreau announced his starters for the next two games as Steve Gromek and Bob Feller with Bearden as the first man out of the bullpen. When sportswriters pressed him for a seventh-game starter, he said "Nobody!"

He was right—because of Bearden.

Amidst the post-game celebration, with players dousing one another with champagne, and hugging each other, Boudreau said, "It was Bearden's Series all the way, all his. Gene was the key to our success."

In the clubhouse after the 4–2 Indians triumph, Bearden was photographed kissing catcher Jim Hegan while his right arm was draped across the shoulders of Bob Lemon.

Boudreau kept on gushing about his knuckleballer. "It's Bearden. It's been Bearden all of the way through the Series and leading up to it. Bearden won the playoff game. Bearden won the third game. Bearden went out there today when we were in trouble and saved the victory for us."

Praise for the previously unknown Bearden that had been growing all season expanded during the playoff and World Series as a national audience got to know him better. At one point, a Cleveland columnist said of Bearden, "He's the knuckle berries."

Bearden was very much the toast of the town of Cleveland after the 1948 season, and even after his late start in the bigs, he didn't turn twenty-eight until the start of the next season. Big things were now expected of him. Bearden had been featured on television, radio shows, and in January, just after the New Year leading up to spring training of 1949, the *Cleveland News* ran about a thirty-part series on his life. If Bearden had been a relative unknown going into the 1949 season, it wasn't going to be the *Cleveland News*' fault if every fan didn't know everything about this spectacular pitcher.

The only problem was that the Bearden of 1948 was gone, replaced by a struggling pitcher who gave away runs as if they were candy canes at Christmas. In his second season, Bearden finished 8–8 with a 5.10 ERA, and it was far into the 1949 season before Boudreau had to explain his reasons and make defenses for why he was still using the man who saved the season in 1948.

"I have to go with Bearden," Boudreau said in August. "With his record last year, the good stuff he has when he can get it over the plate and his attitude toward his job, it would be a crime not to give him every chance to get straightened out. He was the most successful pitcher we had last year. He still can be a big help to us this year."

But Bearden was not a big help to the Indians in 1949. He never got himself straightened out, either. The man whose pitching was so stingy in allowing runs one year, was wild the next.

"Gene Bearden, too, doesn't know what's with Gene Bearden," a sportswriter wrote. "He knows it's bases on balls, but not the why."

Bearden won his first three games of 1949 before things went sour. He pulled a muscle in his leg, kept working hard, but coaches wondered if he wasn't putting too much pressure on himself.

"You know this was the first time I've been hurt playing ball," Bearden said. "I don't know how to act."

As the glow of Bearden's contributions to the 1948 World Series championship faded in the light of day-to-day business, Boudreau's admirable loyalty also had to yield. The Indians put Bearden on waivers in 1950, and he was claimed by the Washington Senators, who after all had had excellent success with knuckleball pitchers. But unfortunately for them, lightning wouldn't strike again.

Although Bearden remained in the majors through 1953, he never again even reached eight victories in a season, let alone a winning record. And just like that, the magic evaporated; his stuff was gone; and Bearden's baffling knuckleball—along with his other pitches—deserted him.

Bearden never experienced another good year in the majors, retiring after seven disappointing seasons (make that six disappointing seasons and one fabulous one). He was only thirty-two when he retired, and finished with an overall record of 45–38. He was eighty-three when he passed away in Alabama, and although his career was abbreviated, his one-year brilliance made him a legend in Cleveland. To date, after sixty-five years, the Indians have never won another World Series.

"He won the pennant and World Series for us," said Bob Feller when Bearden died in 2004. "If it hadn't been for Gene Bearden, Cleveland would not have a world championship since 1920."

Near the end of his life, Bearden managed a hotel in Arkansas—where he had been inducted into the Arkansas Hall of Fame and where a stadium was named for him—and spent much of his free time fishing. Whenever talk of the 1948 World Series title occurs in Cleveland, memories of Gene Bearden and his fantastic knuckleball are revived. He relied on a mysterious pitch and the never-solved mystery is why that pitch abandoned him so soon.

6

HOYT WILHELM: THE LEGEND BEGINS

HOYT WILHELM WAS born in 1922, in Huntersville, North Carolina, and was a right-handed pitcher. By the time he reached the majors in 1952 to play for the New York Giants, he was twenty-nine years old and had been an active combatant in World War II.

As a youngster, Wilhelm had read of the exploits of Dutch Leonard and sought to emulate his throwing of the knuckleball. In 1942, Wilhelm made his professional pitching debut not far from home. He threw for the Mooresville Moors of the North Carolina State League. That was Class-D ball, as low as he could go.

That same year, Wilhelm went into the army, where he remained until 1946. Wilhelm fought at the Battle of the Bulge, was wounded, and among the medals he collected was a Purple Heart.

It was not until 1946 that Wilhelm returned to baseball, like so many hundreds of others who lost time in the service fighting for their country. Before 1947 was over, Wilhelm had passed through the Boston Braves' hands and ended up in the Giants' minor-league system. It took five more years toiling in the minors before Wilhelm earned a call up to the majors.

Until that point there was no team in baseball that would have bet on Wilhelm becoming an outstanding big-leaguer whose longevity out-lasted just about everyone who played the game. Wilhelm turned thirty on July 26, 1952, right in the middle of his rookie season.

But in a startling development Wilhelm went 15–3, pitched in a league-most 71 games (all in relief), led all of baseball in winning percentage (.833), and was tops in the NL for earned run average (2.43).

After traveling such a long road, that season always stood out as one of his most satisfying for Wilhelm. But he was a long way from being finished, or like Gene Bearden, being a one-year wonder. Despite his auspicious starting age, Wilhelm remained in the majors for 21 seasons, became one of the greatest relief pitchers of all time, and is acknowledged by even the best and most famous knuckleball hurlers as the true king of that pitch. He is one of only four knuckleball specialists chosen for the Hall of Fame.

Wilhelm was in the eighth grade when one day the local newspaper in Charlotte, North Carolina, ran a feature story on Dutch Leonard. Included were illustrations of how Leonard held the knuckleball. Intrigued, Wilhelm sought to emulate Leonard. He used a tennis ball as his first practice model, throwing the ball countless times against the side of a barn. As he became better at hurling the knuckler he noticed that when things went right, it floated through the air like a butterfly. The Mooresville team—located fifteen miles from his home—gave Wilhelm a look.

"They cut me," Wilhelm said. In retrospect this was a little bit like the early rejection of another North Carolina athletic legend. Michael Jordan was cut from his high school basketball team as a sophomore and demoted to junior varsity.

Wilhelm was sent home, discouraged, but not surrendering. He kept practicing his throwing with a friend and two weeks later Mooresville called back to retrieve him. The war then interrupted Wilhelm's game playing, but when he was discharged he went right back to Mooresville at the bottom of the minors.

"Nobody wanted me," he said. "Only thing I can say is maybe it was because I was a knuckleball pitcher. Nobody thought too much of me."

Wilhelm had every right to wonder why he couldn't cause more excitement when scouts passed him by. He spent three long years in Class-D, while compiling a 51–18 record.

Even in the late '40s and early '50s, long before there was a player draft, scouts were on the lookout for young men with strong arms who could blow their fastball past batters. Knuckleballers had seen success, but they were rare and the built-in prejudice against slow-ball pitchers did not help Wilhelm advance. Managers were always concerned that a knuckleball pitcher could not throw his way out of a jam without being guilty of throwing a wild pitch or fooling his own catcher into a passed ball. The ripple effect of such miscues could result in base runners advancing and even scoring the winning run. There was also the fact that coaches and managers didn't know much about the knuckleball, so they preferred to steer clear of it.

"The knuckleball is a natural pitch for me," Wilhelm said. "I have been throwing it since I was a kid. It's not something I tried to pick up to go with my other stuff. The knuckler is about all I ever had. I wrap the first two fingers over the top of the ball and dig in with my fingernails. I throw it as easily as you would make an ordinary pitch. There is no strain on my arm. It's just like anything else: if you do it long enough it becomes second nature."

Wilhelm kept on throwing and after spending almost all of his time as a starter in the Giants' minor-league system, Leo Durocher promoted him to the majors as a reliever. At that point, Wilhelm didn't care how he reached the major leagues as long as he did.

"The bullpen, that's where they usually put old men," Wilhelm said. "I'd have been happy to make the team as a water boy."

Wilhelm was 9–2 later in the summer when the Giants were in need of longer relief. Briefly, Durocher even mulled starting Wilhelm. They trailed the rival Brooklyn Dodgers in the pennant race a year after catching them from behind and stealing the pennant on Bobby Thomson's "Shot Heard 'Round the World." Wilhelm had impressed Durocher repeatedly and that made the field boss consider him for a new role.

"I believe Wilhelm could give us a chance for six–seven innings," Durocher said, "and that's something we haven't been getting from most of our pitchers. The kid has been marvelous and I am only afraid his arm is ready to drop off."

In retrospect that was one of the funniest things Durocher ever said. Wilhelm's arm drop off? He did not start, but Durocher had yet to learn that Wilhelm's arm almost never tired and that he was witnessing only the very beginning of a two-decade-long run of excellence marked by one of the sturdiest arms in baseball history.

It took a few years for observers to really appreciate Wilhelm and what he could do with the knuckleball. If it can be said that he made the knuckler dance, it was more like one of those 1920s dance marathons than the twist, cha-cha, or other temporarily hot dance step introduced to teens while Wilhelm was in the majors.

Long-time Baltimore sportswriter John Steadman captured in prose some of the characteristics of Wilhelm's favorite pitch, writing, "What Hoyt Wilhelm does with a baseball is an incredible act of legerdemain which would do credit to Houdini. It's a now-you-see-it, now-you-don't kind of pitch. Here it comes all fat and ready to hit. But right out over home plate it has a way of mesmerizing strong men. They look as inept trying to meet it as a paralyzed drunk trying to find the keyhole at 3 a.m. There has never been a knuckleball like Hoyt Wilhelm's."

Wilhelm had shifted leagues to the Baltimore Orioles when those observations were made. Steadman also took the trouble to consult with the Boston Red Sox's superb outfielder, Ted Williams, in 1961, just after Williams retired following 21 seasons with Boston. No one made more of a science out of hitting than Williams. Williams won six American League batting titles with a lifetime .344 batting average (eighth all time) and smacked 521 home runs (twenty-first all time).

Besides the knuckleball regulars such as that entire crew of Washington Senators, Williams had batted against knuckleball protagonists like Ted Lyons, Murry Dickson, and Early Wynn, as well as others who had dabbled with the pitch. Williams was an authority on hitting, as well as gifted with 20-10 vision, and he instantly rated Wilhelm the best of all knuckleball throwers he had faced. (In 15 plate appearances against Wilhelm, Williams went 4–11 with one RBI, four walks, one strikeout, and a .364 batting average.)

"Out in front of all of them," Williams said. "He was the best I ever tried to hit. Don't let anybody ever tell you they saw a better knuckleball than Wilhelm's. The thing that distinguishes him from the others is that he'll throw a greater percentage of tough knuckleballs. I have never seen him throw a knuckleball which flattened out. It always seems to do something."

Roughly since 1920 there has always been a premier knuckleball pitcher in the majors who gathers considerable attention because he stands out as different from the flamethrowers. Occasionally, there are a few at a time. Sometimes there is just one. Wilhelm was the standout once he broke through with the Giants. One by one, that Senators crew flaked off, and Dutch Leonard, Roger Wolff, Mickey Haefner, and John Niggeling went into retirement.

Wilhelm made his first of five All-Star teams in 1953, and it pretty much fell to him alone to keep the torch of the knuckleball art alive for much of the 1950s. There has never been a time when the knuckleball has been viewed as universally glamorous in baseball, but there have been periods when an individual has made it seem exotic to throw and a marvelous way to confuse batters.

Certainly, Wilhelm at his best—which was nearly all of the time—was one such example. By making the All-Star team in 1953, Wilhelm's worth was finally recognized. From a win-loss perspective, however, his 7–8 mark was not one of his better years. As a third-year man in 1954, when the Giants won the

National League pennant and upset the Cleveland Indians in the World Series, Wilhelm finished 12–4 for a league-leading .750 winning percentage and an ERA of 2.10. Throughout his career, Wilhelm was always difficult to score upon.

By the end of the 1953 season, Leonard, Haefner, Bearden, Niggeling, and Wolff were gone from Major League rosters. Al Papai showed up with his knuckleball in 1948, saw limited action for a couple of years, disappeared from the majors in 1950, and then resurfaced for seven games with the Chicago White Sox in 1955.

While it seemed to just be the *Wilhelm Show*, a new crop of knuckleballers were on their way to join him. Bob Purkey made his MLB debut in 1954; Barney Schultz came along in 1955; Wally Burnette in 1956; and Eddie Fisher, a future Wilhelm teammate with two teams, broke into the majors in 1959.

"He had the best knuckleball of all," Fisher said of Wilhelm. "It moved all over."

One of the main characteristics of the knuckleball is that it moves from Point A, the pitcher's hand, to Point B, home plate, slower than molasses running down the side of a tree. Knuckleball versus fastball is the true tortoise and hare race. Fisher swears that Wilhelm's best knucklers traveled slower than just about any pitch in history. It was as if a pitching machine was set on pee wee speed.

"Wilhelm probably didn't break 50 mph some of the time," Fisher said. "It looked like it wouldn't get to the plate."

Since the knuckleball looked like so much cotton candy floating up to the plate, position players played around with trying to throw one. They were half in jest and half-serious as they toyed with knucklers on the sideline. During the '50s, one player stood out above all others amongst fielders as a guy whose value was considered to be elsewhere, but who had a fine knuckleball. That player was superstar Mickey Mantle. The New York Yankees Hall of Fame centerfielder got considerable enjoyment out of teasing others with his knuckleball. This was not merely legend, said Fisher—who would know—but the real deal.

"Mickey Mantle had a very good one," Fisher said. "He could throw it."

While Fisher made it sound as if Mantle might well have had success if he turned pitcher and relied on the knuckler, a knuckleballer who came along a few years later wasn't so sure.

"Mickey Mantle had a great one on the sidelines," said Joe Niekro. "But most knuckleball pitchers would rather pitch from level ground because we don't get on top of the ball and we don't push off the rubber. So the real trick is pitching with control from a mound."

It was always said that the great Mantle was a five-tool player who could do anything on the diamond. But he was never truly tested to determine if he could have been a six-tool player. Generally, knuckleball specialists are one-tool players. They are not known for running fast, fielding, hitting for power, hitting for average, or making long throws. They do one weird thing well, and that singular skill is what keeps them in the big time.

Wally Burnette gave it his best with the Kansas City Athletics for parts of three seasons in the American League, but was out of the majors by 1958 with a 14–21 record. His case just demonstrated that, despite desire and some knuckleball talent, it could not carry everyone.

Hoyt Wilhelm was the exemplar of the early '50s, the knuckleball champ whose work was as magnificent as the best painter using a canvas. Maybe because it took him so long to reach the majors, or maybe it was his natural temperament, but Wilhelm was also blessed with a calmness that kept him cool during challenging relief situations. It also could be that a player who relies on the unreliable knuckleball is someone who has to expect the unexpected.

Sometimes the unexpected with the knuckleball can be a pretty good thing.

On September 20, 1958, after being shuttled from the Cleveland Indians to the Baltimore Orioles off of waivers, it wouldn't have been surprising if Wilhelm was in a grumpy frame of mind when he took the mound against the New York Yankees. He slumped that season and the Indians didn't figure to miss him at all after he struggled to a 2–7 mark. However, it should be noted that was despite a 2.49 earned run average.

The season was winding down when Wilhelm got the call to start against the perennial pennant-winning Yankees in a nationally televised game. Don Larsen was the starter for New York, the only author of a perfect World Series game in history against the Brooklyn Dodgers in 1956. Larsen and Wilhelm threw up dueling zeroes on the scoreboard into the seventh inning, when Bobby Shantz relieved Larsen.

In the bottom of the seventh, Orioles' catcher Gus Triandos came to the plate. During the ensuing seasons the lumbering Triandos, perhaps one of the slowest runners in the sport's annals, would become well known for his linkage with Wilhelm and his adventures catching the knuckleball, but they were less than a month into their partnership at the time of this game.

Triandos didn't have to run hard this time at-bat, only trot, as he smote a solo home run off of Shantz for a 1–0 lead. By then the 10,941 fans in Baltimore's Memorial Stadium realized they were witnessing a pretty special game.

Wilhelm kept the Yankees on edge but, in the eighth inning, New York left-fielder Norm Siebern, a .303 hitter, smacked a sharply hit ground ball towards Baltimore second baseman Billy Gardner. Gardner grabbed the ball and made an off-balance throw to first to halt Siebern. That was the only chance for the Orioles.

Wilhelm walked two men, but was sitting on two outs in the ninth when New York lead-off hitter Hank Bauer, the right-fielder, came up to bat. The Yankees had not been no-hit for six years, but Wilhelm was unaware until then that he was pitching a no-hitter. Somehow, busy with his job and his concentration, he had overlooked that minor detail until the potential last batter.

"It didn't hit me until I had two outs in the ninth," Wilhelm said. "Hank Bauer was the hitter. He bunted twice foul."

It wouldn't take much for the Yankees to tie the game or go ahead, so Bauer wasn't simply trying to break up the no-hitter. He was still playing for the victory.

"That was the way Bauer played the game," Wilhelm added. "It had rained the day before and the second one went foul by a foot. If it hadn't, I'd have fallen trying to field it. Now I had two strikes and it hit me how close I was to a no-hitter. I couldn't get my arms to work to throw the next pitch. Finally, I did. Knuckleball. He popped it to the second baseman."

It was a fantastic moment for the pitcher who had labored so long in obscurity and who at the time was struggling for one of the few moments early in his career. The regular season ended soon after without Wilhelm figuring in another decision in 1958, but the no-hitter was an exclamation point. If ever a confidence booster's timing was perfect, this was it, and a no-hitter completed in one hour forty-eight minutes against the best team in the league was a masterpiece to remember. The next year he returned for his first full season with the Orioles and pitched better than ever.

The knuckleball had not gone away, it was only on vacation. At thirty-five, Wilhelm was not showing signs of age, but rather regrouping for the next phase of his sterling career. After a winter of rest Wilhelm was sufficiently rejuvenated to become a full-time starter for Baltimore in 1959. His role changed, even if his out pitch did not. The knuckleball was still Hoyt Wilhelm's best friend.

7

BOB PURKEY AND BARNEY SCHULTZ

AS WAS THE case with so many knuckleball pitchers, the rise to the majors and establishing himself as a serious big-league thrower took some time for Bob Purkey. Purkey was a somewhat chubby-cheeked hurler who grew up in Pittsburgh and signed with his hometown Pirates in 1948.

However, it took six years for him to reach the majors, and after compiling a staggering-along record of 16–29 with the Pirates, who apparently never took a shine to his knuckler, Purkey was traded to the Cincinnati Reds. As Pittsburghers would find out, they gave up on him too soon. Purkey won 11 games in 1957 before being traded for Don Gross. He had been used sparingly with the Pirates as a starter, but flourished in that role as soon as he became a Red. He worked hard to improve and succeed, and his efforts were noticed by Reds pitching coach Tom Ferrick.

"Purkey's always studying the batter," Ferrick said during the 1958 season. "When he's on the mound and when he's in the dugout and another pitcher's working the game. If a batter moves up in the box, Purkey will spot it. The same thing goes if the batter moves back, and he'll adjust those pitches accordingly."

In 1958, Purkey's first season in Cincinnati, he finished 17–11 and made his first All-Star team. In 1961, when the Reds won the National League pennant, the right-hander won 16 games (and was voted to his second All-Star team). The next season, 1962, was Purkey's greatest. He finished 23–5 with a 2.81 earned run average (and, you guessed it, was voted to his third All-Star team). Purkey spent 13 years in the majors, which included a stop in St. Louis, and won 129 games in all.

As usual, the knuckleball made it seem as if Purkey was eminently hittable. Then the batters discovered otherwise.

"His ball might look as big as a grapefruit coming up to the plate," Ferrick said, "but it's not as easy to hit. Just look at his record."

When Purkey showed up with the Reds in spring training the first thing he noted was how solid Cincinnati's infield was. If the hitters were going to smack his knuckler hard on the ground he figured he had the supporting cast to scoop up the rollers.

"I like to throw a knuckler because the hitters don't like it at all," Purkey said.

Purkey made a strong first impression and by watching him throw every day his teammates came to understand what made him so hard to hit. Purkey also threw a sinker, so he felt he had batters coming and going, looking for a side-to-side movement and a drop. One thing he did not do was fan many guys. His pitches did not explode past hitters, only bewilder them.

"When he gets a strikeout it's generally because he's gotten a batter to bite on a bad pitch," Ferrick said. "Take a boxing match. You won't find a smart boxer trying to slug it out with a puncher. Purkey's smart enough to know he can't overpower a hitter so he becomes a cutey. He uses everything he has, including his head. Best of all he makes them hit the ball on the ground."

The Reds only recorded a 76–78 record in 1958, but they did field a laudable infield that consisted of George Crowe at first, Johnny Temple at second, Roy McMillan at short, and Don Hoak at third. Temple said backing up Purkey was a fun assignment.

"He breaks a lot of bats," Temple said.

The San Francisco Giants seemed to have a particularly challenging time getting hold of Purkey pitches. At one point his streak against them, which began in 1956, had kept them scoreless for 42-straight innings. Someone suggested that the Giants were his personal pigeons, but Purkey reacted in a horrified manner. He was never boastful anyway and insisted this skein was all about luck, as the Giants hit the ball right at Reds fielders.

"Can't win without a run," Giants manager Bill Rigney stated blandly after Purkey pounced on his men, 4–0.

Actually, Purkey extended his streak versus San Francisco to 46 innings before the Giants finally scored on him. Purkey laughed when he read newspaper stories that called him a "change-up" specialist, because he knew what the writers were really talking about. Unlike most of his contemporaries, Purkey had some success setting down Willie Mays. "How can that man throw a ball by me?" said the future Hall of Famer of the slow-motion knuckler that ruined his timing at the plate. Mays hit just .265 against Purkey with six home runs, but 10 strikeouts.

Purkey was a different pitcher with Cincinnati than he had been with Pittsburgh. His stuff (knuckleball included) was pretty much the same, but with a full-time starting role he blossomed. He won between 16 and 23 games four times and his earned run average was always solid. He was a key contributor in 1961 when the Reds won a National League pennant for the first time since 1940. It was Cincinnati's first appearance in a World Series since the Reds won it all under Bill McKechnie twenty-one years earlier.

However, 1961 was the season of the "Bronx Bombers," when Roger Maris broke Babe Ruth's single-season home-run record by smashing 61, Mickey Mantle slugged 54, and the team set a mark with 240. Nobody was going to stop the Yankees that year. They won the Series in five games, and Purkey lost Game 3, 3–2. He also pitched in relief in Game 5, and his 11-inning, two-appearance stint gave him a 1.64 postseason ERA, which was his only appearance in the World Series.

Purkey's true gem of a season was the next year when he was brilliant with that .821 winning percentage, 18 complete games, and 288 1/3 innings pitched. Things went well from the start of season and he went 13-1 before suffering his second loss.

He was even making sportswriters in other towns notice his skills and won praise wherever he pitched.

"The Reds regard him as just about the biggest bargain they ever got and he is respected in the trade as a pitcher who gets more mileage than most out of his mound equipment," a Milwaukee sportswriter penned. "The Reds purloined Purkey from the Pirates in exchange for a sore-armed left-hander named Don Gross in 1957."

Purkey was just about the last pitcher who would compliment himself when things were going well. Pulling words out of his mouth to get him to describe his fast start was harder than it was for a dentist to pull teeth. Persistence paid off and eventually Purkey drifted around to praise of his knuckleball as the cause of his winning ways.

"I've been throwing my knuckleball more than I usually did early in the season," Purkey said of his successful progress in 1962. "It's helped me get the best start I've ever had, but I'm not really thinking about winning 20 games, much as I'd like to do it."

Perhaps the most humorous incident that year for Purkey occurred when he summoned a local sportswriter to review his old scrapbook. In it a youthful Purkey smiled out from a picture and headline that described him as a "young smoke-baller." Purkey immediately laughed at the notion, but still defended his more up-to-date fastball.

"I don't have blazing speed," Purkey said. "But my fastball does move. And, believe me, without it I couldn't win."

Unlike many future knuckleball specialists, Purkey was not all-in on the pitch. If he was having an off-day and the knuckleball paid him no more mind than a two-year-old toddler, he deployed other pitches.

"The only thing impressive about Purkey is that he wins," said Cleveland Indians manager Birdie Tebbetts, who was the Reds' manager when Purkey joined Cincinnati.

Purkey gave credit to Tebbetts for aiding him in making the switch to full-time starter.

"A great deal of my success began when I went to Cincinnati," Purkey said. "Birdie Tebbetts was the manager there and helped me tremendously with his theory of pitching. He had a knack with me. When I got into trouble and he came to the mound he always managed to say the right thing. You develop your pitches by stages. The knuckler made it all the easier for me to win games, not only because I can get it over, but sometimes the batter is looking for the knuckler and I give him something else."

Of course, Purkey surpassed 20 wins with room to spare, en route to 23 victories. That season made him even more popular in Cincinnati than he already was, especially with team management. The Reds came through with what was described as "a very substantial" salary increase during the off-season, though as a sign of the times the thirty-two-year-old was believed to be making something between $30,000 and $40,000 with his new contract. That is roughly meal money for current players.

"I'm very happy and satisfied," Purkey said of the publicly unspecified terms of the deal.

More than a half century ago, that is what the market would bear for an ace knuckleball pitcher.

Purkey said his two biggest thrills were being part of the Reds' 1961 pennant-winning team and winning 23 games in '62. He did occasionally wonder what his career would have been like if he stayed in Pittsburgh, as the Pirates won the 1960 pennant and World Series.

"I thought I was a good pitcher with the Pirates," Purkey said on a visit back home near the end of the 1962 season. "And if I had stayed here maybe I might have won 20. But the Reds gave me my chance and I'm grateful to them. I'm a better pitcher right now than I ever have been . . ."

That was a legitimate statement in 1962, but a year later Purkey was searching for explanations. As nearly perfectly as things went during that spectacular season, that was how rottenly things went in 1963. The same pitcher finished 6–10 with an earned run average of 3.55. Purkey was even thrown out of a game by an umpire for the first time in his Major League career.

By midseason, Purkey, his coaches, and manager were searching for answers. A key element in the slump was a shoulder injury suffered in March, but the shoulder wasn't bouncing back very quickly—and neither was Purkey's control. By June he had just one win.

"I could see the buzzards overhead waiting to swoop down on my dead arm," he said. "Of course I'm concerned about it. I've been worried about myself since the day the shoulder went bad. I tried to say I wasn't worried, but it wasn't true. I don't have any pain now. The knuckler never was much good in the first part of the season. I always had to wait until late June for it to become real effective. Ever since the shoulder went bad the fastball has been a problem. I mean it starts with the delivery. I don't think I'm throwing it the same. It has no life, no zip. I throw it and it does nothing. My arm seems to lack resiliency."

The season became a throw away, and only a year after recording the best record of his career, Purkey was verbally defending his future. As the 1964 season approached, a determined Purkey sent a message to Reds owner Bill DeWitt, stating simply: "Don't write me off. I'm not finished."

During 1963, simply reaching for an object hurt Purkey's shoulder, but he rested thoroughly in the off-season, going months without picking up a baseball. And Purkey was right, he was not finished. Although he never again approached his mastery of 1962, he studied game films of his excellent showings of 1962 and saw how his form had changed. He made adjustments and won 11 games in 1964 and 10 in 1965, though that second total was for the Cardinals.

Purkey was traded to St. Louis during the off-season following his 1964 comeback for Roger Craig and Charlie James. The Cardinals gave up good value for the thirty-five-year-old, but were coming off a World Series championship and hoped to repeat. They added Purkey to a staff that already had had a knuckleballer in Barney Schultz.

St. Louis general manager Bob Howsam called Purkey "a winning-type pitcher with lots of heart," following the trade.

Not that there wasn't some iffiness in teaming Purkey and Schultz together. Purkey was one season removed from his debilitating shoulder injury. Born in 1926, Schultz was thirty-eight and although he had been brilliant in relief for the world champs in 1964, nobody knew what he had left. The balding Schultz definitely looked his age. Only months before he contributed mightily to the Cardinals' stretch run during a very tight National League pennant race, Schultz was temporarily relegated to Jacksonville of the International League. The reason given at the start of the season was that he was a victim of numbers for the 25-man roster. He was almost old enough to be the father of some of the prospects on that Florida minor-league club in AAA.

Schultz was a full-time knuckleball thrower. It was all he had, and when he was on, it was all he needed. Schultz, who was born in New Jersey, didn't make the majors until he was twenty-eight in 1955. During a seven-year big-league career he never started a game. He was a reliever, first, last, and always. Lifetime, his record was 20–20. The most games he even won in a season was seven, and in 1964, when he was such a critical addition to the Cardinals' bullpen, his record was just 1–3. While his record was sub-.500, his ERA was 1.64 to go along with 14 saves, and the Cardinals knew that they could use Schultz in tight spots.

Manager Johnny Keane said that Schultz was his indispensable reliever in late September.

"If you pitch him in short stints he can work almost every day," Keane said. "I have known him to pitch nine straight days."

Indeed, when with the Cubs before joining the Cardinals, Schultz pitched in nine straight games, at the time a Major League record. He won both games of a doubleheader against the Philadelphia Phillies during that stretch. Also with the Cubs, Schultz struck out seven out of eight Braves hitters he faced in a game.

Schultz said his knuckler was better than ever that year and it was about time, it might be said, for someone who had toiled for 20 different teams in 13 leagues before gaining the spotlight in 1964.

"I popped my wrists more," Schultz said, "as in a fastball. I cut down on my strikeouts, but got 'em out . . ."

It really was no accident that Schultz received the chance to be the Cardinals' reliever in the clutch as the season wound down. He and manager Johnny Keane had worked together during numerous minor-league stops, so Keane had seen Schultz at his finest and fully trusted him. Schultz made big news when he stymied the Yankees for three innings in the 1964 Series opener.

"I pitched for John six years in the minors," Schultz said, "and he knew things about me you won't read in the record book."

Schultz broke into the minors as a multi-pitch thrower, but incurred an arm injury during his second season of pro ball in 1945. That took the whiz out of his fastball and from then on he counted on the knuckleball more than anything.

"I could always grip a knuckleball," said Schultz, who used two fingertips on the ball, with two more at its side, "and I was fooling around with it from the time I was thirteen years old. After I hurt my arm I had to use it more and more." As a youth he played knuckleball catch with a neighbor, who he said had the best knuckler he ever saw.

Periodically people asked Schultz what kind of advice he could offer to young pitchers who wanted to learn the knuckleball. His approach was different than other knuckleball specialists who believed a knuckleball thrower had to turn his entire fate over to the pitch. Schultz took the opposite stance.

"I try to impress the fact that they've got to learn control with their main pitches before they can think about throwing the knuckleball because it's a very difficult pitch to control," Schultz said.

Not very many people asked Schultz about his close personal relationship with the knuckleball until the twilight of his career when he starred for the Cardinals during the 1964 pennant race and in the World Series. Then everybody wanted to know all about it. The Yankees' Mickey Mantle was not one of them. He didn't want to hear another word about Schultz after the Series opener.

"Knuckleballers," Mantle said. "I hate 'em all."

However, Schultz was not as unstoppable in the third game of the Series when Mantle touched him for a home run in the ninth inning to win the game.

Mantle didn't have much more time to despise Schultz because the pitcher retired after the 1965 season, going 2–2 in his last year. Starting in 1967, Schultz became the Cardinals' minor-league pitching coach and spent 1971–75 as St. Louis' Major

League pitching coach, as well as some time coaching for the Chicago Cubs. All of that indicated that he knew more about pitching than just the knuckleball, even if it was what made his career.

One of his personal quirks, given that many knuckleball throwers are careful to throw the pitch with the exact same motion as often as they can, is that Schultz threw the knuckler overhand, sidearm, and with a three-quarters motion. He said he could even throw it underhand, though that was not something any manager would want to see. Eventually, Schultz reached the point where he threw knuckleballs 95 percent of the time.

"I can throw other pitches," Schultz said, "but when I'm getting the knuckler over, why throw anything else?"

In a sense that could well be the signature comment on the knuckler for all of those knuckleball-tossing pitchers.

8

HOYT WILHELM: THE LEGEND
CONTINUES

IN 1985, HOYT Wilhelm became the first relief pitcher
to be enshrined in the National Baseball Hall of Fame in
Cooperstown, New York, and there was no doubt, no dispute,
that the knuckleball carried him down the path to glory.

Wilhelm pitched in a different era, but some of his statistics
stand the test of time. For one thing, he was still employed as
a big-league pitcher when he was forty-nine. That is the kind
of thing only Satchel Paige (who was a rookie at forty-two)
could appreciate. Wilhelm won 143 games, with 19 of them as
a starter and 124 in relief, as he pitched two or three innings at
a time (as opposed to relievers in today's game, who rarely pitch
more than a single inning and sometimes for just a single batter). He totaled 227 saves under the modern definition of the
term, and compiled a 2.52 earned run average in 21 seasons of
Major League pitching.

The key to Wilhelm's success was that he hardly ever gave up any runs. And what gave him entrée to greatness was the knuckleball.

By the end of the 1950s, Wilhelm was established in the bullpen of the Baltimore Orioles, for whom he had played for five seasons. Then at age forty, he joined the Chicago White Sox for six more seasons. Perhaps the Orioles were faint of heart and didn't believe Wilhelm could keep on mowing batters down in his forties. They were wrong.

A syndicated story about Wilhelm that appeared in 1969 when he was forty-six carried the headline "Old Butterflies Never Die," and the subhead "Hoyt Can Last Forever Throwing Like Grandma."

That may not have been the most flattering of descriptions, but Wilhelm was still making hitters look like Little Leaguers with their wild swings, so perhaps it was payback.

"I'm not tryin' to embarrass anyone," Wilhelm said. "I'm just tryin' to get 'em out. I don't have any better idea than the hitter which way it will break. I don't even try to fool hitters. With the knuckleball, it's not how hard you throw it. I'm not like other pitchers. I don't have that constant strain on my shoulder and especially the elbow that a guy who throws the curve or slider does." *(Fool* being a relative term in Wilhelm's vocabulary.)

By the end of the 1969 season, Wilhelm had stamped his name on a variety of big-league marks, including extending some that he already owned. Wilhelm was not only as proficient as anyone in history with the knuckler, he was also ahead of his time as a prized reliever. During his career most pitchers were not interested in becoming relievers. If the manager sent a hurler to the bullpen, that generally signified one of two things: it was a sign that you were not good enough to start, or punishment for failure as a starter.

Not only did Wilhelm give relievers fresh cache, but added luster to the reputation of knuckleball pitchers. His pitch did not make it easy on catchers, however. In Baltimore, Gus Triandos took the heat when Wilhelm's pitches bounded away from him.

When Wilhelm was with the Orioles, the team was managed by Paul Richards who invented an oversized catcher's mitt for the benefit of the backstops. The idea was that if the glove was as big as a hubcap it would provide a better chance to lasso those wacky knucklers.

The original was called "Big Bertha," and it was 45 inches in circumference. It may have made nice bedding for an infant. You can now see this glove at the National Baseball Hall of Fame Museum in Cooperstown. Wilhelm didn't care one way or another about the larger target; he was going to throw his knuckler and let it do what it did. It was for the catcher's benefit, not his. When Wilhelm shifted to the White Sox, manager Al Lopez—a former catcher and sympathetic to those who played the position—also supported use of the king-sized mitt.

However, baseball's Playing Rules Committee did review the matter and decreed that, yes, a glove could be too large. In 1965, the maximum circumference allowable became 38 inches. You can call that the "Hoyt Wilhelm Rule," although he never per-sonally wore any of the big mitts.

Wilhelm pretty much shrugged when the bigger mitt was introduced and pretty much shrugged when it was outlawed.

"I don't know what their idea is," Wilhelm said of the max-imum applied. "Who's on the [Playing] Rules Committee anyway? They don't make many rules changes, but when they do, they don't make sense. What possible harm can the big mitt do? After all, I've only been throwing to the big mitt for about three years and I had some good years before it came along. There will probably be a few more passed balls, but what harm does a passed ball do if the other team doesn't score on it?"

Catchers have never had a lot of fun trying to keep up with the knuckleball, whether it was thrown by Wilhelm or others. A primary catcher for the White Sox during Wilhelm's stay was J. C. Martin.

"It was exciting," Martin said of catching Wilhelm, "because you never knew where the ball was going. Seriously, it could do a 90-degree break and then double back. If you didn't wait, you couldn't see it. You'd have to snatch it when it was right on top of you. It's the best pitch I've ever seen a relief guy throw."

Adding insult to injury, Eddie Fisher, another acclaimed knuckleballer, was on the White Sox staff with Wilhelm and also caught by Martin. In 1965, Martin was charged with 33 passed balls (Martin had 24 passed ball the previous year, with both Wilhelm and Fisher on the roster). That was the Major League record for twenty-two years. The record was broken by Geno Petralli of the Texas Rangers, who had 35 passed balls in 1987. Knuckleball pitcher Charlie Hough was on that team, and might have had something to do with Petralli breaking Martin's record.

"Hoyt had the most consistent pitch (knuckleball)," Martin added. "The other guys had good ones, but every so often they'd throw one that would spin and then they'd get hit. Hoyt's always worked."

After the giant-sized catcher's mitt was banned, White Sox manager Al Lopez and general manager Ed Short sent their own design for a substitute to the Wilson Sporting Goods Company, so that they could use a glove that more resembled a catcher's mitt (and would be approved by Major League Baseball). Even so, Martin wasn't so sure he could live without the big mitt after getting used to it.

"I believe you need all the leather you can get back there in order to block that pitch," he said. "Sometimes, when you had to move the big mitt, it would block your vision, which was bad. But I'd like to have all the glove I can handle."

Martin's opinion was worth soliciting. After all, it was his name that was written in the record books next to those 33 passed balls.

Wilhelm's knuckler kept on working as he aged and switched teams. The White Sox made good use of him long after the Orioles forgot how important he was to their team. As the seasons passed it was easy to lose count of how many times Wilhelm was compared to "Old Man River" who just kept rolling along.

Some baseball people insisted that not only did Wilhelm's effectiveness never wane, but his looks didn't change either. He also stayed in shape, maintaining a weight of around 190 pounds on his six-foot frame rather than slipping into pot belly mode the way some other aging hurlers do.

There was good reason to rave about Wilhelm during his days with the White Sox. In the mid-to-late 1960s, he was the oldest player in the majors and one of the oldest of all time, but his knuckler remained an oiled and cleaned weapon. In sequential years as a reliever for Chicago (1963–68), Wilhelm's earned run averages read this way: 2.64, 1.99, 1.81, 1.66, 1.31, and 1.73. Most pitchers would like to have a seasonal mark like those on their resume just once in a career. Wilhelm was indeed amazing, and the older he got, the harder it was for batters to hit his knuckleball cleanly.

During the 1964 season when the White Sox won 98 games and chased the Yankees down to the wire for the American League pennant, Wilhelm won 12 games and saved 27. He was forty-one and got a raise.

"He had a great year no matter if he had been twenty-one or thirty-one," said White Sox general manager Ed Short. "But when you realize he's forty-one, his performance has to be termed nothing less than miraculous. Just break down his 1964 performance chart and it staggers you to think what the man accomplished. He really had a tremendous year for us."

A couple of years later Wilhelm was still doing the same thing; still extinguishing fires when he came out of the bullpen. At forty-three in 1966, he went 5–2 with six saves despite missing the early part of the year when a broken finger sidelined him during spring training.

"Really, I believe I am as good as I ever was," Wilhelm said. And his manager Eddie Stanky agreed. "He may be forty-three," the field boss said, "but he has a young arm. There's no end in sight for him. He may be around a long time yet."

When a baseball player is in his forties, the clock is usually ticking year-round and often at an accelerated rate. He has already bested Father Time to a degree and the odds of coming back for more each spring training are getting longer and longer. Wilhelm was an anomaly; a guy who didn't fit the pattern. Even among knuckleball pitchers and their notorious longevity, he was the champ. He didn't have to save up for retirement because it seemed unlikely he would ever retire.

It was noted in spring training of 1967, when Wilhelm returned to the White Sox for another go-around, that there were a dozen players who weren't born when Wilhelm made his pro debut. He was a contemporary, but his age made him "Pops" to them. Wilhelm was acknowledged for his calm demeanor, including during stressful times on the mound when he might be called upon with the bases loaded. While he was always calm on the mound, the one thing that could make him a trifle testy was being bugged about when he was going to give up the sport.

"Everybody keeps asking whether I'm about ready to hang them up," Wilhelm said. "But that hasn't even entered my mind. The way I feel, I don't know why I shouldn't go on for a few more years. My legs are strong and my arm feels good. So why quit? As long as I'm physically capable of throwing the knuckler up there and getting the hitters out, I'm staying in the game."

Those who make it to the big leagues know they have a gift, and once they are there, practically none of the players want to quit and start life in the 9-to-5 world; becoming outsiders from the team, the ballpark, and the game. Wilhelm was no different, except that he was because his body didn't fail him at thirty-five or forty. He could just keep playing the sport at a high level long after 99.99 percent of all players in the game's history retired.

"I'm not going to set any goal for myself," Wilhelm said. "I'm just like the manager going down the stretch in a pennant race who says he's going to play them one at a time. I'll just see how I'm doing from year to year. Anybody who has taken a look at my pitching figures last season can't seriously suggest that I'm washed up. I had the best earned run average of my life (1.66).

If it hadn't been for that silly injury in spring training there's no telling how great a year it might have been."

That very season, Wilhelm improved on that earned run average with a 1.31 mark, his career best. The Pulitzer Prize-winning sports columnist Jim Murray said, "You can't read his earned run average with the naked eye. You have to put it on a slide under a scope in a laboratory because it's just bigger than a paramecium."

At the time, the all-time record for the most games appeared in by a pitcher belonged to Cy Young. Young was almost superhuman and started nearly 40 games a year for 22 seasons. When Young retired in 1911, he held the mark for most games pitched in at 906, with 815 of them being games he started. A frequently worked reliever was an unheard-of-concept at the time.

In 1968, Wilhelm was on his way to 1,000 games pitched in and didn't see why he couldn't main his busy schedule long enough to surpass the great Young.

"The way I feel right now, I don't see why I should not be able to do it," Wilhelm said.

Sure enough, Wilhelm passed the 1,000-game mark in 1970, on his way to 1,070. In 2014, Wilhelm remained sixth on the all-time list, passed by five other relief pitchers, including leader John Franco, who pitched in 1,252 games. As of that season, 22 pitchers had shot past Young and all of them were basically full-time relievers except for Dennis Eckersley, who pitched in one more game than Wilhelm, and was both a reliever and starter.

Wilhelm's run in Chicago ended after the 1968 season, when the White Sox didn't protect him and he was taken by the Kansas City Royals in the expansion draft. He said he didn't mind, but it didn't matter much since he never played a game for the Royals. Three months later Wilhelm was traded to the California Angels for Ed Kirkpatrick and Dennis Paepke. Wilhelm spent most of the 1969 season with the Angels and recorded a 2.47 ERA. With a month to go in the season, he was traded to the Braves—where he was even better, going 2–0 with a 0.73 ERA.

Between 1970 and 1972, when he retired, Wilhelm spent time with the Braves, Cubs, and Dodgers. It was a bit like musical chairs. Though he had always been successful, it seemed as if no team wanted to be the one Wilhelm was with when he finally hit the wall. Wilhelm did incur some injuries and was released by Atlanta, but there were still other takers willing to see if he could still put anything on the ball as he encroached on his forty-ninth birthday.

"I feel great," Wilhelm said leading into the 1972 campaign. "My legs are strong and I don't think my arm is going to give me any trouble this spring."

Newspapers were portraying Wilhelm as the Everyman hero to older Americans who could identify with someone their age striking out players half as old. The 1,000-game mark was a notable one, but Wilhelm wasn't all that impressed with himself. Perhaps he could read the future, but even at the time he said, "Somebody will pitch in more than that someday."

He was right, too. And although Wilhelm acted as if he could pitch forever, the end was on the horizon. Wilhelm retired as a player in December of 1972, at the same time the Braves named him manager of their Class-A team in Greenwood, South Carolina. The knuckleball was shelved, but not his baseball career. The management hire represented a respect for Wilhelm's baseball knowledge more than the mastery of his knuckleball, as the farm system was not bulging with knuckleball wannabes.

Wilhelm spent two years as a minor league manager and then switched to the role of pitching coach out of preference and coached for several teams.

"The most important thing (in young pitchers)," he said, "is still talent and control. I look for good control in a reliever. I was always in one-run situations. You can't be worrying about a guy out there who walks guys."

Requests did not flood in asking Wilhelm to teach the knuckleball and he said he wouldn't do it even if they did.

"It's an unorthodox pitch," he said. "You have to have a knack to throw it to start with, and I don't know how many people do."

Wilhelm, who pitched until he was nearly fifty, was elected to the Hall of Fame when he was sixty-one, in 1985.

"That's great," was Wilhelm's first reaction. "I think that's the ultimate for any player that's played a few years in the big leagues. It's a great thing."

Neither Wilhelm's arm nor knuckler ever failed him when he needed them, but his heart did. On August 23, 2002, he passed away of heart failure at age seventy-nine. Appropriately, former teammates took the occasion to rave about Wilhelm's connection to the pitch that made his career.

"He had the best damn knuckleball I've ever seen," said one-time White Sox teammate Tom McCraw.

9

CATCHERS AND CRAZIES

WHEN AMERICAN SOLDIERS go into combat and perform heroically, the United States Military and government present them with honors.

It's possible no baseball player deserved a medal more than former Chicago White Sox catcher, J. C. Martin, for his own work in the trenches. Martin spent 14 seasons in the majors between 1959 and 1972, the first nine with the White Sox, and is now more than forty years into retirement. But he hasn't forgotten the most strenuous assignment of his career.

Martin caught Hoyt Wilhelm, Eddie Fisher, and Wilbur Wood—three prominent knuckleball pitchers—during his days on the South Side of Chicago, though happily for him, not more than two of them at a time in the same season. With the passage of time Martin can speak humorously about his days as a face-mask-, shin-guard-wearing target for that trio, but he doesn't recall them as the best days of his life, either.

"It wasn't very pleasant," said Martin, who is in his late seventies and lives in Advance, North Carolina. "Nobody really wanted that job. It was a rogue pitch. Nobody knew what it was going to do. It created havoc. I didn't have to fight for that job. Everyone shied away."

Since Wilhelm, Fisher, and Wood were on his side, Martin had to do his best to tame their knuckleballs. Sometimes he felt like a signal man just waving at a passing train. Sometimes he felt like a pin cushion, with the ball bouncing off his arms, legs, and chest protector. More than once Martin uses the word "rogue" to describe the knuckleball, as if it were a surprise gigantic wave in the ocean coming at him. It was sink or swim, though.

Certainly, Martin appreciated Wilhelm's skills. The Hall of Famer was a tremendous pitcher, but that didn't mean it was always easy to knock down those floating knucklers without a butterfly net.

"Wilhelm was probably the best reliever ever," Martin said. "But with the knuckler, you didn't even have normal ground balls when you hit it. It bounced funny. It was a dangerous job. All of a sudden he would throw a pitch that made a double break. It was just awful to keep track of it. Batters hated the knuckler. I saw some awful swings by the batter."

New York Yankee centerfielder Mickey Mantle, the switch-hitter who toyed with the knuckler on the sidelines, might never have been inducted into the Hall of Fame if he had a steady diet of Wilhelm's pitch.

"Mickey Mantle didn't want to hit left-handed against knuckleballs," Martin said.

Martin, who also played some first base and third base (probably a relief to him), spent some time with the New York Mets and Chicago Cubs as well, the transfer of teams rescuing him from regular battery-mate work with those knuckleballers.

Catching the knuckler also made for some funny moments while Martin was squatting behind the plate and that little corner of the field included byplay among him, the umpire, and the hitter.

"One time the umpire called a strike and the hitter turned around and said, 'C'mon, that was out there,'" Martin said. "The umpire said, 'At some point in time it crossed the plate.' It was really comical to see the pitch and the speed it was. It usually came in at 70-something miles per hour."

Before Wilhelm played for the White Sox, he was a star for the Baltimore Orioles, where he became acquainted with popular Oriole catcher, Gus Triandos. Triandos, of Greek heritage, was sometimes called the slowest-running player in the majors, but he was normally quick enough as a fielder behind the plate.

Triandos was a four-time All-Star and hit a solo home run in Wilhelm's 1958 1–0 no-hitter over the Yankees. The knuckler taxed him, however. Many years later he reminisced, "Catching Hoyt was such a miserable experience. I just wanted to end the game."

Although that 2009 comment sounded like a lighthearted one, it really wasn't. Long before Triandos issued that statement, he'd said, "For Christ's sake, if the hitter can't hit 'em, how do you expect me to catch 'em?"

Orioles' teammate Ron Hansen said Triandos took quite a beating trying to block Wilhelm's knucklers. "I remember seeing black-and-blue marks all over Gus' chest," Hansen said.

It was Triandos who was the beneficiary of the oversized catcher's mitt Paul Richards designed to help his receivers receive Wilhelm's tosses.

"That glove came from Baltimore to the White Sox," Martin said. "I got to use it one year. The owners outlawed it and we got a new one that was still a lot bigger than a regular catcher's mitt. What made it reliable was that it was almost like a first-baseman's mitt. It had no padding. You could catch the knuckler one-handed."

Martin was provided with a better tool of the trade, but he learned—as did his successors—that the knuckleball still did what it wanted on a given throw and that no glove was going to provide all of the answers.

Larry Bowa, a five-time All-Star shortstop over 16 seasons, mostly with Philadelphia, and later a manager and long-time coach, said the Phillies sometimes gave up on hitting the knuckler when Danny Ozark was manager. He said Ozark rested the big swingers on the team.

"Let the subs get the 0-fers," Bowa said. "Someone's swing can get messed up for a week."

There are so many aspects of the knuckleball that are idiosyncratic. The ball floats rather than spins. It can break twice on the way to the plate. It is thrown at middle school fastball speed. It is wacky, bizarre, and unpredictable. Being a knuckleball pitcher is almost like being part of a cult.

R. A. Dickey, who in 2014 was the only full-time-rotation active Major League knuckleball pitcher, pointed out in the *Knuckleball* documentary he was featured in that a split finger-nail injury can wreck a knuckler's outing.

"It may be the only sport for that to even matter," Dickey said. "To the masses, it's a circus pitch."

At times he has been called "Tricky Dickey," as if he is the second coming of Richard Nixon.

The knuckler has been called a fluke pitch, a freak pitch, and a trick pitch. Whether the knuckleball artist is named Dickey or not, the pitch is tricky to handle.

"You have to throw out everything you learned as a catcher," said former Boston Red Sox player Jason Varitek, who was teammates with knuckler Tim Wakefield for 15 years.

Not all baseball players are created equal—even at the Major League level—and they have different specialties and talents. A rare few have the reliable skill of catching a knuckleball pitcher while making fewer mistakes. Doug Mirabelli was such a player for the Red Sox, and he became known as Tim Wakefield's personal catcher for that reason. Not that Mirabelli thought it was easy, either. Wakefield's long career, pitching until he was forty-four and winning 200 games, was one of the best by a knuckleball pitcher.

Many knuckleball pitchers, as has been widely documented, turned to reliance on the knuckler because they had to when their other stuff dissipated, failed them, or didn't live up to expectations. Charlie Hough, a 216-game winner with the knuckler, said he didn't even aspire to be a pitcher.

"Most of us would have loved to have done something different," Hough said. "I wanted to play third base. I couldn't hit. I couldn't field. I couldn't throw."

So he became a knuckleball pitcher.

Wakefield is one of those knuckleball pitchers to admit that without the weapon he was toast, his big-league career virtually buried before it started.

"I'm thankful that it found me," he said, sounding a bit like someone who was wandering the street only to be touched on the shoulder by an angel with a solution to all of his problems.

"It was an act of desperation. It was either that or to go home and find a job."

Baseball is a funny game, as player-broadcaster Joe Garagiola wrote as the title of one of his books, and nothing is weirder or funnier than listening to hitters and pitchers try to describe life with the knuckleball.

A knuckleball, said the late Pittsburgh Pirates slugger Willie Stargell, is "a butterfly with hiccups." That's a pretty good image.

The case was made pretty vigorously in the well-known *Knuckleball* documentary that managers hate the knuckleball. Of course, many managers are control freaks, so that's a bad match-up right there. But they worry about what happens when a knuckleball pitcher has the bases loaded in a one-run game. They fear a wild pitch or a passed ball costing their team the game. That would explain a comment made by former Dodger manager Tommy Lasorda: "You don't want a knuckleballer pitching for you. Or against you."

Wakefield said he once walked 10 batters in a game and got the win. Dickey, listening in, said, "You're my hero."

Talk about solidarity. That was apparently an acknowledgement that something of the kind could happen to Dickey one day, too.

Going way back in time, Wakefield was actually a first baseman before he turned to pitching and the knuckler, and he paid attention when a scout told him that while he had the talent to become a pro it was doubtful that his bat would take him higher than AA ball.

"I was very reluctant," Wakefield said.

When he realized the choice was between being released and starting over as a pitcher he applied himself. But few learn the knuckler overnight and many can never become proficient enough to make the last leap from minors to majors. Even after Wakefield broke in with the Pirates and had some success, he relapsed. (In Wakefield's first full year as a pitcher [1992], he went 8–1 with a 2.15 ERA. The following season he went 6–11 with a 5.61 ERA.) So he did what most young knucklers do: he called upon Phil Niekro, and it was Dr. Phil to the rescue with some sound, if scary, advice.

What Niekro told Wakefield made it seem as if he were passing on the words of either a daredevil or a hypnotist. Basically, the only way Wakefield would make it as a pitcher was to cut all ties to other pitches. The order to Wakefield was to "cut the rip cord, buddy, and go into freefall, we'll catch you." The message was to forget his curveball and slider. It had to be all-or-nothing with the knuckler. Wakefield put his faith in Niekro and said letting go was a calming experience.

Niekro had to be reassured he was on the right path, too, as he endured his own ups and downs with the knuckler. Bob Uecker, the long-serving Milwaukee Brewers broadcaster who was catching for the Atlanta Braves when Niekro was younger, was the man who helped put him on the full-time knuckleball path. Uecker essentially told Niekro that he had to throw himself into the knuckler all of the way if he was going to succeed with it. Other pitches were extraneous and in the way.

At the time, Paul Richards—the same guy who invented the Gulliver-sized catcher's mitt for Wilhelm and Triandos—was the general manager of the Braves. He made a trade that plucked Uecker from the St. Louis Cardinals, doing so with Niekro in mind. The June 1967 swap was a trade of catchers, with Gene Oliver, a better hitter than fielder, going the other way.

"Ueck became the first in a long line of catchers tailored especially for my needs," Niekro said, "good defensive catchers with a great sense of humor . . . nobody was happier for him than Joe Torre, our everyday catcher, who gave Ueck the ol' white carpet treatment by laying out a path of towels right to his locker.

"He [Uecker] ingrained in my mind that I shouldn't be afraid to throw the knuckler. What happened to it after it left my hand was not my responsibility, but instead his. As a result, he gave me that extra bit of confidence that I needed to get my career over the top."

One of those catchers who nurtured Niekro from his early days was Bruce Benedict, who said he learned to roll with the pitches, so to speak, through the shared seasons with Niekro on the Atlanta Braves.

"The knuckleball is unique," said Benedict. "Some nights you have no chance. I always referred to it as an 'it.' It was me against that thing."

Where Niekro, the knuckleball, and Benedict appeared, passed balls tended to follow, and if not passed balls, then wild pitches. Benedict was proud of his fielding, but he had to resign himself to the circumstances. He never knew what was coming his way once Niekro released the ball.

On August 4, 1979, Niekro was charged with six wild pitches in one game, the National League record (although tied by J. R. Richard of Houston, strangely, during that same season). As part of that same game against those same Astros (a 6–2 win for the other guys), Niekro threw four wild pitches in the fifth inning, equal to the National League record. The knuckleball was the culprit, naturally.

Benedict was behind the plate in the fifth, but was relieved afterwards and did not catch the entire game.

"Phil and I are tied for most wild pitches in an inning," Benedict noted thirty-five years after the occasion. "I'm doing my best to erase that. I get amnesia."

Benedict was born in Birmingham, Alabama, in 1955 and attended the University of Nebraska at Omaha after high school, where a fellow teammate dabbled with the knuckler.

"We called him Knucklehead Nick," Benedict said, "but my first real taste of it was with Phil." Benedict also caught Jim Bouton with the Braves' AAA Richmond team when he was making a comeback and relying on the knuckler.

Niekro rode the knuckler to the Hall of Fame, but for Benedict, riding in the sidecar, it wasn't always a bump-free journey.

"Phil could beat you with that pitch alone if he could get it over," Benedict said. "If he could get it over the plate he could beat you. I heard teams say that playing against him would mess them up for a whole week. I'm just guessing, but at its slowest, I'd say Phil threw the knuckler between 58 and 65 mph."

Attempts at amnesia or not, Benedict has not completely wiped the slate clean of that infamous 1979 game against Houston that featured wild pitches galore.

"I was a young player," he said. "The intimidation factor came into play some games. There were some games the knuckler was larger than life. There were times that catching the knuckler made for more work. Some you can kind of zone in on. I waited until I thought it made its last move and then I tried to catch it as close to my person as possible. Hitters that had the best success had shorter, quicker strokes."

Benedict played 12 years in the majors and has done some coaching and scouting, as well as operating a baseball academy for young athletes. The knuckleball is not a regular part of the regimen or routine for the most part. He still remembers some batters being so put off by Niekro's knuckler at its best that he can chuckle over the ramifications.

"George Hendrick (a four-time All-Star outfielder with power) wouldn't even play in the game sometimes if Phil was pitching," Benedict said. "Other batters would smirk and go, 'You've got to be kidding' when they saw the pitch move. My thinking was, 'That's your problem. I'm busy here.' There were so many hitters that had no chance. I saw some guys swing at the ball and miss and have it hit them."

Benedict and Niekro were pals on the team and still stay in touch. Benedict said despite the snafus, the weird bounces, and his own misses, Niekro never blamed him if the knuckler went bounding off towards the on-deck circle or the dugout.

"He never said, 'Man, I can't believe you missed that ball,'" Benedict said. "You couldn't let it hurt your feelings when you missed it. When he speaks at banquets and I'm there, he calls on me to stand up and says, 'I would not be in the Hall of Fame without him.' We had a great time with it. I caught a lot of his wins."

Benedict used an outsized mitt to catch Niekro and he said it must have met Major League specifications because no one ever questioned its legality. He still has the big mitt as a souvenir and sometimes trots it out as a prop at speaking engagements and even celebrity golf tournaments.

"I've got a huge one," he said. "It must be twice the size of a regular glove. Make that half as much bigger. It's quite the novelty."

As is the knuckleball, of course.

The reminder that J. C. Martin caught Hoyt Wilhelm, Eddie Fisher, and Wilbur Wood—and sometimes more than one of them in a season—elicited catcher empathy from Benedict.

"Oh, lordy," was his first comment. "That type of thing makes me wake up in the middle of the night. You have to have a short memory about it. I haven't caught a knuckler in a long time."

Neither has Martin . . . but he hasn't forgotten about them, either. Dependability is one difference between the successful knuckleballs of Wilhelm, Fisher, and Wood, and others who have given it a try, he observed. Many can throw a knuckler for a brief period, but not many pitchers can throw complete games with it.

"It really is an oddball pitch," Martin said, "a rogue pitch. A lot of people can throw the knuckler when there's no pressure on them, but they can't keep it up, the speed and consistency. Wilhelm was consistent. Wood had the stamina and the strength to go nine innings with it."

The knuckleball also could be deceptive to the uninitiated who had not been exposed to its nature very often. Once, in spring training, when the White Sox were in Sarasota, Martin watched career minor-leaguer Jim Napier step in to catch Wilhelm (he thinks) while not wearing a mask. Coach Ray Berres offered a warning, but Napier did not heed it.

"About the third pitch the knuckler hit him right in the face and they had to carry him off the field," Martin said. "People would look at the pitch from the sideline and say, 'I can catch this guy bare-handed.' They couldn't. It was awful."

That's just another illustration of the dipsy-doodle habits of the knuckleball that could make it tough on a catcher, even one wearing all of the protection allowed.

KNUCKLEBALL

"When the bases were loaded and the game was on the line and they were throwing the knuckleball, there was tremendous pressure on me," Martin said. "I didn't cost us any games. That's one thing I was proud of. They all threw a lot of innings. That will make you old in a hurry. That's how I got all of my gray hairs."

10

EDDIE FISHER AND FRIENDS

DURING EDDIE FISHER'S heyday as a pitcher, he wasn't always the best-known Eddie Fisher in the United States. His career extended from 1959 to 1973, with the most notable years being his association with the Chicago White Sox in the 1960s.

Eddie Fisher the singer, who was born in 1928, ten years earlier than the hurler, sold millions of records during his own heyday in the 1950s and 1960s, and made bigger news than the pitcher by marrying Debbie Reynolds and then Elizabeth Taylor. Although this was not a big deal (except to him) at the time, Fisher, who died in 2010, was also the father of Carrie Fisher, the actress of *Star Wars* movie fame.

It was a fairly safe assumption that if the headlines about an Eddie Fisher appeared on the entertainment page, the Eddie Fisher being referred to was the singer. If the Eddie Fisher in the headlines appeared on the sports page, it was almost surely about the pitcher. Eddie Fisher 1 had the glamorous actress wives. Eddie Fisher 2 had the knuckleball. No known references could be unearthed referring to Eddie Fisher 1 throwing the knuckler, and no insults were directed at Eddie Fisher 2's wife. The singing Eddie Fisher did throw his ex, Ms. Reynolds, a curve, though, by marrying her best friend, Elizabeth.

When Fisher was with the White Sox and was summoned to pitch, the team organist played an Eddie Fisher song to welcome the right-hander to the mound.

Fisher the pitcher found his way to the majors with the San Francisco Giants. Mostly a reliever throughout his career, he seemed to follow Hoyt Wilhelm as an act. The two men played for the Giants, White Sox, and Baltimore Orioles, though not often overlapping. Maybe the Orioles and White Sox felt that as long as they had an oversized catcher's mitt they might as well get some use out of it.

Eddie the pitcher may not have had the same soothing voice as Eddie the singer, but he did produce hits in his own way. After limited appearances with the Giants, Fisher started to make an impact with the White Sox. In his first season in Chicago (1962), he won nine games and posted an earned run average of 3.10.

Over the next few years Fisher was a solid man out of the bullpen, appearing in a large number of games, getting a handful of decisions, and keeping his ERA respectable. In 1965, he flourished, going 15–7 with a 2.40 earned run average in an American League-leading 82 appearances. Fisher also finished 60 games that year, the most in the league.

Still on the front end of a long career, Fisher was mostly a reliever with the occasional spot start thrown in when his team needed him.

The six-foot, 200-pound Fisher was born in Altus, Oklahoma, (where he still resides), and attended the University of Oklahoma.

Fisher wanted to throw the knuckler as a Sooner, but his coach told him to put it off.

"In high school and college I was throwing the knuckler on the sidelines," Fisher recalled recently. He was undefeated most of his time as a Sooner until losing two games as a senior. "My college coach at Oklahoma wouldn't let me use it."

"During one game my coach, Jack Baer, came out to the mound to tell me that I had to throw strikes," Fisher said. "I said, 'I am throwing strikes, but they're hitting them. I've got a knuckleball I'd like to try.' He didn't say anything. The next batter hit a pitch off the wall and coach said, 'You can take that knuckleball and shove it,' or something close to that."

Fisher spent four years at Oklahoma and didn't really have much expectation of playing professional baseball, despite his collegiate success. He graduated, but was offered a five-day try-out with the Corpus Christi team in the Texas League. He did not make a strong first impression.

"In my first game I gave up two home runs in one inning and the catcher came out to talk to me," Fisher said. "I told him I had a knuckleball I wanted him to call. He said, 'You'd better try it because what you've got so far is not working.'"

Fisher came that close to disappearing from the scene before he even got a sniff of the majors. The knuckleball rescued him that day and jump-started his pro career. After employing the knuckler he began setting down hitters for Corpus Christi and the club signed him to a contract. After several years of experimenting with the knuckler as a back-up pitch, suddenly he had to count on it to take him where he wanted to go in professional baseball, or he might find himself in the regular working world.

"I didn't have any instruction in the beginning," Fisher said.

"I had heard of Hoyt Wilhelm throwing it." It was not until later when Fisher and Wilhelm played together with the White Sox that he picked up pointers from the veteran. "I actually had the same grip as Hoyt Wilhelm. But I gripped the ball hard and he gripped it loose. He helped me a lot."

What Wilhelm impressed upon Fisher was the blind-faith routine; the use-it-if-you've-got-it aspect of throwing the knuckler. "He said, 'If you're going to use it, you have to go with it all of the time,'" Fisher said. But that was after Fisher earned his way to the top level of the sport using his self-taught knuckler. It was already part of his repertoire when he made the Giants major league roster in 1959. However, it was estimated that he opened with using the knuckler 20 percent of the time before upping its frequency to about 80 percent in the mid-'60s.

"He [Wilhelm] kept hammering away at me to throw the knuckler more," Fisher said. "He insisted it was my 'out' pitch and he finally convinced me. When I first threw the knuckler in the minors, or even at the start in the majors, I'd use it only when I was ahead of the hitter."

Fisher appeared in 59 games in 1964, 82 the next year, and 67 in 1965 (the latter two being tops in the American League). His arm didn't get weary from overuse and Fisher said he benefited from being on the mound frequently.

"Working often is mighty important to a knuckleball pitcher because it helps his control," Fisher said. "The knuckler is a finely-tuned pitch. You have to keep throwing it in order to retain mastery of it. Wilhelm and I throw knucklers every day. When nobody else is around we throw it to each other. We'd be out there in the bullpen almost every day, and as a couple of guys who threw the knuckler, we'd talk shop."

Not every pitcher has that luxury of a pal on the staff that sees the pitching world the same way and can offer insight into the use of a quirky pitch like the knuckleball. With hardly anyone in the sport throwing knucklers, not many times do knuckleballers end up teammates.

While Fisher and Wilhelm were doing their thing for the White Sox, one pitcher, Frank Lary, who is not especially remembered as a knuckleball specialist, was winning games for the Detroit Tigers. A two-time All-Star, Lary, who did not break into the majors until he was twenty-four in 1954 because of military service, won 21 games in 1956, and 23 games in 1961 as he almost single-handedly uplifted his team against the great Yankees team of that season.

Lary did not arrive in the majors with a knuckleball, but adopted it in the mid-1950s, and doing so immediately transformed his effectiveness. Members of the Tigers' hierarchy, from then-manager Bucky Harris to Hall of Famer Mel Ott, boss of Detroit's farm system, are the ones who lobbied Lary the hardest to take on the knuckler as a bonus pitch. Lary barely saw action in 1954 and had a losing record in 1955, so he was listening to experts talk about what he could do to take the big step into making himself a real big-league pitcher and winner.

"What have I got to lose the way things are going?" he asked himself.

Detroit catcher Bob Wilson saw the difference right away.

"Before he started using it [the knuckleball], batters used to wait him out all of the time," Wilson said. "They knew what to expect—fastball, curve, slider—and about when to expect it.

They're getting those pitches, but they know that when Frank gets a couple of strikes on them he's going to come in there with that knuckleball. They don't want any part of it, so they start taking their cuts earlier now."

Lary was so effective against New York that he gained the nickname, "The Yankee Killer." This was because of his 27–10 record against New York between 1955 and 1961, when the Yanks were the best team in baseball. He was a rare All-Star starter who supplemented his stuff with the knuckler as opposed to making it his number 1 pitch.

Lary won more than 20 games twice. He started using the knuckler after years of fooling around with one playing catch in the outfield with teammates. After he mixed it into his go-to list of pitches he found success.

"I never threw it hard because I was afraid I'd hurt my arm," said Lary, who won 128 games in the majors and his now in his eighties. "One day I told [catcher] Frank House to call for it a time or two and he did. I found myself striking out hitters with the good eyes using my knuckler. I made Ted Williams mad. I tried it on Mickey Mantle and he didn't get a hit off it."

For Lary, the knuckler was a pitch to keep hitters off-balance. He threw it about ten times a game.

"Once that fellow learned the knuckler," Williams said, "he was able to keep you guessing. You never know what he's going to throw, and he's got the guts to fight you all the way."

Another contemporary pitcher of Fisher's and Lary's who used the knuckler was Harold "Skinny" Brown, although he is not always listed as a full-time knuckleball man. A six-foot-two, 180-pound right-hander, Brown, now eighty-nine, made his Major

League debut in 1951 with the Chicago White Sox. As history shows, the White Sox were always generous to knuckleball pitchers. Brown, whose stay in Chicago was brief, spent 14 years in the majors—a majority of them with the Orioles—another team that was a knuckleball sympathizer.

Brown's lifetime mark was 85–92 with a 3.81 earned run average. In 1959, 1960, and 1961—overlapping with Fisher, Wilhelm, and Lary—Brown produced his finest work, winning 11, 12, and, 10 games in successive seasons. Brown was known for his excellent control and was both a starter and reliever during his career.

Definitely not a full-time knuckleballer, Brown liberally used a fastball and slider, mixing speeds to keep batters off-balance. But the knuckler was the natural for catching hitters off-guard. Brown first developed the pitch in high school, but ran into a roadblock during his time in the minors. Hard to believe, but the person who refused to face the pitch was a teammate catcher who didn't want to catch it. Paul Richards, the executive who seemed to be everywhere knucklers popped up—either with the evolution of the oversized mitt or in Baltimore or Chicago, which housed the players who specialized in it—was on the scene with the Seattle Rainiers, too.

Richards, said Brown, told him to "Pitch your own way. Throw what you want to throw, not what the catcher wants you to throw. It's your future, not his. If you get hammered, it counts against you, not him."

Brown stuck with the knuckler, calling for the pitch when he needed it most.

Once Fisher mingled with Wilhelm, though, he was a knuckleballer all the way, only occasionally mixing in other pitches.

When he began his Major League odyssey, Fisher was twenty-two and trying to fit in with the Giants. Brought up to the big club from AAA Phoenix, his placement on the roster was noted, as was his heavy use of the knuckler.

Immediately, Fisher was asked to analyze his knuckler, particularly since he was coming off a one-hitter for Phoenix.

"It has no pattern," Fisher said, offering lecture lessons like a long-time vet on the pitch. "The wind determines the break of the knuckler. Sometimes it breaks in. Another time it darts down and out. I throw it like a fastball, but off the nails of the first two fingers. So far I've had good control of it, especially if there's a cross wind, which I understand is the situation here."

"Here" being Candlestick Park, where the wind blew much the same as it did to Dorothy in *The Wizard of Oz*.

And yes, Fisher's knuckleball came to town with a reputation of being hard to handle for catchers. That's because Al Steiglitz, the receiver he left behind in the desert, was still healing from fifteen stitches above the right eye necessary because of a warm-up pitch from Fisher, as well as five stitches on his right index finger. Steiglitz was probably as happy as Fisher that he was called up from Phoenix to the Giants.

"Poor guy," Fisher said as he waved good-bye to Steiglitz, who was more likely to ask for a trade out of self-preservation than accept a promotion from the Giants.

Fisher made good in his first game, beating the Pirates, 4–1, on June 22, 1959. Afterwards, surrounded by the press wishing to pump up his debut, Fisher admitted his frayed nerves.

"I was nervous going to the mound," he said. "I thought, 'This is it. My first time out here, I hope I don't boot it.'" Fisher's first opponent was Pittsburgh shortstop Dick Schofield, and in

Fisher's mind, the at-bat took an eternity to play out. "I said a little prayer and went to work on Dick Schofield. As long as I live I'll never forget him. It seemed as if he were up there an hour before he flied out to center. The moment [Willie] Mays caught the ball the pressure seemed to lift. But it was three innings before I got my breath and started to relax."

While Fisher had been discouraged from using the knuckler in college, by the time he had reached the Giants, manager Bill Rigney understood that he relied on the pitch. "I threw the knuckler about 25 percent of the time," he said. "Actually, I didn't have as good a control of it as usual, but my fastball, curveball and slider were in the groove."

Veteran catcher Jim Hegan, nearing the end of his long Major League career and who appeared in only 21 games for the Giants that season, was tabbed by Rigney to handle the young hurler that day.

"Fisher's fastball surprised me," Hegan said. "I didn't think he was that quick. Usually, a knuckleball pitcher has more breaking stuff than speed. His is a sneaky fast one. If he can keep that knuckleball over—and continue to use his speed, slider, and curve—he has the stuff to win."

Then and now Fisher understood that the knuckleball was not for everybody. Not every pitcher who tried it could use it to win in the big leagues. He had the gift.

"There are not a lot of guys that had success with it," he said. "It takes a certain feel to take the spin off. I won my first game with the Giants and I won my second. The only way the pitch will work is if you take the spin off. It's got to be done with the fingernails or the fingertips and very few people have that touch. It's like reaching out and pulling the shade down on the window—not too hard, but gently, just right. I threw it down the middle of the plate and I hoped it didn't stay there."

Fisher estimated that the speed of his knuckleball was probably between 62 and 65 mph, which is pretty average for a car on a state highway. Wilhelm's was slower, for sure, he said.

Those first two wins with the Giants came rather easily, but Fisher only went 2–6 as a rookie with a 7.88 earned run average. The knuckler and he both needed some seasoning. Fisher's work with the butterfly didn't blossom and mature until he was with the White Sox and in the company of Hoyt Wilhelm. Then he did good work for the Orioles.

"Just being around a guy who is that successful with the knuckler has helped a lot," Fisher said. "I came to the Sox with an average knuckleball. I thought it was pretty good, but [it was] nothing like Hoyt's. I learned how to use the knuckler by watching Wilhelm in a game. I go with the pitch more now."

White Sox manager Al Lopez joked that his club obtained Wilhelm because he was sick of losing to him. What Fisher had to do was gain confidence in the knuckler even when he was behind in the count. Lopez and Fisher agreed that a pivotal moment occurred when Fisher was behind 2–0 in the count to Detroit Tigers slugger Rocky Colavito during a 1963 game. Fisher abandoned the knuckler and Colavito made sure that the ball abandoned the ballpark when he smashed it for a three-run homer. Lopez removed Fisher from the game and said it was because he attempted to fool Colavito with a slider instead of his best pitch.

"I yanked him," Lopez said. "He should have thrown the knuckler. That's his out-pitch."

Fisher had some good times in Chicago, but didn't stay long enough. Fisher the baseball player often heard jokes from fans when he signed autographs because he had the same name as the singer. After a stay with the Orioles (1966–67), Fisher pitched one season for the Cleveland Indians in 1968. He did not enjoy that stopover because he believed that the Indians manager, Alvin Dark, was prejudiced against knuckleballers. Then Fisher joined the Angels where he appeared in 52, 67, and 57 games over three seasons and was hungry for more. The knuckleball, as both he and Wilhelm expressed, only got better with more use. Rest was for wimps, not relievers, in their minds.

"The knuckleball pitcher is a special breed of cat," Fisher said. "He needs work, a lot of it. Hoyt Wilhelm told me once that the more he pitches, the better he is and I couldn't agree more. I really believe that I could pitch in a hundred games in one season. I have the kind of arm and the kind of temperament . . . and I throw the right kind of pitch."

Fisher never did fulfill that goal of appearing in a hundred games in one season. For a time his career-high 82 was the Major League record. He was always available, though, and near the end of his big-league career he returned to the White Sox for a couple more seasons, the team he is most closely identified with.

Interestingly, after spending most of his career coming out of the bullpen—this being his second stint with the White Sox in 1973—he started more games than he relieved before ending his career at the tail end of that season with a 2–1 mark and a 1.29 earned run average for the St. Louis Cardinals. Fisher had always wanted to be a regular starter, but teams thought he was more valuable as a reliever.

In 1973 Fisher spent some time in a White Sox rotation that included Wilbur Wood— another knuckleballer. Wood threw lefty and Fisher righty, so it was a complex challenge for opponents to cope with the duo. Fisher, who pitched in 690 games during his Major League career, pitched a complete game victory in 1973—his first complete game in ten years.

Fisher was grateful to manager Chuck Tanner, pitching coach Johnny Sain (who endorsed him, even if he didn't teach him about the knuckleball), Wilhelm, catcher Ed Herrmann, and Wood. Fisher admitted Wood was an inspiration.

"When you see Wilbur out there winning with his knuckler, it gives you confidence. You feel that you can do the same thing."

When Fisher was sold from the White Sox to the Cardinals with a month to go in the 1973 season, he said he came prepared for St. Louis.

"I stole the White Sox's knuckleball mitt and took it with me," Fisher said.

But even with that attractive piece of equipment, he claimed the Cardinals' catchers sought to avoid him as if he were carrying an infectious disease. The Cards had Ted Simmons, Joe Torre, and Tim McCarver.

"Not a damned one of them would catch a knuckleball," Fisher said.

They were catchers who may have understood that Fisher was their ally, but the knuckler was not their friend.

11

WILBUR WOOD: THE EARLY YEARS

WILBUR WOOD WAS a prized commodity for the Boston Red Sox out of high school. Not only was he a local star, from nearby Belmont High, but he was a left-handed pitcher. Since he was in their own backyard, the Red Sox couldn't miss on signing Wood.

That was just fine with Wood, because he grew up a Red Sox fan and thought there would be nothing finer than pitching for them. Boston scouts liked his fastball and the way he mowed down the hitters, and believed he had potential to be a front-of-the-rotation guy. The Sox signed Wood as an amateur free agent in 1960, and he made his big-league debut in 1961 at age nineteen.

Not only did the Red Sox make the best offer, but Wood was influenced to sign with the local club by Tom Brewer, a solid right-hander for the Sox who lived in a house nearby and was friends with his family. Brewer told Wood what he could expect.

"I started out at $1,000 a month in the minors," Wood said.

Those were actually pretty good wages for a player fresh out of high school at the time, as some made as little as $400 a month in the low minors.

The Red Sox were not very good in those days. Ted Williams had just retired and Carl Yastrzemski was just breaking in as a rookie. The team was in dire need of pitching. Wood, who stood six feet tall and weighed 180 pounds, was thrown into a few games as a teenager. He pitched four innings in his debut against the Cleveland Indians on June 30, 1961, and hit the mound at Fenway Park during the next home stand. He appeared in six games—five of them in relief— and walked away from the season with a 0–0 record with 13 innings on his resume and a 5.54 earned run average.

The big thing was stepping onto the mound in his hometown in front of friends and family while wearing that Major League uniform.

"Of course you're all excited," Wood said. "You can't wait. It was all fastball, curveball. I had the knuckleball in my back pocket."

Although that ERA was somewhat unsightly, it didn't really matter to the Sox. Wood was just supposed to quell his nerves and get the feel of Fenway Park and what it was like to face Major League batters instead of high schoolers. The only problem was that after 1961 came 1962 and 1963 and the results were pretty much the same. Wood was living in the minors, making cameo appearances in Boston, and not pitching very often or effectively.

After three years, he got a longer trial in the big leagues during the 1963 season. Still just twenty-one, Wood pitched in 25 games and had six starts, but finished with a 0–5 record. He threw 64 2/3 innings and his ERA was a much-improved 3.76.

While his ERA had dropped considerably, the only W connected to him was the one that began his first and last name.

Self-awareness was also starting to take hold. Wood spent most of his summers in AA or AAA in the Red Sox organization and between those roles and his brief showings with the Sox, evidence indicated he should be worried.

"I was fastball, curveball. I thought I was a few yards short on my fastball," Wood said many years later. "After a few years I knew I had to change."

To Wood, that meant he had to add a new pitch, an out-pitch that would expand his weaponry and keep him in the majors. As a youngster of about twelve or thirteen, when Wood played catch with his father in their backyard, he fooled around with a knuckleball.

"That's when it began," Wood said. "I was pretty young. Something like that. My father had a palm ball that he threw with no spin on it. I had a knuckleball, but I didn't throw it much in high school. I didn't need to. When I played semi-pro ball in the summer I'd throw it then."

When a Red Sox scout came knocking on his door in 1960 to sign him out of high school, Wood did not give his knuckleball a thought and neither did they. The Sox wanted the fastball-throwing southpaw. After those first shaky seasons, Wood had some doubts about his core pitches being able to carry him. The Red Sox seemed to run out of patience, however, during the 1964 season. Wood appeared in seven games, went 0-0, and was sitting on a ghastly 17.47 earned run average at the time. In their minds, he had shown no improvement.

In Wood's mind, he had been begging for help from the organization, explaining that he knew how to throw a knuckleball, but that he needed some expert advice. The Red Sox pretty much shrugged that off, as they were still decades away from Tim Wakefield and seeing firsthand the success a knuckleballer can have in Boston. As has been demonstrated numerous times throughout baseball history, managers generally are not knuckleball experts—nor are very many of their pitching coaches. Those who understand the pitch have used it to good effect and those who have succeeded with it are limited in number. There was no one like that around the Red Sox in 1964.

"There wasn't anybody in the Red Sox organization who knew about the knuckleball," Wood said. "I had no one to talk to about it."

In September of that year, the Red Sox sold Wood outright to the Pittsburgh Pirates. That was essentially code for considering him a failure. It was then that Wood committed to the knuckleball full-time. He felt that he had to, or he would soon be out of baseball. He became a born-again pitcher. However, he still had basically the same problem: There was no one with the Pirates who was a knuckleball pro, either, or, for that matter, associated with their high-minor-league teams. Wood was learning that the knuckleball man could live a solitary existence.

"No one knew about it over there, either," Wood said of Pittsburgh. "I went to the Pirates' Columbus, Ohio, AAA team and I started throwing the knuckleball anyway."

So many knuckleball pitchers who made breakthroughs— and their coaches and managers say the same thing—called the knuckler a pitch of desperation. That description absolutely fit Wood, who was facing the unemployment line as the next stop, and the shattering of his big-league dream. No one had to tell him. His view of reality was uncluttered.

"I told myself, *You'd better do something different, or you're going home to look for a job*," Wood recalled.

Wood got into three games (starting two) with the Pirates at the end of the 1964 season and lost two of them, but did finish with a respectable 3.63 ERA. The Pirates kept Wood around for the 1965 season and he made 34 appearances, all but once out of the bullpen. His ERA dropped to 3.16 and he finally won his first big-league game. Wood recorded that win in late August when he pitched the sixth inning of a 4–2 triumph over Houston. Still, Wood did not pitch in the majors in 1966. That year, Wood pitched for the Columbus Jets in the International League, a team operated by the Pirates. He finished 14-8 as a full-time starter at AAA. As soon as the season ended, the Pirates shipped him to the White Sox for a player-to-be-named later. That player turned out to be Juan Pizarro. Pizarro had won as many as 19 games in a season and was a two-time All-Star, but at age thirty, his skills had just begun to fade.

Wood's time with Columbus in the International League during the '66 season was not wasted. He posted a 14–8 record with a 2.40 earned run average. That was like an advertisement that he could help some big-league team willing to give him a chance.

When he carried his duffel bag to Chicago, Wood was still trying to find his skills and make them work for him. He was a one-time prospect who was living on the edge of baseball oblivion. He once possessed what was believed to be a great future, but instead was staring at a bleak one, and only at the age of twenty-five. It was pretty much now or never for Wood when he joined the White Sox. Until that point in his Major League career he had done nothing except collect a few stories he might someday be able to tell his grandkids.

There was one major change in Wood's life when he became a member of the White Sox. This time he was joining an organization that had a long history of good experiences with people who threw the knuckleball. Ed Cicotte was damned for his involvement in the "Black Sox" scandal, but was credited as being the innovator of the pitch. Ted Lyons' knuckleball got him into the Hall of Fame during his twenty-one-year career with the Sox. Eddie Fisher had done yeoman work with the knuckler starting in 1962. And one of Wood's new teammates was Hoyt Wilhelm, the grand master of the pitch.

What a relief it was for Wood to talk about his knuckleball grip and delivery and have someone around who not only didn't gaze at him as if he were speaking Mandarin, but who could jump right in and help. Fisher was in Baltimore by then, but having Wilhelm as a knuckleball partner was like having a personal pitching coach in the clubhouse.

"When I got to the White Sox in 1967, Hoyt was there," Wood said. "He talked to me a lot and he was the one who said I should junk all of my other stuff and go exclusively with the knuckleball. It was obvious by then that my fastball and curveball were not going to cut the mustard in the big leagues."

Unlike his previous five seasons, 1967 wasn't one to forget. Wood made a good impression on White Sox manager Eddie Stanky to earn a spot on the roster and continued playing well. He got into 51 games, finished 4–2, pitched 95 1/3 innings, and for the first time in his career, Wood recorded a sterling earned run average of 2.45.

Wilhelm liked what he saw, but felt Wood had it in him to be even better. For years Wood had relied on his fastball and curve, which blew away the hitters in high school. They even got him noticed by the Red Sox. But the fastball and curve were getting batted all over the lot in the majors and often enough in the minors, too. It is terribly difficult for an athlete who has known the kind of success that lifts him to the top 2 percent of fellow players to give up on his bread and butter. It was almost like getting fatherly advice about a girlfriend—it had been nice so far, but the relationship wasn't going anywhere anymore and you certainly weren't going to marry her.

Wilhelm wanted Wood to break up with his gal and immediately get hitched to someone else. No wonder it was a challenging mental transition.

"It was a bad moment," Wood said. "But it was something that had to be done. I had to change. By 1968, I had fully committed to the knuckleball."

But once he agreed and followed the then-forty-three-year-old future Hall of Famer's advice, Wood settled into his new life as a knuckleball pitcher.

"I've thrown the knuckleball almost as long as I've been pitching," he said. "However, it's never been more than just an extra pitch I'd toss once in a while just to get the batter off stride a little. But since talking with Wilhelm, it's become my main pitch. And I've certainly had good luck with it. Wilhelm, of course, is one reason for it because he not only has sold me on using it more, but also has improved it by giving me some tips on how to throw it.

"I had a tendency to drop down with my arm when I threw the knuckler and Hoyt has me throwing it strictly overhanded.

It breaks down more consistently that way, whereas if you get down close to sidearm, it will break laterally, in the same plane, and you'll get killed."

Wood also learned that the White Sox catchers were not afraid to call for the knuckler. J. C. Martin, Duane Josephson, and Jerry McNerty may not have enjoyed trying to follow the flight path of the butterfly, but they had more experience than most in doing so after catching Wilhelm and Fisher for so long.

"No matter how great your knuckler is, it won't do you a bit of good if the catcher doesn't call for it," Wood said, "and the main reason he doesn't call for it is that he can't catch it."

Martin knew he was in for combat when summoned to catch the knuckleball guys, but unlike other catchers, he developed an admiration for them. He, as much as anyone, understood that they were throwing the knuckler because they *had* to do it. Without the pitch they could not have survived in the majors. While the majority of pitchers relied on velocity, this trio relied on trickery. The fact that Martin could actually catch a knuckler better than most at his position, he believes, extended his career.

"It kept me in the big leagues," Martin said. "It made me appreciate [the three knuckleball pitchers] because they didn't have that blinding speed. Those guys I caught relied on nothing but their knuckleball. I have to admire those guys. Those guys were great pitchers. Wilbur, he could go out there and pitch all day long."

After starting in 8 of his 51 appearances in '67, he became the closer for the White Sox in '68. That was his true breakthrough year, when he appeared in a Major League-leading 88 games. That year Wilhelm pitched in 72 games with a 1.73 earned run average and a 4-4 record. Wood finished 13–12 with a 1.87 ERA and 13 saves. Wood won the 1968 award as the best relief pitcher in the American League, as granted by *The Sporting News.*

"That year they were about half the pitching staff," Martin said.

In fact, Wood was pitching in so many games that sportswriters were clustering around his locker all the time asking if he was tired. After appearing in his 78th game of the season, with three weeks to go, Wood answered the question again. "My arm doesn't feel a bit tired," he said.

Wood had made a quantum leap in performance and it was being noticed by everyone around baseball. "He is an amazing pitcher," said White Sox manager Stanky.

What Wood had shown the White Sox in AAA before they traded for him was his ability to throw strikes. Coming out of the bullpen with men on base, he couldn't afford to be wild. Wilhelm would have been the closer in '68, Wood said, but his arm was bothering him a bit. Bob Locker was a third member of the bullpen triumvirate, appearing in 70 games with a 2.29 ERA.

"We had some pretty good pitching out there," Wood said. "They went after me as a middle man, but the transition to closer was easy for me when I did it. There was nothing to it once I had had some success with the knuckleball."

Wood was obviously in the right place at the right time, with a team that understood the knuckleball better than others, and with a mentor who was an all-time great. He didn't underestimate the value of those catchers, either, contributing to keeping those errant knucklers alive.

"These guys had all caught the knuckleball," Wood said. "They were experienced. They had seen it all. I got in my fair share of games. I was fortunate I ended up with the White Sox."

At that point, after being sent to the minors five times by big-league teams, Wood's ambitions were modest. His first goal, he said, was to play five years in the majors. Then he half-jokingly, half-seriously, said maybe he could stay in the majors as long as Wilhelm; in other words, playing well into his forties. Besides Wilhelm, Wood was grateful to White Sox pitching coach Marv Grissom. Grissom may not have been a knuckleball specialist, but he did coax Wood into altering his motion.

"I used a full windup at the start of last season," Wood said of 1967. "Then, about mid-season, I went to a half-windup. In spring training this year, Grissom talked me into not using any windup at all."

It took some time for Wood to make the transition from a failed Red Sox to a star White Sox. The gap in-between was not so terribly long—a couple of seasons—but the journey from the high-hopes high schooler to a Major League regular actually took eight years.

From the time Wood was signed by Boston when he was barely old enough to shave to the time Wood emerged as invaluable to the White Sox, he was pushing thirty. He was hopeful, but given the way his big-league adventure had played out he couldn't tell that his finest years with his grandest accomplishments lay ahead. Of course, it was all attributable to the knuckleball.

12

PHIL NIEKRO: ANOTHER KNUCKLEBALL METHUSELAH

MOST OF THE known knuckleball world should probably thank Phil Niekro for his assistance. Not *the* Phil Niekro, the Hall of Fame pitcher whom everyone knows, but his father, Phil. Following the chain of command and the passing on of wisdom from one generation of baseball player to the next, everyone whom "Dr. Phil" helped when he was starring for the Braves and since he retired, owes a debt of gratitude to the man who taught him how to throw a knuckler.

Growing up in Ohio of Polish heritage, Phil Niekro was the son of a coal miner who loved baseball and showed his oldest son (and also younger son, Joe) how to toss a knuckleball. Philip Niekro, the older pitcher, was a hotshot thrower when he was young, possessed of a wicked fastball that left batters gaping at his speed as they walked back to the dugout.

"No one ever called me Junior," Phil Niekro said. "We had different middle names."

Phil Niekro, the Major League pitcher, was born in Blaine, Ohio, on April 1, 1939, and has become so identified with the knuckleball that his nickname is "Knucksie." Father Philip played semi-pro ball and represented a coal mining team for many years called Lorain Coal and Dock. There were stories written about his prowess, and young Phil read how his dad struck out 16 or more guys in a game on occasion (in fact, Phil the elder struck out 17 men in his first game). Dad also played first base when it was not his turn on the mound.

However, then Philip hurt his arm at age eighteen and lost his speed. Phil believes the injury occurred on a cold spring day. Dad adapted, discovering the rudiments of throwing the knuckler from another coal miner named Nick McCay, who had played minor-league ball and picked it up along the way.

"I was too young to see him pitch when he had his fastball," Niekro said of his father. As a seventy-five-year-old, the retired pitcher who lived close by thought back to his beginnings as a knuckleballer while sitting in a quiet spot inside the ballpark of the Atlanta Braves' AAA farm team in suburban Atlanta.

"But by the time we were living in Lansing, Ohio, where I grew up, and I was old enough to play catch with him, he had the knuckleball. One day he threw me one and he kind of giggled when he did it. I said, 'What's that?' He showed me how to hold it and we just started throwing it. I just got hooked into it. It was something we did every day in the backyard, just throwing knuckleballs to each other. I didn't really know what it was."

In a book about his life, Phil Niekro said that his father had a formidable reputation in the area going back to his youth. "Folks used to come from miles around to see him play and he was always the highlight of the show," Niekro wrote in

Knuckleballs. "Old-timers in the area still say that my dad was the finest pitcher they'd ever seen, even after seeing the likes of my brother Joe and me, and after watching a slew of big-league games in Pittsburgh, which is only about 70 miles to the north."

Philip was featured in a magazine story about people who worked in the coal mining industry, and the articles explored how enthusiastic the Niekro clan was about baseball. Dad used to work a long shift, but his sons were waiting for him to get home so they could play catch—Phil's first glove was a Dizzy Dean model.

"The boys got all their baseball from their dad," said mother Ivy Niekro. "Philip would get off that streetcar and all you could see were eyes and teeth . . . that's how dirty he used to get. But he never complained. He played baseball with the boys every evening while they were growing. Joe was awfully small then and Phil was only six or seven."

Phil turned six in 1945 and Joe was not born until November of '44. When he was a tot, Phil called his brother Joe, "Jo-Jo." He said his mother and sister Phyllis did the dishes while the boys played catch.

It is interesting to realize that even then when Philip was a pitcher that there was a certain amount of knuckleball prejudice against the pitch that practically nobody understood.

"Years ago," Philip Niekro said in 1980, "you weren't allowed to throw the knuckleball. They said it was hard on the arm. Actually, it's the easiest pitch on the arm. You don't have to whip it, you just throw it natural . . . just let it roll off your knuckles."

Sports of all kinds—not just baseball—were big in the Niekro brothers' neighborhood when he was a kid. One of Phil's closest friends and neighbors was John Havlicek, who became a Naismith Basketball Hall of Fame star for the Boston Celtics.

"John and I would choose up sides in our hometown for pick-up games," Niekro said. "We'd take a bat like kids do to choose teams. I didn't play grade-school ball or Little League. I was a year too old when it came to my hometown. I could get guys out with the knuckleball even then. I went out for the high school team when I was a freshman and I pitched four years with a knuckleball. My younger brother Joe played Little League. Joe fooled around in the backyard with the knuckler, too, when he was growing up. I think it was kind of a family tradition. I just kept throwing the knuckler. Nobody told me I couldn't do it."

Niekro competed for Bridgeport High School in Ohio and was signed by the Milwaukee Braves as a free agent in 1958. That was before the Major League draft took effect. Philip Niekro handled the negotiations at the house for his son and he was adamant that he get a decent amount of money out of the deal—decent being of quite a different standard in the 1950s.

"Dad drove a hard bargain," Phil Niekro said. "He wouldn't let me sign without a bonus, and the Braves finally agreed to give me $500. 'Takes me a month in the mine to earn that kind of money,' Dad said to me later with a satisfied smile. 'Baseball is more than just fun, son. Remember, you want to earn your dollar. You got to work for it.'"

While Niekro did have to add some polish to his game, he also began running into both knuckleball prejudice and knuckleball encouragement as a young pitcher. Teams do not scout knuckleball pitchers. They look for strong arms that deliver the ball with velocity, and athletic players who will blossom and only get better. A knuckleball confuses scouts. They can't project and they feel sheepish recommending a player who might be throwing 65 mph. Of course, in the late '50s and early '60s, pitch speed measurement was in its infancy.

During his second year in the minors, Niekro was playing for the Jacksonville Braves of the Class A South Atlantic (or Sally League), and his manager was Red Murff. Murff had the rare distinction of becoming a thirty-six-year-old rookie just a few seasons earlier and later signed Nolan Ryan for the New York Mets. In 1960, he was the Jacksonville boss and Niekro looks back at his association with Murff as a turning point of his career.

"He came up to me and said, 'Niekro, you know if you get that knuckleball over the plate, you can pitch in the big leagues.' No one had ever told me that before. I had so much respect for him that what he said really took hold. I thought, 'Well, if he believes it, then maybe it's true.' And before that year was over I was moved up to Louisville, which was the AAA team of the Braves."

It was not as if Niekro was riding a rocket ship to the majors, however. The knuckleball that had been pinpointed by one savvy baseball man as his ticket was viewed with suspicion by others. Niekro bounced between minor-league stops for a few years, spent some time in the service, and, finally, in 1964, made his Major League debut. He was twenty-five by then and his Major League season amounted to just two appearances. In 1965, Niekro went 2–3 with a 2.89 earned run average in 41 games.

The Braves moved to Atlanta for the 1966 season, and Niekro began building his long-time connection to the community when he compiled a 4–3 record. His ERA spiked to 4.11, however, and he was shocked to be told he was headed to AAA Richmond where he spent half the season.

"I was told that they were going to send me to Richmond because they didn't have a man to catch my knuckleball," Niekro said. "I thought that was not my problem. I told them to go find somebody who could catch it. You know, coming up through the minor leagues I never thought about the catcher. I was thinking, *I'm just trying to make the majors.* The better I got I didn't worry about it too much. I said, 'There's got to be a catcher someplace who can catch the knuckler.'"

In 1966, the Braves' primary catcher was Joe Torre, who was then a four-time All-Star (and would make five more All-Star teams), smacking 36 home runs, driving in 101 runs, and batting .315 in 148 games. His back-up was Gene Oliver, who had been known for his hitting, but batted just .194 that season. Ed Sadowski, the team's third catcher, only got into three games.

For the 1967 season, though, the Braves swapped Oliver to the Philadelphia Phillies for Bob Uecker. Uecker, although he has made a comedy career out of saying how he never could hit, could field the catching position better than Oliver, and most importantly at this point, could handle a knuckleball. (During his six seasons in the league, Uecker had a career batting average of .200.)

"When Paul Richards came over from Baltimore to become general manager of the Braves, he traded Gene Oliver just to have Uecker come over and catch the knuckleball," Niekro said. "I don't think they cared if Uecker only hit .140."

Which was a good thing, because that's pretty much what he did—Uecker really *did* hit .146 that year during his last season in the big leagues. And Niekro flourished with Uecker's help.

While his won-loss record was just 11–9, Niekro led all of baseball with a spectacular 1.87 earned run average.

"Uecker was going to call the knuckleball in situations where the other guys weren't," Niekro said. "They were worried about the start of an inning in a close game or with a man on third. They wouldn't call it. So Bob came over and he made the adjustment. He really turned me around. He's the first catcher who really called the knuckleball in situations where other catchers wouldn't. His attitude was, 'Balls can't get by me.' He felt we might lose some games because the knuckleball got past him, but we would win more than we lost. I led the league in ERA. He led the league in passed balls. I think catchers in the Braves' organization began thinking if they could catch Niekro's knuckleball they might get to the big leagues."

Among those who followed Uecker—who was out of the majors after 1967 and beginning his brilliant broadcasting career—were Bob Didier, Paul Casanova, and Bruce Benedict. It wasn't exactly as if Niekro had a personal catcher who only played when he pitched, but those guys could cope with the knuckleball better than some others.

Benedict, who spent twelve years in the majors, from 1978 to 1983 catching Phil Niekro knuckleballs, developed a good sense of humor about his years on the run chasing the pitches that got away.

"I was a very young player. There are two theories about catching the knuckleball and none of them work." Sometimes, Benedict said, he might try to catch a knuckler with a different approach, but that didn't always work, either. "I'd go to catch it with one hand and have it hit me on the other hand."

The 1967 season established Niekro as a regular in the Braves' rotation. Unfortunately for him, this was before the Braves became a National League dynasty, when they began clicking off division titles with the regularity of the school bell ringing each day. Instead, the Braves were a mediocre franchise and any time a winning record was achieved it was noteworthy. Atlanta had trouble stocking the lineup with enough key players even as Niekro blossomed into one of the reliables. After 1967, he won 14, 23, 12, 15, 16, 13, 20, and 15 games in consecutive seasons, taking him up through 1975 when he turned thirty-six, an advanced age for a starting pitcher. Twice he was named to the National League All-Star team (1969 and 1975). The 1969 season may have been Niekro's finest, with a 23–13 mark and a 2.56 earned run average.

In 1971, it became public knowledge that, in his spare time, Niekro dabbled as a poet. He sometimes wrote poems during airplane flights on Braves road trips.

"I started fooling around with it a few years ago just to kill time, but I've found it's a helluva way to express yourself. Sometimes you just can't think of the right things to say until you get by yourself and sit down and write. I got started writing a couple of lines on Christmas cards to my family or friends. I wrote a few things people said they liked, so I just kept doing it. Only recently I started saving everything I write."

It was not difficult to imagine baseball teammates teasing Niekro about being the second coming of Carl Sandburg instead of the second coming of Hoyt Wilhelm, since everything that happens to an individual is fair game in a locker room.

The *Atlanta Journal*, the old afternoon Atlanta paper, ran one of Niekro's poems. He said his writing focused mostly on his wife and family, and even his hometown. Naturally, a sports-writer wanted to know if he wrote a poem about the knuckle-ball. Niekro said no, he hadn't tackled that topic. It was probably just as well. It might have proven as elusive to describe in poetic language as it did in post-game interviews.

One of the great moments of Niekro's career, a milestone for any big-league pitcher, occurred on August 5, 1973, when he tossed a no-hitter to beat the San Diego Padres, 9–0, in Atlanta.

On that day, Niekro, who was thirty-four at the time, walked three and struck out four. San Diego's Dave Roberts was also safe on an error. Niekro had the lead from the first inning on, and a big lead by the sixth. The no-hitter was the first for the Braves since they had moved to town from Milwaukee. Also, at the time Niekro's father was suffering with health problems and his oldest son felt it was likely to cheer up his dad.

The win "came at the best time in my life," Niekro said of his father being hospitalized in Ohio with blood clots in his lungs. "I didn't think about that during the game, but when the game was over, I thought about how this might lift his spirits."

Niekro said he never looked up at the scoreboard after the third inning, but his progress was charted by an increasingly quiet dugout. Following tradition and superstition, teammates ignored Niekro, not even speaking to him as the innings sped by with San Diego hitless.

"I'd look at someone and they would look right through me," Niekro said. "All there was were blank stares. Then when I was going out to the mound I saw my wife [Nancy] in the stands. She looked the same way, just a blank stare."

Niekro's catcher on the day of the no-hitter was Paul Casanova, who happened to hit an inside-the-park homer that was overshadowed by his pitcher's gem. Not that Casanova minded all too much. He was more excited about calling the game and catching the no-hitter than by his unusual offensive feat.

"My biggest problem was just catching it," Casanova said of the 95 percent knuckleballs Niekro threw. "It's tough. I caught him one inning in St. Louis last year and didn't catch many. I'm just as excited as Niekro. It's my first, too. A lot depends on catching. A lot of the time the catcher is the only friend the pitcher has out there. It was beautiful, just beautiful."

* * *

Over the years Niekro became one of the most renowned knuckleball throwers, as well as a student of the history of the pitch. Most of what he read credited Ed Cicotte as the inventor, and he was aware of certain other knuckleball historical facts.

"I don't remember much about Eddie Cicotte other than that he was one of the original guys," Niekro said.

But in his mind, the player who most popularized and raised awareness of the knuckleball was Hoyt Wilhelm.

"Wilhelm, to me, was the best," said Niekro, who is often lumped together with Wilhelm as one of the two best all-time knuckleballers. "Hoyt Wilhelm is really kind of where most people in baseball relate to the start of the knuckleball. I'm sure there were guys before that, but Gene Bearden had just one year, (Jesse) Haines was good. There were some guys. But to me Wilhelm is the start of the knuckleball."

By 1975, Niekro had two 20-win seasons on his resume—his 20 victories in 1974 led the National League. He also recorded a 2.38 ERA that year while pitching 302 1/3 innings. By then he was an institution in the city of Atlanta, generous with his time for community causes, and he was one of the cornerstone figures of the franchise in addition to sluggers Hank Aaron, Davey Johnson, and Dusty Baker.

Leading up to the 1975 season, the Braves signed Niekro to a $100,000 contract. He was the first Braves pitcher to earn that much. It was a far cry from that $500 bonus his dad dickered for with the Braves so many years earlier. Phil Niekro had made a living in the game.

13

JOE NIEKRO: LITTLE BROTHER
MAKES GOOD

JOE NIEKRO HAD the same genes and upbringing as his older brother, Phil. He came out of the same family that knew and understood the knuckleball. So it figured that sooner or later Joe would turn to the knuckler—which he did—and that sooner or later the knuckler would become his primary weapon—which it did.

He also told stories about how his father was a fastball blazer before an arm injury turned him to the knuckleball, and how he and Phil were anything but.

"He was big and strong," Joe said of his dad. "If they had radar guns in those days, they say he threw it 100 miles an hour. Phil and I can't bring it 100 combined."

Joseph Franklin Niekro was born in 1944 in Martins Ferry, Ohio, and grew up to stand six foot one and weigh 185 pounds. He was a right-handed thrower and like brother Phil attended Bridgeport High. Unlike Phil, by the time Joe Niekro became available, he was grabbed in the amateur baseball draft, at the time a new way of distributing talent amongst the big-league clubs. Joe was drafted by the Chicago Cubs in the third round.

However, one thing that Joe Niekro did differently between Bridgeport and the majors was attend West Liberty College in West Virginia, gaining experience as a college pitcher instead of in the low minors.

It takes a good memory to recall Niekro's stay with the Cubs, but he did some good work for the team in 1967, his rookie year, going 10–7 with a 3.34 earned run average. The next year, Joe finished 14–10, but things went sour in his third season with the Cubs and he was never again a factor for them.

After his good start in the bigs, Joe Niekro began to struggle. In 1969 he finished 8–18, combining his final throwing for the Cubs with his efforts for a new team, the San Diego Padres. He moved on to the Detroit Tigers and went 12–13 in 1970. But over the next seven years, with the Tigers, Atlanta Braves (overlapping with Phil), and joining the Houston Astros, never again did Joe Niekro win that many games in a season. He was a fastball and slider pitcher, and those tools were not getting the job done for him in any way beyond allowing him to retain a job in the majors.

When Joe spent two seasons in Atlanta, his brother Phil helped get him reacquainted with the knuckler. Yet it was not until 1977 that Joe regained the touch that he once had and began winning more games than ever. The Astros were the beneficiaries when Joe went 13–8 in 1977, and then followed up that season with marks of 14–14, 21–11 (the win total led the National League), and 20–12. Niekro was a 1979 All-Star and in true knuckleball fashion he kept right on winning for the

Astros through his late thirties and into the start of his forties. In his first nine seasons to age thirty, Niekro was a better pitcher the older he got—after turning thirty—than he was as a younger man. His 20-victory seasons both were recorded when he was older and he pitched in the majors until he was forty-three.

* * *

Once again it was the knuckleball to the rescue. Joe, like Phil, always had a knuckleball in his background, but conventional pitches carried him through high school, college, and his first years in the majors. The day came, though, when he needed another pitch to survive, and given his father's and brother's background with the knuckler, it was natural that he chose the old standby. He began working it into his repertoire in 1972 and relied on it more and more as time went by.

"I guess most people have thought of me as a knuckleball pitcher all along," Niekro said in 1976, "but I really didn't start throwing it until a few years ago."

Niekro said he spent his Cubs years throwing a fastball, curve, and slider, and only toyed with a knuckler on the sidelines, not in games. Joe Niekro was tempted to add his knuckler into the mix, but when he brought the idea up to manager Leo Durocher, the suggestion was not greeted with a smile.

"He told me that if I wanted to work on a knuckleball he'd be glad to send me back to the minors, but he didn't want me messing around on his team. I never brought up the subject again."

Niekro tried out his knuckler in winter league ball in Puerto Rico and it was met with more enthusiasm. The ball showed so much movement that Niekro shifted from making the knuckler solely a practice pitch to a sometimes-game pitch. It took a few years to perfect the knuckler and to trust it, but by the end of the 1976 season, Joe knew that whatever time he had left in the majors from age thirty-one on, it was going to be through the assistance of the knuckler.

A sportswriter asked how long he could pitch and Niekro responded in knuckleball-thrower fashion. "Look at my brother," he said of Phil, six years older. "He's thirty-seven and going strong. I can get my knuckleball over the plate most of the time and it's just not the kind of pitch that wears you down."

Following his good start with the Cubs, Joe Niekro endured many trying times. Not only did he move between five Major League teams, but four times those teams dropped him to the minors. That kind of typical up-and-down, knuckleball-hurler experience convinced him to adopt devotion to the pitch and give it a full-time chance.

"At one point when the Tigers sent me down," Niekro said, "I thought about quitting. I didn't even want to get out of bed." His wife kept his spirits up and preached repeatedly that he would be back in the majors. Hard to believe, but when he joined AAA Toledo in the Tigers' chain he immediately pitched a perfect game.

After the 13–8 production of 1977, the Astros were believers. Joe signed a multi-year contract carrying him through the 1981 season. Joe's success, following on the heels of Phil's, brought additional attention to Philip, back home in Ohio. Reached on Father's Day of 1979, the elder Niekro said, "I'm proud of them and happy they don't have to work for a living." That sentence offered perspective between life as a coal miner and life as a ball player. "But a lot of times I wish they weren't pitchers. It's too hard on my nerves."

Philip noted that the original family name in Poland was Niekra. No matter, as the Niekro brothers were proud of their heritage and Phil said he knew just about every bar in the country where he could hear polka music when he traveled as a player.

Joe even occasionally told Polish jokes. During a period of time when he was being shuffled between long relief and short relief, he said, "The one thing I never wanted to be was a utility Pole."

Joe Niekro did not completely forsake his other pitches in favor of the knuckleball, but when the knuckler was cooking he didn't need anything else either. Once, in an exhibition game, he struck out the first five batters he faced on the Twins, but catcher Cliff Johnson missed all five, recording five passed balls.

"It was the greatest knuckleball I've ever had in my life," Niekro said, "and I get knocked out on strikeouts."

But as time went on more and more of those super knuckleballs were thrown in games that counted and his teammates noticed, almost feeling sorry for opposing batters, but at the least thankful that they didn't have to bat against Joe Niekro's knuckler.

"He struck out Bob Boone [of the Phillies] on one knuckleball that even God couldn't have hit," said then-Astros infielder Art Howe.

Despite not surrendering full use of his other pitches, Niekro definitely considered himself a member of the knuckleballers' fraternity.

"I wouldn't be here today if it weren't for me developing the knuckleball," he said in 1979. "I've started soaking my arm in ice after some games. I've seen all the other hard throwers do it." The latter comment was another joke.

Phil Niekro admitted that his brother approached the knuckler a little bit differently, employing those other pitches more than he ever used any of them.

"That's the difference between Joe and me," Phil said. "He beats our team [the Braves] every time he faces us and the reason is that he keeps our batters guessing constantly as to whether he's going to throw the knuckleball, slider, or fastball. I may be a good pitcher, but Joe is a great pitcher. And he's a great man."

With the Astros, too, Joe Niekro had a catcher in Alan Ashby, who could handle the knuckler, although Ashby teased, "If I can catch it, it's not at its best."

As the 1979 season wound down, the close Niekro brothers found themselves in an unusual position. The Astros needed a win to remain in pennant contention and they were playing Phil Niekro's Braves. The opposing pitcher: Joe Niekro. Joe had already won 20 games, and if Phil gained the victory, he would have 20 wins too. That would make them the first brothers in National League history to reach the 20-victory mark in the same season. Phil got the win, the brothers got the milestone, but the loss was costly to the Astros.

Phil earned the win, but he wasn't happy afterwards. He didn't enjoy the distinction being gained at the expense of his brother's team.

"That's one of the few times I really didn't want to go out and pitch in that situation where a team was trying to stay in the race," Phil said. "I'm not proud of what I've done."

Joe won 21 games that season and 20 the next. He also posted seasons of 17, 15, and 16 for the Astros into the mid-80s. By the time the Niekros passed their fortieth birthdays, even their teams began wondering about their futures.

In 1985, when he was forty-five, Phil pitched for the New York Yankees and won 16 games. Joe, turning forty, joined him there for a short while. In 1987, Joe moved on to the Minnesota Twins. He did not see the trade coming and thought he would have had a better chance to make it to a World Series for the first time by staying with the Yankees.

For the sake of a book, the brothers sent letters back and forth to one another throughout the 1987 season. The book was titled, *The Niekro Files*. Phil Niekro turned forty-eight on April 1, around opening day and Joe sent him a "geezer" present of a tricycle with a wire basket and highlighted by an orange warning flag to let motorists know he was coming.

"I can just see you riding that trike, keeping up with the other pitchers who have to run," Joe said.

After a tough early season start, Yanks boss George Steinbrenner brought in Hoyt Wilhelm to work with Joe Niekro on his knuckler. Yes, Dr. Wilhelm made house calls, too.

"He's really helped me, Knucks," Joe said in his letter to his brother. "He's got me throwing my knuckleball higher in the strike zone. I was throwing them too low. I call Hoyt my guru, my roommate in the clubhouse." Joe said his education should have been complete after learning the pitch from his father and picking up pointers from Phil and Wilhelm.

"Working with Hoyt Wilhelm has helped. I had my doubts when he first told me to throw the knuckleball higher in the strike zone. As you know, you don't want to put anything up in the hitter's eyes."

During that season the Niekro brothers were chasing a somewhat unknown, but still notable record—most victories by a team of brothers. The record holders were Gaylord and Jim

Perry with 529 wins, and the Niekro brothers had the mark within sight by June 1.

At the time Phil was pitching for the Cleveland Indians and on that date he was the winning pitcher in a 9–6 decision over the Detroit Tigers. The Niekro brothers had 530 wins in the bank.

"We got it, we did it, it's over," Phil wrote to Joe after the game. "God bless, America, let's polka. We, the Niekros, Phil and Joe, are the winningest brothers in baseball history. God, I can't tell you how proud I am to be able to say that. I want this record to belong to Bridgeport High School, the Sportsman's Club, Lansing Grade School, St. Joseph's Schools, all the coaches we played for, all our relatives, and the little town of Lansing. Ninety-nine percent of the people in Ohio don't know where Lansing is, and two brothers, sons of a coal miner and his loving wife, won 530 games in the big leagues. What makes 530 special for me, though, is doing it with a brother like you, Joe. I love you Joe, go get 531."

Phil had been rooting for his brother to get the record-breaker because he already had 300 wins. Joe got the record-tying win instead. Gaylord Perry won 314 games. Jim Perry won 215 games. The Niekro brothers did keep winning for a little while. Phil concluded his career with 318 victories; Joe ended up with 221 wins. Their combined 539 wins remains the Major League wins record for brothers. It is unlikely to be threatened any time soon.

When Joe reported to the Twins, one of the first things he learned was that catcher Tim Laudner had never caught a knuckleballer. Kent Hrbek, one of the team's top players and the clubhouse clown, put a large wastebasket in front of Laudner's locker with a note reading, "Good luck."

Reluctant to leave New York, Joe Niekro received an enthusiastic, standing-ovation welcome from Minnesota fans when he began warming up for his first Twins start.

"It made me feel so warm inside I was afraid I might burn a hole through my T-shirt," he said.

Joe almost burned a hole through his cap a little later in the season, this time from embarrassment and irritation. An umpire caught him with an emery board and sandpaper in his uniform pockets and the American League suspended him for ten days. Possession of such a utensil is pretty much prima facie evidence of scuffing the ball. Niekro said he always carried the stuff because he might have to file a nail during a game and as a knuckleball pitcher that can be critical to his success. Niekro had never before been suspected of scuffing baseballs to make them squirm. Usually, the knuckler did that on its own.

"I feel like I ought to be wearing black-and-white convict stripes—sounds like my old Yankee uniform," Joe informed Phil when his suspension commenced. Joe said he had been carrying the same things around in his uniform for sixteen years and no one ever told him it was wrong to do so. He referred to the emery board as "the lethal emery board." "Overall, it's been a nightmare."

Niekro thought he might get an endorsement contract for emery boards, but that did not pan out. One thing about the Niekros is that they always had a good sense of humor. During the suspension, Joe appeared on *Late Night With David Letterman*, wearing a carpenter's apron loaded down with Vaseline, emery boards, a nail file and toenail clippers, and carrying a power sander.

At one point later in his career, Joe wore a T-shirt apparently for the benefit of sportswriters that read "I'm Joe, Not Phil."

It should be noted that Phil also had a T-shirt that read, "I'm Phil, Not Joe." Phil Niekro said people would come up to him and say, "Hey, Joe, how are you doing?" And he would go, "I'm Phil." They did have a family resemblance, but that was all. "Not that we're twins or look alike," Phil said. Maybe they were just knuckleball twins.

The trade to the Twins that Joe originally wasn't keen on enabled him to play for a pennant winner and World Series champion in 1987. Niekro pitched two innings in Game 4. Phil flew in to be present and witnessed Joe's effort. It took more than twenty years of big-league pitching but Joe Niekro made an appearance in a World Series and got to drink champagne after his team won the title in seven games.

"That was one of the highlights of my twenty-two years in the Major Leagues," Niekro said. "I was thrilled to finally get the chance. I had almost resigned myself to the fact that I might never get into a World Series. I treasure the memory."

When the Twins put out a series of bobblehead dolls of the 1987 champion players, Joe Niekro's had a nail file in the back pocket.

Joe Niekro retired from active duty following his 1988 season with the Twins. He went 1–1 as a forty-three-year-old and his lifetime record was 221–204 with a 3.59 earned run average. The Niekros had been teammates for a short while in their long careers, but in retirement Phil was asked to manage the Colorado Silver Bullets woman's professional baseball team in the 1990s, and Joe joined him for a couple of years as the pitching coach.

Unfortunately, Joe Niekro suffered an abrupt and tragic end to his life. Seemingly healthy, he died suddenly of a brain aneurism at age sixty-one in Tampa, Florida, in 2006. It was a complete shock to Phil. He was walking on a beach at Amelia Island, Georgia, with a grandson.

"The phone rings and I pick it up and I can't hear him clearly, but it's Lance (Joe's son)," Phil said. "I could hear, 'Dad, helicopter, Joe, Tampa.' That's all. By the time I got up to the cottage he called again and said, 'Dad's on a helicopter on his way to Tampa Hospital.' My wife and I drove there and by the time I got there he was on life support. I stayed there with him and the doctors said, 'He had an aneurism. He just blew it all out. You will have to tell us when you want to pull life support."

The devastating news took a while to digest, but the family made the decision and Joe Niekro's funeral was held a few days later. Joe's daughter Natalie started The Joe Niekro Foundation, which donates money to aneurism research and treatment.

Phil had been so close to his brother that the events were difficult to process.

"I tell people that as close to Joe as I was, when I saw him, whether it was the next day or two months, the first three words out of his mouth were, 'I love you,'" Phil Niekro said. "And those are the first three that came out of my mouth. When we saw each other the last three words were 'I love you.' I also tell people that when I won my 300th game I was given a gold belt buckle with diamonds; it's got 300 of them, which is a hell of a gift, but the best gift that my brother Joe left me with is those three words, 'I love you.'

"Once I talked to group in Cooperstown and I told them that. Afterwards a man came up to me and he started crying.

I told him I was sorry, I didn't mean to offend him. He said, 'No, no. I lost my wife about five weeks ago and I didn't tell her I loved her.' And we both cried then. I learned that if you go away someplace, even two or three days to go fishing, there are no guarantees. Joe was as healthy as anybody. I say I can't leave the house without telling my wife or my boys that I love them."

14

WILBUR WOOD EMERGES

DURING A DISCUSSION about his career and Chicago White Sox history in the mid-2000s, Wilbur Wood said if it wasn't for the knee problem that ended his big-league career he could suit up and throw his knuckleball right then. Wood was in his mid-sixties at the time.

The comment was worth a chuckle, but that's the difference between knuckleball pitchers and other pitchers. Usually, the knuckleball pitchers have other body parts fade away that aren't their arms. Their chronological ages are one thing, but their throwing arms' ages are something else. A fastball pitcher with longevity might not even be able to comb his hair when he becomes a senior citizen. A knuckleball pitcher might be looking for a tennis partner.

Wilbur Wood started out as a promising fastball pitcher from Massachusetts, just down the street a few miles from Fenway Park. The Boston Red Sox jumped at the chance and signed him, but he did not blossom into an excellent pitcher until he joined the Chicago White Sox.

Wood, the successor to knuckleball specialists Hoyt Wilhelm and Eddie Fisher with the White Sox, posted some of the most amazing statistics from the mound since the early days of the live ball era. For younger baseball fans raised in the oh-so-conservative 2000s, when pitchers hardly ever throw complete games and relievers rule, some of Wood's numbers border on fiction, even fantasy.

Even some older fans whose memories have faded have difficulty comprehending some of the things the southpaw accomplished as a White Sox starter after making the switch from the bullpen. And all of it was possible because Wood's key pitch was the knuckler and didn't put any strain on his arm.

Between 1971 and 1975, Wood started 42, 49, 48, 42, and 43 games, the last four totals leading Major League baseball. During those seasons, he won 22, 24, 24, 20, and 16 games. These days the league leader may or may not win 20 in a season. Wood's 24-win seasons led the AL both years (and all of baseball in '73).

Now comes the fun part. In 1971, Wood threw 334 innings. A typical work load for the league-leader now would be 250 innings or less. But that was a slow year for Wood. In 1972, he threw 376 2/3 innings, the most in the majors since Walter Johnson in the 1920s (although Mickey Lolich had a cuckoo year in 1971 when he threw 376 innings). In 1973, Wood threw 359 1/3 innings. Both in 1972 and 1973 he led the league in innings pitched. In 1974 he threw 320 1/3 innings and 291 1/3 in 1975.

A three-time All-Star during this career, Wood was a throwback to the days of the early twentieth century, when pitchers pitched often, finished what they started, and piled up innings as if collecting wood for the winter. Oh yeah, and in 1973, his record was 24–20. By the standards, patterns, and methods applied to modern-day pitching, it is unlikely that very many of those numbers Wood recorded will ever be seen again in the baseball world.

Wood's knuckleball was humming in those days; or better yet, floating with abandon. His turning point was, as it was for so many in the knuckleball fraternity, when Wood devoted his game to the sink-or-swim philosophy with the tricky pitch. When the Pirates let him go it was a hard message to swallow and it took a pep talk from Wood's wife telling him he should try the knuckler for a year to see if he could still make it in baseball.

Before Wood became a full-time White Sox starter in 1971—averaging two starts a week—he led the American League in appearances for three straight seasons, with 88 (led all of baseball), 76, and 77 games, respectively. During the 1971 season he started at least eight times on two days' rest.

"Everybody thinks I should be more tired, but I'm not," Wood said. "I feel no difference, physically or mentally, between two and three days' rest. Sometimes I don't know myself how much rest I've had."

In today's game, everyone counts how much rest a starter gets, and it is expected that the pitcher will not pitch more than every fifth day. Wood threw the knuckler about 85 percent of the time by 1971. His pitching coach, the otherwise knowledgeable Johnny Sain, who admitted not knowing much about knuckler behavior, did insist, however, that pitching with just two days' rest should make a difference even for a knuckleballer.

"It's not all that easy to pitch with two days' rest," Sain said. "There's a physical and mental strain. But Wilbur is ideal because he keeps a cool head. He has an excellent emotional level. He acts the same whether he wins or loses."

Manager Chuck Tanner thought that Wood might be able to pitch often enough for him to win 35 games, but that never occurred. Wood was just grateful that Tanner made him a starter.

"I always knew I could do it. But nobody would listen."

Another argument that Wood found difficult to win was his belief that his arm could handle the task of pitching both ends of a doubleheader. He finally reached the point of convincing Tanner to give it a try—with some conditions. In July of that season in 1973, Wood took his regular turn on the mound for the first game of a doubleheader against the New York Yankees. Tanner told him that if he won the first game he could start the second . . . only the Yankees jumped on Wood that day, scoring six runs early. He did not give up on the notion, however. The feat had been accomplished before, the most recent time being August 28, 1926, when Cleveland's Emil "Dutch" Levsen won both games of the doubleheader over Boston, 6–1 and 9–1. Levsen had a brief career and the highlight was his throwing those 18 innings that day. No evidence suggests he was a knuckleball pitcher. Wood had previously won both ends of a doubleheader, but only in relief, something that had been achieved many times before.

Fascination with how Wood was able to pile up such crazy stats grew during the 1971 season. It was that year one of his personal habits was revealed in *The Sporting News*. "The secret is out on Wilbur Wood," a blurb read. "The White Sox's knuckleball artist bites his fingernails—except the two he uses to throw his specialty. 'I need those two to get a proper grip,'" Wood said.

One writer jokingly suggested Wood was looking for "new sweatshops to conquer," and that his three-day rest between starts was virtually a vacation for him. Chuck Tanner was forever being lobbied by Wood for more work.

"He asked me if I'd let him pitch against Kansas City with one day's rest," Tanner said. "I said I'd see. When the time came, I decided against it. He said, 'But you promised.' I said I didn't promise. I said I'd think about it. He was very disappointed. With his easy motion, there's not much strain."

Still, Tanner remained hesitant to commit sending Wood to the mound twice in a day for a full dose of nine innings, even if he sounded like a believer.

"Heck, I just don't mean Wilbur can pitch both games," Tanner said. "I mean, he can win 'em, too."

Wood won 22 games in 1971 with a 1.91 ERA and, in 1972, his huge year, he won 24 for the first time, throwing those 376 2/3 innings with 49 starts and a 2.51 ERA.

"I aim for the heart of the plate and hope for the best," is what Wood said about his knuckler. He also graciously thanked Hoyt Wilhelm just about every time he did an interview with a sportswriter for making him the All-Star he now was.

"I never can thank him enough," Wood said of the influence of Hoyt Wilhelm and his advice when Wood first joined the Sox.

Wood was certain, though, that it was important he had developed the rudiments of throwing the knuckler when he was a kid and said he had seen many desperate pitchers switch to the knuckler later in careers with little to no success. Taking it up cold and late made it much more difficult to master, he believed.

"This is why so many older pitchers fail with the knuckler," Wood said. "Most of them are over thirty when they first try it. At that age there's no way you can control the knuckler as a brand new pitch. He [Wilhelm] said he didn't know. I have long since learned that if he doesn't know, nobody does. He is not an authority on the knuckleball. He is *the* authority. No man, living or dead, ever knew as much about that pitch as Hoyt Wilhelm."

Wood determined over time that he got maximum bang from the knuckler by throwing it 90 percent of the time to hitters, and if he mixed in other pitches too often, he lost knuckleball effectiveness.

"The fastball is no faster and the curve doesn't break any sharper," he said. "They just look faster and seem to break sharper to hitters who have gone half-nuts looking at knucklers."

The fundamental aspect of the knuckleball is its lack of spin, and each knuckleballer brings a slightly different grip and philosophy to their livelihood pitch.

"Other than the position of the first two fingers," Wood said, "the big thing is to keep all your fingers off the seam so the ball won't rotate more than one-and-a-half times on its way to the plate. Wilhelm's knuckler doesn't even rotate that much. The least spin beyond a revolution and a half will keep the ball from breaking and make it act like a hanging curve. Brother, when your knuckler spins they'll hit it a long way—a long, long way. That means anybody, not just a power hitter."

That's the thing about the knuckleball. Even when a pitcher like Wood wins 20 games in a season—and does it more than once—everybody still wants to know how he is pulling it off. Sportswriters don't ask fastball pitchers the same questions knuckleball pitchers get. It is just assumed that their best stuff is a speedy blur and a hitter can't track it. With a knuckleball pitcher there is a sense of the occult, as if wizardry is involved and the batters really should get it if they just concentrated.

"If I get a piece of the strike zone, they have to swing," Wood said. "And as long as they swing, I've got them."

For a while in 1972 it seemed possible that Wood might hit 400 innings, an astounding figure out of date since the Deadball Era. Then when Wood's wins stopped piling up so quickly, people immediately began piling on, suggesting that he must be overworked, tired from pitching so much. It was an easy conclusion to reach, whether true or not. Tanner remained an adherent of Wood's style and supported him.

"We have never ordered Wood to work with two days' rest," stated the White Sox manager. "In every instance we always ask him first whether he wants to work with only two days' rest. It's entirely up to him. As a matter of fact, when [Johnny Sain] approached him recently about the two-day business, he told us, 'Don't worry about it because if I ever feel tired I'll let you know about it immediately.'"

If Wood ever was mired in a slump, it may have only been attributable to the vagaries of the knuckleball. Some days the knuckleball cooperates and some days it doesn't.

Wilhelm was gone to the Dodgers for the last chapter of his career by the time Wood rose to real prominence, but Eddie Fisher came back to the White Sox for a second stint in 1972. That meant an extra arm that could keep the catchers hopping. Catcher Ed Herrmann had to cope with Wood *and* Fisher, while trying to develop some semblance of a strategy.

"I look for the knuckleball about five to seven feet in front of home plate," Herrmann said. "The last break should begin about then. But you never know. It might break again. Still, with the big glove (38-inch circumference) I can at least get a piece of the ball. My first goal catching Woody was to go a full game without a passed ball. My ultimate goal is to catch a game without dropping the ball."

Wood was as active as any knuckleball pitcher in history, but he said he never heard of a knuckleball specialist needing arm surgery, specifically Tommy John surgery (before it was named for the Yankee pitcher), the way so many young pitchers do today.

"You get as stiff as anyone, but you don't tear things," he said. "You're not putting additional pressure on [your shoulder]."

Wood said that his switch to a starter from the bullpen was a natural outgrowth of personnel changes and Chuck Tanner's outlook. Rich "Goose" Gossage and Terry Forster were young bullpen specialists on the team and Tanner did worry about the possibility of errant knuckleballs costing the White Sox runs in late-inning situations. Wood said he was also a holdout for a bigger contract—he guessed he probably got another $1,000 or $1,500 out of his persistence, peanuts by today's standards, and was going to be traded to the Washington Senators. But the deal never came off.

"So now they're stuck with me," Wood said. "I got off to a pretty good start and pitched well."

Despite the periodic spectacular success of some pitchers like Wood, Wilhelm, Phil Niekro, and those earlier Hall of Famers Ted Lyons and Pop Haines, there is never a mass search of amateur ball seeking the next great knuckleballer.

"There aren't too many throwing it now," Wood said. "It's not a pitch you suddenly wake up and say, 'I'm throwing a knuckleball.' Guaranteed that at a tryout no scout will look for a knuckleballer."

Wood feels he is safe predicting no Major League pitcher will ever top his 376 2/3 innings in a single year again. It has been forty-two years since he did it and it might well be forty-two more without it being challenged.

"That was the fun about pitching the knuckleball," Wood said. "When I was throwing the ball on two days of rest in a four-man rotation, I loved it."

Wood's pitching and wooing of Tanner in allowing him to start both games of a doubleheader reached the status of nagging after a while until one day during the 1973 season, Tanner finally consented. Finally, Wood had his chance to fulfill a long-held goal . . . and nothing went the way he hoped. On July 20, the White Sox were scheduled to play two against the New York Yankees at Yankee Stadium. Wood, already 18–12 on the year, drew the opening-game assignment.

And he got slaughtered. The Yankees battered him for six runs (five earned) on four hits, and Wood did not get a man out. His stat line for the first game read zero innings, and the final score read 12–2 New York. This was one time where no one could suggest that Wood was tired from pitching in the first game so, after consultation between Tanner and Sain, they sent Wood out for the second game a few hours later.

The Yankees won that one, too, 7–0, and Wood was shoved around to the tune of five hits and seven runs (five earned) in 4 1/3 innings. So Wood pitched in both ends of a doubleheader as the starter, lost two games in one day, and had one of the worst pitching days of his life (Wood went into the doubleheader with a 18–12 record and 2.66 ERA. He left the day with a 18–14 record and 2.98 ERA).

"We were kind of short on pitching," Wood said years later, "and I wanted to do it. I should have kept my mouth shut."

At one point during that season, Wood said he received a phone call from Phil Niekro, asking Wood if he thought Niekro could do it and Wood said sure.

"I told him he was crazy not to do it," Wood said. ". . . if a pitcher can do it—and a lot more can if they tried—he ought to. Best way to make money is to win, right?"

Midway through the 1973 season, Wood hit a rough patch and gave up several hits and runs. (For the month of June, Wood went 1–8 with a 4.43 ERA, ballooning his season's earned run average from 1.98 to 2.65.) Newspaper reporters were asking what was wrong with him. But he straightened himself out quickly and by the end of July it was noted that he was on a pace to win 30 games. It turned out neither extreme was reality for long and Wood finished that season with his 24–20 mark. (Besides his troubles in June, from August 1–24, Wood went 0–4 in seven starts with a 5.69 ERA, giving up 26 earned runs in 41 1/3 innings.)

At the peak of his prowess—when he was near the top of American League statistical lists for several years running—Wood earned the nickname "Wilbur Wonderful" from sportswriters. His swift start, winning 10 times in the White Sox' first 33 games, gained him plentiful national attention and projections made over the 162-game season hinted that he could win 50 games in a season. Nothing like that ever came to pass, of course, but it was eye opening to even discuss such a thing. Also mentioned was Denny McLain's 31-win season of 1968 by way of comparison. For a while it seemed as if only Wood had a level head.

"You know and I know that in this business the (expletive) can hit the fan at any time. There's so much luck involved. There can be an injury. So you can't look ahead and worry about 30 wins when you have 14."

Wood notched his fourth straight 20-win season in 1974, and one of his new teammates that year was future Hall of Fame third baseman Ron Santo, who spent all but one of his 14-year career with the Chicago Cubs, finishing up with the White Sox. As soon as they renewed acquaintances—they had previously met at All-Star games—Santo teased Wood about how infrequently he delivered fastballs.

Santo asked Wood how many fastballs he thought he pitched in a season and Wood replied, "Not any more than I have to. There is no point in making this game easy for the batters."

Also in 1974 the White Sox presented Wood with a molded replica of his knuckleball grip, an interesting little trophy acknowledging his success with the team. As the years passed, Wood did not present a very svelte frame in his uniform. He developed a bit of a pot belly, although he insisted it did not hinder his pitching even if it disqualified him from most modeling gigs.

"Having a big middle doesn't bother me," Wood said. "My ego I mean. And I don't think it's hurt me as a Major League baseball pitcher."

Wood's 1975 season represented a bit of a drop-off from his previous four. He won 16 games, finishing 16–20 (his losses leading all of baseball) with a 4.11 earned run average. What he did not know was that his best days were behind him.

Wood began the 1976 season—when he was thirty-four—with a 4–3 mark and a solid 2.24 earned run average. He appeared to have regained his sharpness. Then in a game on May 9 versus the Detroit Tigers, outfielder Ron LeFlore smashed a line drive right back to the mound with two outs in the bottom of the sixth. The forcefully hit ball creamed Wood on the left knee and smashed his kneecap. He was removed from the game and immediately underwent surgery. The prognosis was so bleak that many predicted he would never pitch again.

That was the end of Wood's 1976 season, but he did return to the White Sox the next year. He was not his usual self, going 7–8 with an ERA of 4.99. He admitted that LeFlore's line drive worked against him mentally and that it was difficult for him to again get comfortable on the mound.

Wood worked the entire 1978 season for the White Sox, going 10–10, which wasn't horrible, but his earned run average of 5.20 was. After the season the White Sox tried to ditch Wood, but he thwarted waiver deals to the Milwaukee Brewers and Pittsburgh Pirates, thanks to his number of years with the team. He was only thirty-six when he retired—young for a knuckleballer—and far removed from his own goal of pitching well into his forties the way his mentor, Hoyt Wilhelm, had.

He still wanted to pitch, but was also ambivalent once the White Sox told him they didn't need him anymore. The knee injury is what finished Wood's career prematurely. He ended his 17-year career with a 164–156 record and a 3.24 ERA, and proud of the fact that he never had any arm problems.

* * *

After retiring, Wood returned to the Boston area where he owned a seafood market and later worked as a pharmaceutical representative. He gardens, and in 2013, said that a White Sox oversized catcher's mitt that was used for him and that he kept was donated to the Special Olympics.

Although Wood did make that statement that he could still pitch in his sixties, in 2014, when he was seventy-two, he no longer made the same claim. He said he could probably throw one knuckler and that's all. At long last perhaps his fingertips were telling him no more.

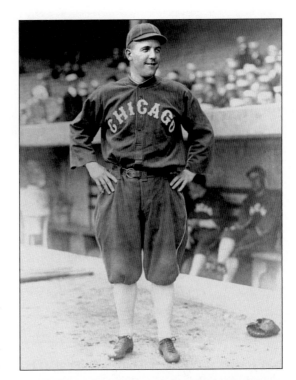

Ed Cicotte was infamous for being a key member of the Chicago White Sox that fixed the World Series in order to lose to the Cincinnati Reds in 1919, but is given credit for inventing the knuckleball.

Photo courtesy of the National Baseball Hall of Fame and Museum

Ted Lyons (right) is one of only a handful of Hall of Fame knuckleball pitchers. Lyons (shown with fellow hurler Paul Gregory) was the mainstay of the Chicago White Sox pitching staff between 1923 and 1946 and won a team record 260 games.

Photo courtesy of the Boston Public Library

Emil "Dutch" Leonard had the unique experience of being part of a four-member Washington Senators rotation of the 1940s which featured a quartet of knuckleball experts.

Photo courtesy of the National Baseball Hall of Fame and Museum

Hoyt Wilhelm is considered the guru of the modern era of knuckleball pitching and became a Hall of Famer for his performances with the Giants, Orioles, White Sox, and other teams as he pitched until age 49.

Photo courtesy of the National Baseball Hall of Fame and Museum

Gus Triandos was catching for the Baltimore Orioles when he accepted the difficult assignment of handling Hoyt Wilhelm's knuckler. Triandos benefited from the introduction of an oversized catcher's mitt to aid his fielding.

Photo courtesy of the National Baseball Hall of Fame and Museum

J. C. Martin was a catcher who had more headaches than most because, as a receiver, he handled knuckleball throwers Hoyt Wilhelm, Eddie Fisher, and Wilbur Wood, all with the White Sox.

Photo courtesy of the National Baseball Hall of Fame and Museum

Wilbur Wood was another White Sox hurler specializing in the knuckleball and used the pitch to win 20 or more games in a season four times.

Photo courtesy of the National Baseball Hall of Fame and Museum

Jim Bouton was more famous for writing the best-selling baseball book *Ball Four*, but he staged a late-career comeback because of the knuckleball he learned as a kid.

Photo courtesy of the National Baseball Hall of Fame and Museum

Phil Niekro is the winningest knuckleball artist of all time with 318 victories and is one of only a few knuckleball specialists elected to the National Baseball Hall of Fame.

Photo courtesy of the National Baseball Hall of Fame and Museum

Bruce Benedict was Phil Niekro's regular catcher with the Atlanta Braves for several years and Niekro always praises him in speeches as a key player who helped get him into the Hall of Fame.

Photo courtesy of the National Baseball Hall of Fame and Museum

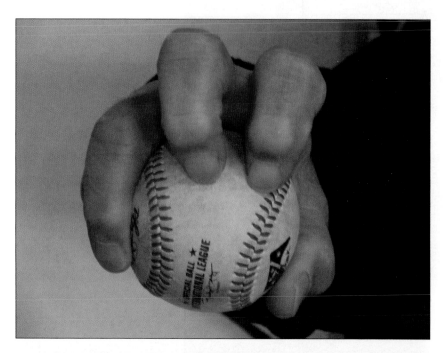

Phil Niekro showing his knuckleball form that he used to win 318 games in his Hall of Fame career.

Photos of Phil Niekro's knuckleball grip courtesy of Lew Freedman.

Joe Niekro was the younger half of the brother team that set the sibling record for most victories in Major League history and, like his brother Phil, learned the pitch from their dad during backyard play.

Photo courtesy of the National Baseball Hall of Fame and Museum

Charlie Hough (seen throwing for the Florida Marlins at the tail end of his 25-year career) won 216 Major League games and became a guru of the knuckleball; a go-to guy for advice to young pitchers learning how to throw the tricky pitch.

Photo courtesy of AP Images

Tom Candiotti had success with the knuckleball, pitching for the Cleveland Indians and Los Angeles Dodgers in the 1980s and 1990s.

Photo courtesy of the National Baseball Hall of Fame and Museum

Tim Wakefield became one of the Boston Red Sox's winningest pitchers in history due to the knuckler, which allowed him to throw well into his forties.

For the last few years, R. A. Dickey, first with the New York Mets and now with the Toronto Blue Jays, has been the only knuckleball pitcher still going strong in the majors. He continues to carry on the tradition of one of the sport's least understood pitches as he becomes yet another in a long line of knuckleballers to pitch into his forties.

15

CHARLIE HOUGH

———————————

ONE THING CHARLIE Hough could not do with his knuckleball was huff and puff and blow a house down. Instead, if he threw a knuckler with all of his might, it might bounce off a wall with a *thud*. That is despite him being six foot two and weighing 190 pounds.

Boy, headline writers had fun with Hough during his 25-season career in the majors, which lasted from 1970 to 1994. One day a sports department wit would refer to his knuckler as the "sincerest form of fluttery." Another day it was referred to as a "magic show."

The point in all cases, as it was for all of the best knuckleball throwers, was that no one could comprehend how Hough could get batters out with such junk that dipped and twirled in slow motion. As some of his fellow knuckleballers were also able to do, Hough pitched into his forties and won a lot of games.

In his case, Hough accumulated 216 victories. As it so happened, he also had 216 losses. But when he was at his best, he was better than a .500 pitcher for sure. Hough was born in

Honolulu in 1948, but came out of high school in Florida from Hialeah High. The Los Angeles Dodgers drafted him in 1966, and although Hough still works for the organization, he made many intermediate stopovers between those employment stints.

While he is regarded as one of the guru marvels of the knuckleball, growing up Hough never would have imagined being associated with the pitch. He also has a sense of humor about the turns his life took. When he was young, Hough said, "I wanted to pitch or play third base for the Boston Red Sox."

Hough never did pitch, hit, play, or work for the Red Sox, but that's life for most people going back to those childhood days when they wanted to be policemen, firemen, or cowboys. Unlike the Niekro brothers or Wilbur Wood, Hough did not have a father teaching him a knuckler while playing catch. It was not long ago, in fact, that he read a book about spitball pitchers and knuckleball throwers that led him to discover more about Eddie Cicotte's creative involvement.

"It basically said that when they outlawed the spitter, some mediocre guys like us threw the knuckleball," Hough said, apparently picking up that interpretation from the *CliffsNotes.* "For me, the first guy I was aware of throwing the knuckler was Hoyt Wilhelm and when I knew about him I was not at all interested in throwing it."

Hough's self-evaluation was that he was not more than a "long-shot prospect" for the Dodgers roster, but in 1967 when he was nineteen he split time between Santa Barbara and Albuquerque in the Los Angeles minor-league chain, winning 16 games in total. He was also sure he was going to get drafted again—this time by the army and sent to Vietnam and so he signed up for the Marine Corps Reserve.

That permitted Hough to go to spring training in Vero Beach, Florida, at famed Dodgertown, but his right pitching shoulder started to give him problems, something he couldn't shake.

"I pitched 1968 and 1969 with a bad shoulder," Hough said. "It never improved."

The Dodgers were kind enough not to give up on him despite the aches and pains that were affecting his velocity, and shipped Hough to the Arizona Fall Instructional League. "Supposedly only prospects went," he said.

Years before Tommy Lasorda became a Hall of Fame manager for the Dodgers he was working in their minor-league system. Lasorda and Goldie Holt were on hand studying Hough's form. Holt was a career minor-league player who later coached for the Chicago Cubs and Pittsburgh Pirates in the majors, but spent years working for the Dodgers as a scout and minor-league talent expert. Holt, who died in 1991 at age eighty-nine, was the one who taught Hough how to throw a knuckler.

First he had to break the news gently to Hough that he was a candidate to learn it.

"He walked up to me as I was throwing and said, 'Have you ever thought of throwing a knuckleball?'"

Of course that was just one way for the organization to inform Hough that he was never going to make it to the majors with the Dodgers any other way.

"I just threw one that didn't spin in about 10 minutes," Hough said. "It came out of my hand right, just on my own. Once you can throw it pretty good, you spend the rest of your life trying to get it over the plate." Lasorda was the other enabler.

"Tommy's idea was for me to learn it and I had to throw it every day."

Hough spent some time as a reliever in AAA throwing and throwing the knuckler—and throwing it well (1.95 earned run average with 12 wins in Spokane), and made his first appearance in the majors for the Dodgers in August of 1970. He was twenty-two, got into eight games, pitched 17 innings with a 5.29 earned run average, and finished with a 0–0 record. The ERA was not a grand announcement of his presence. In 1971 it was similar: four games, 0–0 record, 4.15 ERA. In 1972 the situation was more of the same: 0–0 in two games, finishing with a 3.38 ERA.

Compared to Hough's slow progress, the Daytona 500 was a head-to-head turtle race. By 1973, Hough was twenty-five and wondering if his pitching career would ever gain traction. That season it did. He became a full-time reliever for the Dodgers, appearing in 37 games. He actually won some (and lost some), going 4–2 with a 2.76 earned average

By mid-summer some sportswriters noted that Hough had become a contributor and, more importantly, so had manager Walter Alston.

"His control is better now that when he came up. That's the big difference."

By then, after slowly easing into it, Hough was throwing a knuckler 90 percent of the time, and could speak to his long apprenticeship.

"I'd have to say that a knuckleball takes longer to learn than any other pitch," Hough said that year. "Hoyt Wilhelm didn't pitch in the Major Leagues until he was twenty-eight and he started throwing it in high school. I've been throwing it since 1969 and it's only in the past year that I've gotten to where I'm fairly consistent. I think it takes an awful long time to get a good release point and a good feel for it. Some guys can throw a slider for a few weeks in the bullpen and then use it occasionally in a game. But to get a good knuckleball you have to throw it almost every pitch to keep sharp. You have to keep the spin off the ball and if you change the [angle of the] grip in the smallest degree you get a spin and you've got no chance at all."

Hough said he could tell that Alston had gained faith in his ability.

"You just feel that the manager believes in you. Plus it helps when you believe in yourself."

That 1973 season was the first one of consequence for Hough in LA. Up until then he was no more than a guy changing buses in town. But '73 was the start of something big and long lasting. For the rest of the 1970s, including after Lasorda took over as manager in 1976, Hough played an increasingly larger role.

In 1974, Hough was used in 49 games—all in relief—finished with a 9–4 record and recorded a 3.75 earned run average. The next year his ERA dropped to 2.95, though his record was a poor 3–7. Lasorda's first season in charge from the bench was 1976, and he turned Hough loose in 77 games. Lasorda was rewarded with a 12–8 mark and a 2.21 earned run average. Hough also notched 18 saves.

Hough was called upon to explain the difference in his effectiveness between 1976 and 1977 and he was diplomatic, although run support was an issue.

"Last year [the 3–7 season] I threw as well as I ever have, but it seemed as if when I gave up a run that would be the ballgame and I'd get the loss. This year, it seems if I get into a game, we score."

The circumstances that greeted Hough coming into a game from the bullpen and the way the ball bounced, as much as anything else determined his fate in relief, Hough said. He wouldn't even claim to be a better knuckleball thrower.

"I'll throw it in tough situations now. It doesn't break any better, but it's easier to throw now and I do feel a lot more comfortable throwing it."

By 1976 Hough began making his wish aloud to someday be a starter. He thought he would keep getting better and could be a productive part of the rotation.

"I'm just now developing," Hough said. He even spent time in the Dominican Republic in winter ball trying to gain some experience as a starter. At that point he had never started a big-league game.

Although he was a full-time reliever, Hough looked for more, but never overlooked how the knuckleball had transformed his career from a permanent minor leaguer.

"Without the knuckleball, there's no way I'd be pitching in the big leagues. Without the knuckleball I'd be punching tickets at Hialeah Race Track."

Hough remained in the Dodgers' bullpen through the 1978 season—with just one start before 1979. He started 14 games in 1979, but it was not until 1982 (when Hough was with the Texas Rangers) that he became a full-time starting pitcher. (From 1970–81, Hough's record was 53–49; from 1982–94, it was 163–167.) He won the majority of his games after that, but sometimes wonders what his career might have been like if he started regularly at a younger age.

"Maybe it was the wrong spot for me," he said of relieving. "I don't know if I would have made it otherwise, though. I had Tommy [Lasorda] in my corner. I got to play in three World

Series. I pitched until I was forty-six years old, and not many guys can say that."

Hough appeared in 70 games in 1977, but his record was only 6–12 with a 3.32 earned run average, though he did notch 22 saves. He had some streaks where he was untouchable and some others when the knuckleball failed him. Hough started well that season, with Lasorda calling him "My Hope Diamond," but he had some aches and pains.

Although Hough's route to the majors was circuitous and he endured those first few seasons hardly ever getting off the bench, by the time he was established in the Dodgers' bullpen and had become proficient with the knuckler, he began thinking he could become one of those knuckleball artists who challenged records for longevity.

"In this business you never know when your career is going to be over," Hough said when he was twenty-nine, "but I think I'll be in baseball for a long, long time. I'd like to pitch into my forties because I really love this game. Hoyt pitched until he was forty-nine. Who's to say I won't be able to pitch that long? The knuckleball is a pretty easy pitch on the arm, you know. Really, it's a thrill just to be in the big leagues. I've been very fortunate because I wasn't blessed with that much talent. Fortunately, people like Tom Lasorda believed in me. Before I hurt my arm the best thing you could say about me was that I had perfect control."

By 1977 Hough had been throwing the knuckler for almost a decade, but was still amazed by its properties. He realized the knuckler could be a humbling pitch to count on and he definitely hadn't become a know-it-all.

"I still think I'm learning the knuckleball, too. It's a pitch you learn something new about every year. There are days it breaks and days it doesn't break. You're out to try to find out why."

Employing hindsight and wisdom gained over the intervening decades, Hough said that it was remarkable how little he knew about relying on a knuckleball when he first made the pitch his livelihood.

"When I started throwing the knuckler I had no idea what I was doing. I made it to the majors and I still had no idea what I was doing. The next year Hoyt Wilhelm helped me. He taught me things only a knuckleball pitcher would know, where to stand on the rubber and gripping it. Hoyt Wilhelm and Phil Niekro are the ultimate pitchers of the knuckleball world."

One of the greatest temptations a knuckleball pitcher might face if he has not sold his soul to the pitch is reverting to a fastball or curve to bail him out of tense situations. It's not going to work.

"To throw a knuckleball well, you can't really throw much of anything else. I know that may sound crazy, but you have to learn to deliver the ball so much slower that eventually this fouls up your motion for standard pitches. Actually, you push the ball more than you throw it. Any time I have problems getting the ball over the plate you can bet that the hitter is going to be looking for the fastball. Well, if I show them my fastball under those conditions, they'd probably hit it up in the seats. In fact, I wouldn't be safe if I threw the resin bag.

"So I do the only thing I figure I can do. I throw them another knuckler and hope it catches the plate. Sometimes I get out of jams that way and sometimes I don't. But at least I know I've gone with my best. And a lot of times when they're looking fastball and get the knuckler, they pop it up."

As the years passed, the Dodgers made sure to keep Hough busy. In 1976 he played in those 77 games. A year later he pitched in 70. In 1979, Hough started 14 games in addition to making 28 relief appearances and tossed what was to that point a career-high 151 1/3 innings.

"I don't know if I've ever said no when they've asked me to pitch," Hough said in 1979. "You just go ahead and pitch. They pay you to play. So what if I'm tired, or if the whole bullpen is tired?"

After the 1979 season ended, the Dodgers dipped into the free-agent market and signed pitchers Don Stanhouse and Dave Goltz, acquisitions that seemed to have implications for Hough's future with the team, though nothing was said to him. A career-long Dodger who had been up with the big club since 1970, the thirty-two-year-old Hough began the 1980 season in the bullpen. He pitched in 19 games and was 1–3 with a 5.57 earned run average. That did not help his case.

On July 11, 1980, the Dodgers sold Hough to the Texas Rangers. Although it may not have seemed so at the time, it turned out to be the best move for his career. The Dodgers also should have known that periodic knuckleball slumps are often turned around and followed by periods of great success, as if nothing had ever intervened.

For the rest of 1980, Hough spent most of his time relieving, only now in the American League. In 1981, Hough finished 4–1 for Texas with a 2.96 ERA. It was already looking as if the Dodgers had made a mistake. In 1982, Hough got to live out his long-held dream. He became a full-time starting pitcher, going 16–13 and kicked off part II of his big-league career as a full-time rotation pitcher.

None of this life-begins-at-forty stuff for Hough. For the right-hander with the soft pitch it began all over again at age thirty-four. He threw 228 innings that season—77 more than ever before—and that was just the beginning. Between 1983 and 1988, Hough tossed no fewer than 230 innings and in 1987 led all of baseball with 285 1/3 innings pitched.

In consecutive seasons (from 1982–88), Hough won 16, 15, 16, 14, 17, 18, and 15 games. He was chosen for the American League All-Star team in 1986 and, in 1987, he started a league-high 40 games. It was just another case of an aging knuckleball pitcher showing no signs of wear and getting better as he got older.

On June 16, 1986, Hough nearly closed out a no-hitter against the California Angels. He had it going for 8 1/3 innings before a combination of a muffed fly ball, a hit, and some passed balls cost him the decision, 2–1. Someone immediately asked if Hough had come that close to throwing a no-hitter before and he replied, "With that junk I throw?"

Hough could be self-deprecating—even at that moment of disappointment—but he also had enough evidence on his side with the passage of time to show that when it was working the knuckler was the batter's worst enemy.

"There are times you stand on the mound and say, 'I don't think the guy can hit this,'" Hough said. For more than eight innings, it was true on that near-no-hitter night.

If Hough was a helper out of the bullpen in Los Angeles, he assumed a much more public profile the longer he pitched with Texas and anchored the rotation. One newspaper story suggested the Arlington Texas Chamber of Commerce should either put his picture on the cover of the local phone book or get him declared a historic landmark.

Hough appeared in the 1986 All-Star game, but that was not a day when the knuckler behaved the way it was commanded.

"That's what can happen when the knuckleball is your bread, butter, and entree," Hough said after calling his All-Star selection "one of the highlights of a pretty mediocre career." Hough was charged with a wild pitch and a balk, but added, "I didn't feel like I pitched that bad. It was my typical game. But I guess I really stunk."

Although the AL won 3–2, in his 1 2/3 innings, Hough allowed two runs on two hits, one of them earned, and struck out three.

When he packed his luggage for the game in Houston—his first All-Star selection in 17 seasons—Hough brought along an oversized catcher's mitt to help out whoever drew the assignment to handle him if he got into the game. That someone turned out to be the Boston Red Sox catcher Rich Gedman, who was apologetic. "Charlie pitched good, but I goofed it up," Gedman said. "Wouldn't you be embarrassed? Maybe next time I won't miss any."

There was no next time for Hough in the All-Star game, but he kept chugging along. In 1989, Hough's earned run average began rising—perhaps in tune with his knuckler rising—and he had some losing streaks. Blackie Sherrod, the famous Dallas sports columnist, sympathized in print, calling Hough "Everyman" who more than any other player represented the fans. "His shoulders are stooped with hard winters, he has a cigarette cough, and if he entered a Mr. America contest he would lose his citizenship," Sherrod wrote. And that was in support of Hough.

Hough remained with the Rangers through the 1990 season when he finished 12–12, though he was no longer a consistent winner. That season, Nolan Ryan, whose supersonic fastball made him a sort of anti-Hough, expressed appreciation for what Hough achieved.

"That's something that you just don't develop," Ryan said of Hough's knuckler. "That's something that takes years and years of dedication and work. People can make it move, but you have to be able to control it."

After the 1990 season, Hough was granted free agency and signed with the Chicago White Sox. His next employer took him on when he was forty-three, and he won 16 games in two seasons. In 1993 he joined the expansion Florida Marlins, near his old high school stomping grounds, and wrapped up his Major League career there, though with two losing seasons. No one had to tell Hough what happens to a knuckleballer who struggles with consistency. Batters feast on him.

"It was like throwing twenty changeups in a row," he said once of getting hit hard because of an erratic release point in his delivery.

Hough's last active season was 1994 when he was forty-six. His back hurt, his legs hurt, even when he walked, not just running. His neck hurt after he pitched. Only his remarkable right arm seemed to be in good working order when he pitched.

"At this point in my career, I'm not going to dominate anybody. I'm just trying to pitch a decent-enough game so the boys have a shot at winning."

His body told Hough it was time to walk away—or limp away.

Even after a quarter of a century in the bigs and still an object of interest for any fan of the knuckleball, Hough said he has remained friendly with some of his catchers, especially given all they went through helping him.

"I like them," he joked.

He can also alternately joke and be serious about the knuckleball that was so instrumental to his career. He said he laughed when asked what it took to "master" the knuckleball, as in, "When did you think you really mastered a knuckleball?" Hough's reply: "Maybe next year."

* * *

Hough has been sought as a teacher of the knuckleball, but mostly he helps established knuckleballers such as R. A. Dickey or Tom Candiotti, who called for emergency consultation when something seemed amiss. He even gets requests to teach people how to hit a knuckleball. Not only would imparting such information make him a traitor to his class he also readily admits there is no way to pass on that tidbit.

"A knuckleball thrown well is pretty darned hard to hit. You can't teach someone to hit it."

Many pitchers have tried and failed to emulate the knuckleball success he, the Niekro brothers, Hoyt Wilhelm, and a few others achieved. It's just not something one can pick up in a hurry and some pitchers can never make it work for them.

"Most of the guys I know of who are, or were, trying, looked up and said, 'This isn't working,'" Hough said. "I didn't throw a knuckleball by choice."

And as he moves into his late sixties, he definitely isn't throwing one now. His arm lasted long enough to make a good living, but Hough isn't traveling the country giving knuckleball tossing demonstrations.

"My shoulder's a mess," he said. "I can't throw a ball anymore. I can't throw the ball across the room."

16

PHIL NIEKRO II: NOT JUST ANOTHER KNUCKLE GUY

IN 1975, PHIL Niekro was thirty-six years old. By any measurement applied to baseball, he was not a young prospect. He was not a phenom, but was becoming a phenomenon; an old man of the game who commanded awe and respect because he was becoming "Old Man River" just rolling along.

At a time when most players are coping with the fading of the skills that enabled them to join the elite of the Major Leagues, Niekro was in his own kind of prime. Between 1977 and 1980, Niekro led the National League in starts four straight years with marks of 43, 42, 44, and 38. This meant he was just about matching his age each season since he was 38, 39, 40, and 41 on the calendar as he progressed. In the middle of all that Niekro threw 330 1/3, 334 1/3, and 332 innings in consecutive years, also league-leading figures.

Not only was Niekro one of the best pitchers in the National League in the 1970s, he was also the workhorse of the league;

the possessor of the iron arm that never tired. In reality, he was another knuckleballer blessed with the skill to throw it, manage it, and benefit from it without wearing down his arm. He was just more durable and better than just about all the others.

In 1979, when Niekro finished 21–20, he was almost distraught winning his 20th game because it came at the expense of his brother Joe.

"What if Joe never had another chance?" Phil Niekro said at the time. "I'd have to think I ruined it for him."

As it so happened, Phil Niekro didn't have to carry that burden. Later in his career, Joe played for a World Series winner.

The 1970s and 1980s were not especially good times for the Braves. While they soon would be setting a record for winning 14 straight divisional titles, Niekro suffered with some of the worst clubs in that city. He was the beacon on otherwise weak teams. After the 1976 season, when Atlanta went 70–92, questions began arising about how much longer Niekro could go, even though he finished 17–11 for that squad.

"I'll pitch just as long as I possibly can," Niekro said.

And he never wavered from that statement. The Braves seemingly wanted Niekro to spend the rest of his life with them: pitching, coaching, and maybe even becoming manager someday. He looked as if he could go on indefinitely counting on that knuckler, especially in 1982 when he went 17–4, the best winning percentage in the National League, at age forty-three. In 1983, Niekro went 11–10 for the Braves, but after the season, somewhat shockingly, Niekro was released by Atlanta.

He ended up signing with the New York Yankees for a chapter of his career that he didn't see coming, and at age forty-five, Niekro won 16 games with a 3.09 earned run average. He wasn't by any means finished. That season Niekro surpassed 3,000 strikeouts for his career, meaning that an awfully large number of batters had flailed away helplessly at the knuckler. The most peculiar aspect of reaching the milestone—though not really for a knuckleball pitcher—was that Texas' Larry Parrish swung and missed at a 2–2 knuckler for the 3,000th K, but New York catcher Butch Wynegar missed the ball and Parrish ran to first safely. Niekro said that was the first time Wynegar had missed a strike with the batter making it to first. At the time the 3,000-strikeout club was pretty small, and Niekro joined Nolan Ryan, Walter Johnson, Steve Carlton, Tom Seaver, Bob Gibson, and Ferguson Jenkins on the list.[1] They were all fastball pitchers and Niekro recognized that he was the odd man in the club.

"I don't scare anybody," Niekro said. "I don't really intimidate with this pitch."

Clearly Niekro, whose hair had turned gray and who was still flaunting his Polish heritage by wearing such T-shirts carrying messages like "Kielbasa Power," was focused more on pitching than retiring. People who heard about a forty-five-year-old still at the top of his game may have assumed that Niekro spent all of his waking hours either in the gym or running miles along the Hudson River. Once again the knuckleball was its own animal and did not require the same power as throwing a fastball.

"I'm no exercise freak," Niekro said in the 1980s. "I don't believe you have to run five miles a day. I haven't run yet this year. I'm not into vitamins. I'm not into superstition. I get up in the morning whenever my eyes open. I go to bed when my eyes

---

[1]   Only 16 pitchers have over 3,000 strikeouts for their career, and as of 2014, Niekro was 11th all time.

get heavy and tell me, 'Niekro, it's time to go to sleep.' I don't like pressure. I don't flip out. The last time I was angry, it was with myself."

Perhaps the strangest aspect of the summer of '84 was Niekro being invited back to Atlanta to have his number 35 jersey retired, even at the same time that he was pitching and winning for the Yankees—and could still have been pitching and winning for the Braves.

Owner Ted Turner, who had underestimated Niekro's staying power in letting him get away to New York, definitely tried to make the occasion a friendly one—a make-up call of sorts— at Atlanta Fulton-County Stadium. "We're friends, aren't we, Phil?" Turner said. "Tell them we're friends."

Niekro did get emotional and was gracious, even if he owned another team's uniform.

"I have a different job now," he said. "I don't have a different home, but I have a different job. I guarantee you I'm not leaving the state of Georgia."

He wasn't kidding about that, and more than thirty years later, Niekro still maintained his residence in the Atlanta area. Niekro never wanted to burn any bridges, but he did want to keep on pitching regardless of age.

A milestone much more significant than 3,000 strikeouts was reached in 1985, when Niekro was in his second and last season with the Yankees and finishing 16–12. He beat the Toronto Blue Jays, 8–0, to collect the key victory. In an unusual gesture, Niekro stuck to a plan he had mentioned months earlier. He said if it came down to going for the 300th win he wanted to capture it without throwing knucklers. Few believed he would try to do that since he generally tossed the knuckler 90 percent of the time. But before the game he told catcher Butch Wynegar that's what he wanted to do.

Later, in a book called *Knuckleballs*, Niekro explained why he adopted that tactic, saying he wanted to "show, not only myself, but also everybody else, and all those guys [who thought] that the only thing that kept me in the game all these years was my knuckler, that I was more than a knuckleball pitcher."

Younger brother Joe was a member of the Yankees that season and he came out of the dugout to warm up his older brother before the ninth inning. In the ninth, Phil struck out the last hitter, Jeff Burroughs, with two knucklers to end it, the only ones he threw the entire day. He felt he owed it to the knuckler. He became the 16th pitcher in baseball history to win 300 games.

"I always wanted to pitch a game without the knuckleball," Niekro said after the event. "I wanted to end it the way I started back in 1965."

At the time, since it was early October and the season was ending, and his contract was up, Niekro wasn't sure if he would ever pitch again. His ERA crept up to 4.09 and this time it was the Yankees who felt Niekro would be better off retiring at the end of 1986 spring training. Still, his arm said no.

Dick Young, the famous New York sportswriter, who lamented Niekro's departure from the Yankees, wrote, "Phil Niekro is probably the only player in the history of baseball who pitched a big-league shutout in the game before his release."

It was late for Niekro to go searching for a team, but he signed for the 1986 season with the Cleveland Indians within the week. That was the team he rooted for when he was growing up in Lansing, Ohio. Other teams also put in bids, but Niekro gave

PHIL NIEKRO II: NOT JUST ANOTHER KNUCKLE GUY

the nod to Cleveland. Niekro was forty-seven when the season started, and darn it if he didn't pitch another game without a knuckler during the year, once again stunning onlookers who didn't remember that he had a fastball, screwball, a sinker, and other tools to boot.

"I know I can win without the knuckleball," Niekro said after throwing 6 1/3 innings against the Minnesota Twins. "I've been throwing it all my life, but it's always nice to know you've got other pitches."

Not that anyone really thought so at the time, nor have they remembered him that way since. During that 1986 season Niekro went 11–11. He pitched most of the next season with the Indians, too, going 7–11, before bouncing to the Toronto Blue Jays and back to the Braves to end the season.

That was it for Niekro after throwing a single game for the Braves to conclude the 1987 season. It also concluded his twenty-four-year career with a record of 318–274 and 3,342 strikeouts. Niekro was back in Atlanta for the end, and where he hoped to make a new beginning as a manager. The Braves offered Niekro the chance to manage in the low minors in 1988, but he said he preferred to start in AA or higher. He did manage the Richmond Braves in AAA in 1991, though they posted a 65–79 record.

Instead, Niekro's managing career went in a completely different direction. Between 1994 and 1997, with Joe Niekro as one of his coaches, he was the manager of the Colorado Silver Bullets, an all-women's barnstorming team that was founded by businessmen in Atlanta and sponsored by Coors beer as it traveled the country playing against men's teams.

Niekro was approached by officials at an Atlanta advertising company asking if he would manage. At first he was surprised that the women's team was going to play baseball, not softball, and his wife and daughter lobbied him to take on the task.

Most of the players were former college softball players. The Silver Bullets held tryout camps all around the country and signed up a roster of 23 players, most of whom had been All-Americans.

"They didn't know much about baseball," Niekro said, "and the first year in spring training I was saying, 'Boy, this is going to be a project here.' Our catchers couldn't throw to second base. They never took a lead off base. They couldn't throw the ball from short to first base. I think we won like two or three games the first year, but in our fourth year we had a winning season."

Naturally, the automatic question was whether or not anyone on the team had knuckleball potential with Phil Niekro as the manager and Joe Niekro as the coach.

"The first day Joe came to me and told me all of the pitchers who could make the ballclub," Phil Niekro said. "One was a young lady named Lisa Martinez from California. Joe said, 'I've got a pitcher that throws underhand like college softball. Her ball sinks a foot. She's got a riser and she throws a knuckleball. She's a submariner. What should I do?' I said, "Well, there's nothing in the rules even in the big leagues that says you can't throw that way."

Martinez let go of the ball at her knees and baseball had seen submariners in the majors like Ted Abernathy.

"I said, 'If she can get them out, let's go with it,'" Niekro recalled. "So we kept her."

The Silver Bullets went to the Southern League All-Star game and the manager of the Spartanburg team was around and Niekro urged him to come out and watch the women play. He put

Martinez into the game in relief and she struck out several batters. The guy told Niekro, "I've got this big reliever in Spartanburg and I'd trade you for her right now, if I could, but I can't."

"She played one year and then she got married and I don't think she had any interest after that," Niekro said. "The Silver Bullets could play. It was four really, really interesting years."

That fourth season the Silver Bullets finished 23–22 and Niekro said compiling that winning record was as thrilling as anything he experienced in baseball.

Also in 1997, Niekro was voted into the National Baseball Hall of Fame in his fifth year of eligibility, just long enough to give him pause, though he was pretty confident his 318 wins would one day get him in the door.

"Well, sometimes you wonder," Niekro said of the intervening years. "I thought someday it was going to come. It's a day of a dream."

The year before Niekro had been the biggest vote-getter, but no player had reached the 75-percent-vote threshold. As soon as his enshrinement was announced, Niekro was in demand and he attributed his fame and success to the knuckleball while he found himself still explaining it.

"These two fingers have taken me a long way," Niekro said about the fingertip grip on the pitch. "My whole life has been the knuckleball. If he [speaking of his father] had not taken the time to teach me the knuckleball in the backyard, I would not even have been able to play high school baseball."

Niekro became one of the best pitchers in history by counting on the toughest pitch to employ in the game.

"Few pitchers can consistently control it and fewer still can make a living throwing it," Niekro said. "Yet that's exactly what my brother Joe and I both did. We credit our dad. He's the one that taught me the knuckler—and just about every important thing I know."

Niekro's best friend growing up was future Boston Celtics star and Basketball Hall of Famer John Havlicek, who upon the occasion of Niekro's Baseball Hall of Fame induction told how they used to pocket the six cents bus fare to school and hitchhike and how he caught Niekro's knuckler when they were young.

"I caught him without catcher's equipment," Havlicek said. "Maybe that's why I had such good reflexes."

During Niekro's long career he said how he actually preferred pitching against some of the greats of the game more than he did against lead-off-type, selective, work-the-count hitters, or bottom-of-the-order guys.

"The big guys?" Niekro said in retirement. "I'd much rather face the home-run hitters than the slap hitters. Their strike zones were bigger. Most of them had the heavier bats. Once they got things going, it was hard for them to stop. They wanted to hit the ball out of the ballpark. It seemed like the slower I threw it the harder they swung. If you were trying to hit the ball in the upper deck, I could get your timing off very easily with a knuckleball. They knew it was coming. I knew they knew it was coming. I wanted them to swing at it."

Demonstrating an insightful bit of self-analysis of his 70 mph knuckler, Niekro said he knew he never scared hitters when he wound up and that if "I did hit a batter they'd spit at the ball and throw it back at me."

Yet Niekro won more than 300 games and pitched in the big leagues until he was forty-eight, an almost impossible achievement.

"I was fortunate. I was lucky. I was blessed. Someone's taken very good care of me somewhere along the line."

As time passed and Niekro stayed away from organized baseball, the administration of the Braves changed and officials began wondering out loud why he was not a bigger part of the organization. Invitations to spring training in Lake Buena Vista, Florida, started coming and Niekro and his wife started showing up for a month at a time leading up to the regular season.

"It's more of a vacation," Niekro said. "We don't get paid, but they put you up and give you meal money. If I want to put a uniform on, I can. They ask me to hang around the players, to sign autographs, a little bit of everything. I told them I didn't want to step on anybody's toes down there. Sometimes I go out to the batting cage to help them bunt. They let me throw."

Once, some years ago, though after he retired, the Braves called Niekro and asked if he could throw batting practice one day because they were going to face the Boston Red Sox with Tim Wakefield. Then, as is common, there were almost no knuckleball pitchers in the majors and some of the hitters had never faced one. Niekro answered the call, but informed the Braves he was in California. They quickly sprung for a plane ticket and Niekro returned East.

On game night one of the players, a switch-hitter, asked Niekro if he should bat left-handed or right-handed against the righty-throwing Wakefield.

"Everybody was asking me how to hit the knuckleball," he said. "I said to myself, 'You guys are in trouble if you're asking me two hours before the game about the knuckleball.' I think I could have won that night."

Niekro's permanent residence is in the suburbs of Atlanta, quite close to the home of the Braves' AAA Gwinnett County franchise. When he's not fishing Niekro often watches the minor-league club play. Niekro, who turned seventy-five in April of 2014, said he sometimes tosses batting practice to the twenty-somethings.

"I throw a couple of times whenever they want me," Niekro said. "They let me throw. I'm always open to throw BP whenever I want here. I don't throw the knuckler. Anybody can throw a fastball. I could go out there right now and throw for a half hour if I want to do it. It would probably take me a while to get the knuckler thing going, though."

It would be something to see, the seventy-five-year-old knuckleball grandfather making those fresh-from-college, young draft picks lunge at the knuckler, swinging with all their heart at a pitch they've never seen before.

17

JIM BOUTON MAKES A COMEBACK

MORE FAMOUS FOR being funny in print because of his classic baseball book, *Ball Four*, Jim Bouton discovered a way to resuscitate his pitching career after he lost a few miles per hour on his fastball: throw the knuckleball.

It may be argued after reading Bouton's prose that he was one of the funniest men in baseball history and that, although his Major League pitching career was rather compressed, he did perform excellent work for the New York Yankees in the early 1960s when he relied on a fastball and curve to get the job done.

Bouton was born in Newark, New Jersey in 1939 and played college baseball at Western Michigan University before signing with the Yankees' organization at a time when they were still supervised by Casey Stengel in the dugout and identified with Mickey Mantle, Roger Maris, and Whitey Ford on the diamond.

A rookie at twenty-three in 1962, Bouton joined a Yankees rotation that still kept the team at the top of the American

League. He finished 7–7 with a 3.99 earned run average for a club that won the pennant and bested the San Francisco Giants in the World Series. New York, by then under manager Ralph Houk, won in seven games, though Bouton did not appear in the Series.

The next year, 1963, was Bouton's coming-out party. He finished 21–7—the best of his career—with a 2.53 ERA, and was chosen for the All-Star game as the Yankees again won the pennant. Indeed, Bouton appeared to be the next big thing on the mound for the Yankees, winning 11 games by the All-Star break. He was a traditional pitcher at the time, meaning that his collection of pitches featured the usual stuff.

"I throw the ball hard and I throw a curveball," Bouton said at the time. The curve was his outstanding specialty pitch, ranked amongst the best in the league. "I've got great confidence in it and I use it a lot in the pinch. I think that's one of the big reasons I've got off to such a nice start this year."

Unlike many of those who succeed at the top level of the sport, Bouton was a late bloomer. He said even in high school that he had trouble convincing the coach to use him in games because of his lack of speed and effectiveness. Because of that slow-motion beginning to his pitching career, Bouton experimented with trick pitches of every kind. That explains why, even as a twelve-year-old, he taught himself the knuckleball.

Bouton called his knuckler an early-career "necessity. I was so small I couldn't throw the ordinary stuff up to the plate hard enough to get anybody out. So I decided to throw the knuckleball. I read all about the knuckler in stories about Hoyt Wilhelm. He was with the Giants then. He was my big idol. It worked good, too. And I could get it over the plate."

Actually, much later, Bouton offered a revised version of his knuckleball beginnings, noting that he was first introduced to the knuckler while eating breakfast one day.

"I was ten years old and I looked at the cereal box," Bouton said. "It had a picture of Dutch Leonard on it and he showed you how to grip the knuckler. You should throw it with your fingertips, I learned. I ran out into the yard with my brother Bob and tried it. It was almost impossible to throw a ball without spin. I couldn't make it not spin. It took half a summer until I threw one accidentally. The ball was absolutely dead in the air. It broke and hit Bob in the knee. He was writhing in pain on the ground. I thought, 'What a great pitch.' I spent the rest of the summer trying to maim my brother and my father."

This doesn't mean that Wilhelm wasn't Bouton's idol—he served that purpose for many a knuckler and knuckleball wannabe over the years. But Bouton did a lot of the early work himself.

One way that Bouton developed his knuckler was through a hustle. Not hustling as in "working hard," but hustling as in "pool playing" or the like. He had a friend who admired his skill with the knuckler and together they hatched a scam in junior high. His friend would approach somebody at school or in a playground who didn't know Bouton.

"There was always a new guy," Bouton said.

Bouton's friend would say, "See that little kid over there? I bet you if he throws you five pitches you won't be able to catch the ball."

The stakes were $1 and of course Bouton threw the knuckler, which danced all over the place in ways the sucker had never seen before.

"It would hit him in the chest or the forehead," Bouton said.

Bouton and his friend won their $1, which was decent money for such a limited work investment in the early 1950s. Then the newly won-over pigeon would recruit another youngster to fool and maybe the stakes would grow to $5.

"I had a good knuckler for a thirteen-year-old," Bouton said. "The problem with the knuckleball as a Major League pitcher is it's a long story. You usually come to it as a failure. I had a very good overhand curve and I had good control and then I had the knuckleball."

Bouton's high school in North Jersey was a large one with 2,500 students, many of whom were good athletes in all sports. Bouton was pretty well known, but then his father changed jobs and moved the family to the Chicago area. Bouton did not immediately win the confidence of the baseball coach, frequently warming up in the bullpen, but then not be used.

"My nickname was 'Warm-up Bouton,'" he said.

Bouton loved the sport and felt he was better than he had been able to demonstrate with his high school team. The summer after his junior year he joined an American Legion team.

"I was depressed," he said. "This was my last chance in baseball, really."

Trying to impress the coach, he worked extra hard. On a muddy, rainy day he was raking the infield to smooth it and was asked what he was doing. It was suggested that he play second base, but Bouton said he was a pitcher. He heard the coach say he had five guys better than him, but in the second game of the doubleheader, in the rain, he got his chance.

"It was the greatest moment of my life," Bouton said. "I found myself."

Instead of being a bench-warmer as a senior, Bouton won the respect of his coach. The coach, Jacob Eit, someone Bouton describes as "a very nice man," saw the benefits of Bouton's Legion play. "You had a great summer, son," Eit told him entering the school season of 1957. That year Bouton pitched a no-hit shutout in the state tournament and he used the knuckler as an out pitch when needed.

"I had a knuckleball as squishy as a tomato," he said. "It turned out that even though I had good stuff, I had a knuckleball available. I was not going to give in. I was not going to abandon it."

However, in a sense he did so for a while. His fastball and curve got him signed by the New York Yankees.

"Basically, in the early 1960s I had good, conventional stuff," Bouton said. "I didn't throw a knuckleball in the minor leagues."

As Bouton matured into a six-foot-tall, 180-pound thrower (from the 150 he weighed while playing in Class D), his immediate need for the knuckler diminished. But in his own mind he was still a little guy and he did not want to completely discard this previous savior pitch, although the Yankees told him to do so.

"They didn't want me to become a guy with a trick pitch at my age," Bouton said. "I go along with that, but that doesn't mean I still can't throw a pretty good knuckleball. I practice it on the sidelines on days I'm not pitching. The way I look at it is that it's never going to do any harm to keep practicing the pitch. One of these days, when my hard one isn't quite so hard, the knuckleball may be the pitch to keep me employed a few years more."

That was as prophetic a prediction as any young hurler ever made about his own career without being able to literally look into the future. In the meantime, though, the knuckler was pretty much shelved as Bouton set down opposing batters. He did not overpower them and somewhere along the way one of his catchers, either Yogi Berra or Elston Howard (Bouton can't remember which), bestowed the nickname "Bulldog" on him because he worked so hard to get outs.

Actually, for an additional pitch Bouton detoured into the slider, which worked well for him alongside that fastball and curve. In 1964, Bouton finished 18–13 with a 3.02 ERA and led the American League in starts with 37. New York was swept by the Los Angeles Dodgers in the Series and Bouton lost Game 3.

Bouton demonstrated intelligence on the mound and his teammates respected his efforts and savvy. "He's just a bear-down guy," Howard said. "He's at his best when he's behind on the count and there are men on base. When it's like that, he's just a bulldog—a battling kind of bulldog."

Yankee infielder Phil Linz, who also had been a teammate of Bouton's in the minors, said the pitcher was always thinking ahead about how to become better, even when he was young and out of the Major League limelight.

"There were the losing types and the winning types," Linz said that Bouton postulated. "He said you had to train yourself to think like a winner and he's done that."

When Bouton had a son that year, he started calling young Mike "Little Bulldog," because he wanted the boy to know that "he's got to battle and scratch for the extra comforts of life."

That season one of Bouton's trademarks, a la Willie Mays, was that his baseball cap flew off his head when he was trying to make a play. In Bouton's case it occurred when he bore down and fired a fast one. The cap taking off of its own accord like a plane from nearby LaGuardia Airport was a common-enough occurrence that it was remarked upon regularly by teammates and sportswriters.

First baseman Joe Pepitone urged Bouton to more or less nail the hat on his head, to "go ahead and hitch the cap on his dome with [thumb] tacks." Bouton said, "I think I'll nail up a suggestion box in the clubhouse." Nobody cares too much if your cap flies to the moon if you are winning about 20 games a year.

Hall of Famer Mays' cap tended to blow off in the breeze when he was chasing a fly ball full out or running the bases. Bouton said if he was employing his pitching form properly his right arm brushed the bill of the cap right off his head. That was when he was throwing fastballs. The issue became a moot point later when he counted on knucklers. By the end of the 1964 season, Bouton had not thrown a knuckleball in a game for the Yankees in three years. He had no way of anticipating how that would soon change.

* * *

Although Bouton made his mark by winning 39 games in two seasons, he did not see far enough into the future when he was riding high to recognize that he would never again be as valuable a member of a big-league rotation. Those gaudy early statistics quickly became memories. In 1965, incurring a sore arm, Bouton went 4–15 with a 4.82 earned run average for the Yankees. In 1966, he finished 3–8, although his ERA was a much better 2.69. He made it into just 24 games, though. In 1967, appearing in only 17 games, Bouton went 1–0, but had become a reliever by then, throwing in just 44 1/3 innings. It looked as if his career was doomed and he would never again be a healthy pitcher.

"My arm was dead," Bouton said. "I didn't have a sore arm. When I finished 4–15, looking back I should have rested, but I wanted the ball. I got sent to the minors [in the 1960s] and that's when I realized, 'I'm never going to have that fastball again.'"

And he didn't. Bouton's velocity was gone, never to return.

"I went back to my high school knuckleball," Bouton said. He also said if he did not have the knuckler education to that point he never would have been able to pitch in the majors again, as it would have taken too long for him to adapt. "It would have been too late to learn it then. I got two more years in the big leagues. I couldn't have begun to learn the knuckleball at the age of thirty. Finally, it started to come for me."

In 1968, the Yankees gave up on Bouton and sold him away to a team that did not yet exist . . . except on paper. He emerged at the beginning of the 1969 season as a member of the Seattle Pilots expansion team in the American League. The Pilots lasted for just one year at Sicks' Stadium and then bolted for Milwaukee to become the Brewers. Feeling cheated by organized baseball, Seattle residents protested loudly and eventually landed the Mariners in 1977.

It's possible that if it were not for the presence of Jim Bouton and his energetic pen on the roster, no one would remember the Pilots except those who played on the team. Bouton, who finished the '69 season with the Houston Astros, spent the bulk of the year with the Pilots. As a side job he chronicled in a diary the comings and goings of the expansion team. Bouton's was the first truly candid, inside story of a team's happenings in a clubhouse and off the field and he was mightily resented for telling tales that many felt should have been left private.

The book was wildly humorous and became a bestseller and launched Bouton into a writing career after he retired from the game. It was a more innocent time and halfway through the 2010s decade in another century many of the incidents that produced outrage seem tame. But the book will still make any fan laugh, as will Bouton's follow-up volumes.

Bouton's editor on *Ball Four* was one-time *Washington Post* sportswriter Leonard Shecter, who in his foreword wrote that Bouton's original manuscript ran to 1,500 pages and Shecter's toughest challenge was leaving out so many funny things in compressing it.

It should be noted that the knuckleball plays a part in the first paragraph of Bouton's introduction. He wrote: "I'm thirty years old and I have these dreams. I dream my knuckleball is jumping around like a Ping-Pong ball in the wind and I pitch a two-hit shutout against my old team, the New York Yankees, single home the winning run in the ninth inning, and when the game is over, take a big bow on the mound in Yankee Stadium with 60,000 people cheering wildly. After the game reporters crowd around my locker asking me to explain exactly how I did it. I don't mind telling them."

Things never got that good with the Pilots, who finished 64–98. Bouton appeared in 57 games, all but one in relief, went 2–1 and compiled a 3.91 ERA. He did not get along very well with manager Joe Schultz, whose big-league playing career dated to 1939 and big-league coaching career dated to 1949. In *Ball Four*, Schultz was the butt of many jokes and humorous comments. He was conservative and Bouton was not.

Throwing the knuckler was one way in which Bouton was not conservative. It was all he had to work with by then, but he quickly learned that managers in general become very conservative around knuckleballers.

"They don't appreciate the pitch," Bouton said. "First of all, it looks strange. They're not thrown fast. It's hard to control the knuckleball. You can walk three or four guys. There was always the thought among managers that the knuckleball was sort of a free pass. They could understand a single or a double, but not the walks. The batter had to work for that [a hit]. That was OK."

It might be said that Bouton was a knuckleballer waiting to happen; that there was a certain inevitability that he one day would become connected to it in the majors. He had that kind of image, a player with a few quirks who could identify with a pitch with more than a few quirks. Anyone who throws a knuckler must have a sense of humor, and Bouton was renowned for that aspect of his personality.

He once said of the knuckleball: "It's a wonderful pitch. It defies logic. It flutters up there at grandma speed and renders strong men helpless."

The Seattle Pilots were a blip on the Major League radar screen and Bouton didn't even last in Seattle as long (or as short) as the team. In all, Bouton pitched 122 2/3 innings, and finished 2–3. Two of the 73 appearances were starts. Not being on the manager's favorite people list may have resulted in Bouton's exile and may not have been very surprising.

In late August of that season, Bouton was traded to the Astros for Dooley Womack and Roric Harrison.

"The Seattle Pilots traded me to the Astros for a bag of batting practice balls," is how Bouton analyzed that exchange.

The trade must have been consummated overnight because Bouton got the word he was on the go early in the morning with a hotel room phone call on a road trip to Baltimore. Since the Astros were only two-and-a-half games out of first place he was happy to move to a better team. As he recounted in *Ball Four*, however, his roommate, Steve Hovley, seemed to think it was all a dream and then protested that he could not join the Astros on the road in St. Louis that day because he had a prior engagement at the Museum of Art with him.

"You promised," Hovley said.

When Bouton made his introductory phone call to Houston general manager Spec Richardson, he asked if the team had any receivers with knuckleball experience. Richardson said Johnny Edwards would give it a try. As has just about every knuckleball thrower, the time came in Bouton's career when he met up with a catcher who had no experience catching the dancing pitch and in Bouton's case that guy was Edwards in Houston.

"He never caught the knuckleball before," Bouton recalled years later. "He would curse the ball. He didn't have the big glove."

Ball Four was a sensation when it came out in 1970, and one reason for it was what it revealed about ballplayers as human beings rather than as esteemed athletes. In one passage set in the locker room Bouton watched fellow pitcher George Brunet get dressed. He noted the lack of undershorts being pulled on and asked Brunet if it was an oversight.

"No, I never wear undershorts," Brunet was quoted as saying. "Hell, the only time you need them is if you get into a car wreck. Besides, this way I don't have to worry about losing them."

Mothers always used to say you should wear underwear so you would not be embarrassed in that fictional car wreck, but how many guys have ever worried about losing their underwear?

Then there was the time that pitcher Marty Pattin had a bad game and left the field steaming hot. He kicked over garbage cans and hit the clubhouse door hard on his way in. Bouton and teammate Fred Talbot asked him what he was going to do if he had another bad game. Before that contest they put a hangman's noose in Pattin's locker. Cold. Lucky for all concerned, Pattin pitched well.

After the final month cameo in 1969, Bouton went 4–6 with the Astros in 1970, but *Ball Four* came out, creating massive attention and distractions and Houston sent him to the minors. He was only thirty-one and still hoped to work his way back to the majors. Sitting in his hotel room he fielded a telephone call from WABC-TV in New York. The book's humor, style and the attention it received persuaded the station that he might make a good sportscaster. Bouton was tempted by the offer, but turned it down.

"I said, 'No, I'm still pitching.' Two weeks later something changed my mind."

Bouton embarked on a new career as a sportscaster in New York, one that took him to two networks. He also appeared in some movies and TV shows and lectured widely, telling stories from *Ball Four*. Then he got the itch to pitch again. In 1975, Bouton signed a deal with the Portland Mavericks, a Class A team. He recorded a 5–1 record throwing the knuckler, but dropped pitching again when he was summoned to help make a TV series out of *Ball Four* and act in it. The TV show was ill-fated, lasting only a handful of episodes.

At the time the show was billed as a comedy where the action took place in the locker room rather than on the ball field. It wasn't about the games. The half-hour show had Bouton playing a relief pitcher named Jim Barton trying to hang on in the majors—which sounded transparently true to life in paralleling Bouton's own story. Apparently more people laughed at the book than the TV show.

Proving that a knuckleballer's arm never dies, Bouton made a comeback to baseball, his limber right arm showing enough life to gain him a contract with Chicago White Sox owner Bill Veeck, whose life was more emblematic of being a maverick than the Portland team's nickname. Bouton pitched a little for a White Sox minor-league team with little success, but then played in the Mexican League, essentially the equivalent of AAA ball.

After still another minor-league stint in the Southern League at age thirty-nine, Bouton returned to the majors with the Atlanta Braves and went 1–3 in five starts. The knuckleball allowed him to reach the big leagues again.

"It was just a challenge," Bouton said of why he embarked on a second pitching career.

Bouton left the majors after the 1978 season, but he basically has never truly retired again. His final Major League stats included a 62–63 win-loss record and a 3.57 ERA. When sportswriters check in with Bouton periodically, they learn he is not exactly reclining on a couch somewhere, but is still pitching, throwing the knuckler in semi-pro senior leagues here and there around the Northeast. The *New York Daily News* sought him out in Massachusetts in 1995 when he was fifty-six. He was pitching then. In the spring of 2014, recently having turned seventy-five, he was still pitching.

"I threw this morning," he said to an interviewer in May of that year. "I try to throw 100 pitches every other day. I pitch amateur baseball, senior baseball. The younger guys think they are going to knock it out of the park. They swing from their asses and they pop it up. I have a lot of fun."

Bouton has this theory that every high school baseball pitcher should be required to learn how to throw the knuckleball, partially as a challenge, partially as an emergency back-up system, partially so they can see how the other half lives who can't throw a ball 95 mph.

"The knuckleball," Bouton said, "is about hanging in there, sticking with it, battling through something that may be heartbreaking."

As Bouton might have said, but didn't . . . you never know when you might need the knuckler to bail you out of a game jam or a life jam. It would be smart to listen to a guy who can still pitch when he is seventy-five years young.

18

TOM CANDIOTTI

IT IS HARD to beat a nickname like "The Candy Man," which applied to Tom Candiotti for the obvious reason of his last name. Maybe his pitches were fluffy, too, given his reliance on the knuckleball during his sixteen-year Major League career in the 1980s and 1990s.

Candiotti was born in 1957 in Walnut Creek, California, and after high school ball he played for St. Mary's College in California, a school where his father, Caesar, had also played the outfield. The Kansas City Royals signed the right-hander in 1980, but he was taken from them by the Milwaukee Brewers in the winter meetings draft later that year.

After working his way through the minors, the six-foot-three, 205-pound Candiotti made his Major League debut in 1983 with Milwaukee when he was twenty-five. It was not a bad showing, with a 4–4 mark and a 3.23 earned run average in 10 appearances. Alas, things did not go as well the next season when Candiotti finished 2–2 with a 5.29 ERA. At that point the

Brewers did not appear to have much faith in Candiotti, and he was granted free agency.

Candiotti's career prospects improved markedly once he signed with the Cleveland Indians for the 1986 season and became a teammate of Phil Niekro. Having Niekro around was a tremendous boost for Candiotti's confidence, as he gave him tips on the knuckleball.

At that point Candiotti needed assistance. His career was stalled, and like many others who had good skills but not full-time Major League repertoires, he had to add a new arrow to the quiver.

"My stuff just wasn't good enough," Candiotti said years later. "I had minor success, but it wasn't going to cut it."

After the 1985 season and before he signed with Cleveland, Candiotti played winter ball in Puerto Rico with Charlie Hough. Another of the knuckleball whizzes, Hough took Candiotti under his wing and recommended that his Texas Rangers sign him. Tom House, who was in the Atlanta bullpen and caught the home run that Hank Aaron hit to break Babe Ruth's career record and became a virtual doctor of pitching, was another influence. Candiotti showed enough promise that a few teams made offers. Cleveland felt like the right fit.

"The Indians jumped in," Candiotti said. "I was a minor-league free agent and they offered me the chance to be in the majors. I said, 'I'll take that.'"

He may have been wanted, but Candiotti didn't feel secure joining the Indians, either, after his minor-league sojourn.

"I felt a lot of pressure in spring training. I figured this might be my last chance. If they didn't like what they saw, I might have to go to work somewhere."

Notice that he didn't say "somewhere else," as in another team. He meant trying a new profession. But Candiotti succeeded, and made the Indians' roster.

That also teamed him with Niekro, who was then forty-seven and approaching the end of his illustrious career, though not before winning 11 games for the Indians during the 1986 season.

"I was able to go out and play catch with Phil Niekro every single day and watch him every single day," Candiotti said. "I watched how he did things, changed speeds, and held runners on."

When Candiotti ran into House during that 1986 season, he said the pitching expert told him, "Congratulations." Candiotti replied, "Congratulations on what?" House said, "You have become the 20th knuckleball pitcher in the history of baseball."

That was as good an estimate as any, though unofficial, depending on how such things are measured, but it pointed out to Candiotti right away that what he was doing put him in rare company.

Candiotti had learned the knuckler at a young age, but never used it on his way up to the majors. He turned to it, as others had, when he needed something fresh in his arsenal. He was somewhat surprised at times just how effective the knuckler could be in baffling hitters.

"I've never been a strikeout pitcher. I never dreamed I'd strike out a lot of people. Maybe there's something to this knuckleball stuff. They [batters] can't seem to hit it. I was trying to strike everybody out with it. Knucksie [Niekro] taught me that you want the hitter to swing at it." No knuckleball pitcher would fret, however, if hitters swung and missed instead of making long outs.

The image of knuckleballers is that they throw the ball so softly to home plate that it wouldn't break an egg if it were resting in front of the catcher, but Candiotti said his knuckler was thrown a little bit faster than normal, in the 70s, much like R. A. Dickey throws his today.

"Mine was as hard as possible," Candiotti said. "I threw it as hard as I could."

Niekro and Hough, in particular, became long-term confidants and helpers, guys that Candiotti could approach at any time to evaluate his delivery and form. One game, Candiotti remembers, pitted Cleveland against Texas, Niekro against Hough.

"I was never so nervous in the bullpen. "[Charlie] was always there anytime I needed to talk to him."

That made it hard to root against him in the game. Candiotti was well aware of the knuckleball brotherhood and said when Hough and other knucklerballers were pitching against any other team except his own, he rooted for them.

That 1986 season was a good one for Candiotti. He finished 16–12 with a 3.57 earned run average and led the American League with 17 complete games. He kept busy for 252 1/3 innings. It was the first season Candiotti was a full-blown knuckleball pitcher and he and Niekro were a terrible twosome in the Indians rotation.

"You tend to wonder, 'Would it have been easier if I just had a really good slider and changeup?'" Niekro said. "Maybe I'm just a nut. On the other hand, I feel Tom Candiotti and I are practitioners of what is truly a dying art."

At the time the two other knuckleballers in the majors were Hough and Joe Niekro. Candiotti was very grateful for Phil Niekro's help in advancing his career.

"It's definitely a pitch that younger pitchers should be willing to learn," Candiotti said at the time when he was twenty-eight, "but you have to be especially dedicated. You can't just learn about the knuckleball in a month or two. It's a lot of work, but it's worth it as far as I'm concerned. Phil has been much more than a teammate to me in this regard. He's a teacher, he points the way."

Whenever he was asked about his own knuckler, Candiotti praised Niekro's assistance and how much it meant to him.

"He became my guru. It takes a different mentality to throw the knuckleball and nobody really knows how to teach it. It's tough to label yourself a knuckleball pitcher, to tell yourself you're not good enough to make it otherwise."

Candiotti still thought his other pitchers were OK and he eased into throwing the knuckler an increased percentage of the time on the mound. The best knucklers know that it has to be almost blind devotion for the pitch to pay off.

"You've got to eat with it and sleep with it," Niekro said. "The margin of error is so delicate. You can have a bad knuckleball and have no idea why. With a breaking ball you can usually figure out what you're doing wrong. When a knuckleball ain't there, it's mass confusion."

Candiotti said that he had been a serious knuckleballer for just a year and was still learning a lot about how to handle it. His other pitches were still somewhat of a crutch, but Niekro said that Candiotti threw it harder than he did and that his ball had more motion than his own. It was a good compliment.

"I'm very lucky to be on the same team with him at this stage of my career," Candiotti said. "Phil has slow, slower, and slowest speeds to his. His is much more baffling because a batter doesn't know where it's going."

One thing that Candiotti was still trying to figure out was how to keep his fingernails whole, without cracks or injuring his fingers. The little things really do matter when throwing a knuckler. Everything must be just so. Compared to the macho-type injuries suffered by athletes in any other position, an injured fingernail does not sound like cause for alarm, but it can be. Candiotti experimented with coating his nails with gelatin and even glued a false fingernail on top of one of his to remedy a torn nail.

"Phil tells me that it may be a couple of years before the nails get real hard," Candiotti said. "I guess I'd better eat more Jello."

He did not specify the flavor, but Candiotti apparently did not eat enough of it in 1987. Perhaps it was coincidence, but Niekro was struggling too that year, the last full-time one of his career. It was tough going for Candiotti, who finished with a 7–18 record and a 4.78 earned run average. He did improve late in the season, however, after a consultation with Hough in mid-July. They worked together during the All-Star break for a half-hour session. (From May to June, Candiotti had a 1–5 record with a 4.81 ERA. In July and August, his record was 5–4 with a 3.94 ERA.)

"He noticed that my wrist was slipping off to the side as I threw, causing the knuckleball to move laterally. He told me to straighten out my wrist and he got it to float more up and down, in the strike zone."

At the start of the season, Candiotti was missing the plate. "I was throwing ball, ball, ball," he said. Word got around the league that the strategy was to wait Candiotti out and make him throw strikes. He adjusted by August and that month pitched a one-hitter against the New York Yankees.

It was almost as if a switch had been flipped. After the discouraging 1987 season, Candiotti rebounded and went 14–8 in 1988, 13–10 in 1989, 15–11 in 1990, and 13–13 in 1991. Although he split the '91 season between Cleveland and Toronto, Candiotti's ERA was a career best 2.65.

As was always the case, even with the best knuckleball pitchers, there was a period when things got out of whack and a pitcher had to fight to rediscover his form. The knuckleball was always going to bite back.

"It's just a ball that doesn't spin and it has a mind of its own," Candiotti said. "You're trying to take the spin off of it. It's like a quest to throw the perfect knuckleball. I don't think anybody has mastered the knuckleball and it's never going to happen."

Candiotti moved into the knuckleball world by throwing the pitch about 40 percent of the time in 1986, and inched his way up to throwing it 80 to 90 percent of the time. He sometimes threw a curve as a first pitch to batters to get ahead in the count.

"Charlie [Hough] said if he had a curveball he would throw it, too," Candiotti said. "Early on I viewed myself as going from a pitcher who threw the knuckleball to a knuckleball pitcher."

Pitchers are careful never to talk about "owning" a hitter or having complete mastery over a hitter—at least not while they are still active and a batter can get revenge and make them look foolish for uttering such a statement. But afterwards, well, they might open up a little bit.

"There were some hitters when they were coming up, I was smiling already," Candiotti said.

Some batters could hit him and others couldn't if they used an aluminum bat or Fred Flintstone's club at the plate.

"Eddie Murray," Candiotti said of the future Hall of Famer, "you could see him grind the bat so hard." Murray never could hit Candiotti, going just 7-for-44 for a .159 average against him in his career. Another hitter said, "This is my day to play wiffle ball." Candiotti theorized that some batters relaxed at the plate too much because they knew the knuckler was going to come in much slower and they wouldn't have to focus on a 95-mph heater. Some days the knuckler displayed so much motion that Candiotti had no idea what was going to happen. Once he even threw behind a hitter, not on purpose.

"The ball was just moving," he said. "It was just a nutty day with the knuckleball."

Once, with Hough in the stands, a handful of rows from the field before the game, Candiotti played catch with him when no one else was around.

"We had about 10 or 12 tosses," Candiotti said. "I threw the knuckleball back to him and he gave me a nod. It was pretty cool. None of my teammates would play catch with me."

A few years after Candiotti's one-hitter, he pitched 7 2/3 innings of a no-hitter against the Yankees, but when he lost the no-hitter, he also lost the game, 6–4.

"I feel like drinking about twenty beers," Candiotti said after the costly late-inning turnaround. "I was having such a good time out there. The knuckleball was really dancing."

Before departing Cleveland, Candiotti, who was fond of throwing to Sandy Alomar, broke the catcher's finger immediately after he had come off the disabled list from another injury. When he joined the Dodgers in 1992 (he won 11, though he lost a National League-leading 15 games that season), Candiotti greeted his new catcher, Mike Scioscia, with an arm full of oversized catcher's mitts and said, "Pick your weapon."

The Dodgers gave Candiotti $15.5 million to relocate to the West Coast after his short stay in Toronto, and he stayed with Los Angeles through 1997. His knuckler was as slow as ever—a good thing—which is the opposite of what is said about a fastball pitcher as he ages. During the early stages of Candiotti's stay in LA, noted *Los Angeles Times* columnist Mike Downey compared his tosses to fireball reliever Rob Dibble's. "When, say, Cincinnati's Dibble throws a wild pitch, he could wipe out a family of four. But with Candiotti pitching you could diaper a baby in your lap without a care. If a pitch gets away, your baby could reach up, catch it bare-handed, and fire it back at the pitcher every bit as fast."

Of course, not every one of his knuckleball memories is satisfying. During one game for the Dodgers in 1997, Candiotti hit four Houston Astros with pitches, including Derek Bell in the first inning and second inning to tie a Major League record. Candiotti hit three men in the first alone. Some hitters might take offense, but it was a soft knuckleball hitting these guys, so no riots broke out. It was more a case of "there goes that crazy knuckleball again," rather than the Astros believing Candiotti was trying to wipe them out. On the other hand, years later, Candiotti might well chuckle about that series of pitches.

By the time Candiotti retired after the 1999 season following a return to the Indians briefly, he was forty-one. His lifetime mark was 151–164 with a 3.73 earned run average.

After retiring as a player, Candiotti had the opportunity to first move into the Indians' front office and then in the early

2000s move into broadcasting with ESPN. He then became a broadcaster for the Blue Jays and more recently was a member of the Arizona Diamondbacks' team as a radio analyst.

A few years ago while performing those duties when the Diamondbacks were headed to Boston to meet the Red Sox at Fenway Park and were scheduled to face the game's then-premier knuckleballer in Tim Wakefield, Candiotti fielded a request from manager Bob Melvin. He asked Candiotti to throw batting practice at Fenway because many of the Diamondbacks had never seen a knuckler.

"Mark Reynolds swung at like the first seven knuckleballs and then threw his bat down and said, 'That's enough,'" Candiotti said. "It was funny. Then Melvin said, 'I think this is going to backfire on us.' I think Wakefield pitched something like a three-hitter."

Candiotti said he never felt old on the mound, but when he was still going in his forties and had to run around backing up first base or third base, his muscles did ache.

"You'd feel it the next day," he said. "It was never my arm. In 1981 I had Tommy John surgery, but that was before I threw a knuckleball. When I retired it had nothing to do with my arm. It's the rest of your body that breaks down. With the knuckler it's just not easy to do. It's a very difficult pitch to throw or more guys would do it. A lot of guys play catch throwing the knuckler and you can see very quickly who might have a good one. But it's one thing to *throw* a knuckleball. You have to have a *good* knuckleball."

As evidenced by that cameo appearance throwing batting practice for the Diamondbacks, knuckleball pitchers continue to be at a premium, with few carrying on the tradition. In

2001, when actor-comedian Billy Crystal, a devoted New York Yankees fan, was making the movie *61* about Roger Maris and Mickey Mantle pursuing Ruth's single-season home-run record, he recruited a knuckleball pitcher, not an actor, to play the role of Hoyt Wilhelm. Crystal hired Candiotti to play Wilhelm, which wasn't exactly casting against type. In the flick Candiotti threw a groundball out.

"I'm an official movie star now," Candiotti joked.

While broadcasting remained his livelihood after baseball, Candiotti found fame in a different way. He turned to bowling with a serious commitment and excelled in the game. He rolled a perfect 300 game and averaged more than 200 pins in a league in his off-season Scottsdale, Arizona, home. In 2007, Candiotti was inducted into the celebrity wing of the International Bowling Museum and Hall of Fame.

Candiotti said he was watching the Pro Bowler's Tour on TV when he decided to take up the game. The key was viewing the top rollers throwing curving balls for strikes. *I've done that my whole life*, thought Candiotti.

The ex-pitcher obtained a PBA card and played many games against the top pros. Amusingly, those guys were always asking him to throw a knuckleball down the lane.

"But I couldn't," he said. "It would be fun if I could."

It would be something to see a bowling ball weaving back and forth across the lane and swooping in on the head pin before scattering all ten.

19

STEVE SPARKS

HIS NAME BELIED his primary pitch. Steve Sparks sounded as if he would be the perfect purveyor of the fastball, but he ended up depending on the knuckleball during his nine-year Major League career covering 1995 to 2004. Instead of firing a ball that gave off sparks, Sparks threw a ball that sputtered its way to the plate like a Ford Model-T.

Sparks was born in Tulsa, Oklahoma, in 1965 and played college ball for Sam Houston State. He was drafted by the Milwaukee Brewers, but realized his fastball was too slow at about 82 mph, and his slider wasn't sharp enough to compensate for that limited velocity, so he buckled down to learn the knuckleball starting in 1991.

It took a while, but Sparks made his Major League debut with the Brewers in 1995. By then he was twenty-nine. The knuckleball kept him in the majors hurling for Milwaukee, the Anaheim Angels, and the Detroit Tigers; and it was with Detroit he had his one big year.

Sparks spent more than five years in the minors and it was beginning to dawn on him that he didn't have sharp enough stuff to become a big leaguer. His was the story of many knuckleballers, turning to the pitch as a last-ditch effort to save his career—indeed to even allow him to *have* a Major League career. He did not help himself in 1994 when, in a comic gesture that was more or less a Superman routine, he attempted to rip a phone book in half. The phone book won. Sparks separated a shoulder —his right, throwing shoulder.

It was not the brightest moment of his career, though it was probably the oddest. Sparks says that he always shows up on lists of those who suffered the weirdest or freakiest of baseball injuries.

"I'm always high up on the list." Sparks said he was severely admonished by Sal Bando, the Brewers' general manager, and manager Phil Garner, for the goofy incident.

The separated shoulder at the most inconvenient of times nearly derailed his career after he had made the adjustment to a knuckler to keep it going.

"I had peaked at AA," said Sparks, who became a Houston Astros broadcaster after retiring. "I wasn't going to make it to the Major Leagues."

He worked as hard as he could to develop a knuckler that would get him another look from the Brewers, who were ready to give up on him. Sparks made it into the Milwaukee rotation in 1995 when he started 33 games and finished with a 9–11 record and 4.63 earned run average.

"Looking back I was very appreciative of them giving me another chance. A lot of managers don't like knuckleballers and are prejudiced against them, and it's understandable, I guess, but Phil Garner recognized the niche I provided as far as pitching a lot of innings."

That was true for one year, at least (1995), when Sparks tossed 202 innings. His second year in Milwaukee ended badly, with a 4–7 mark and a shuttle between the majors and AAA. Then an injury kept him out the entire 1997 season after undergoing Tommy John surgery. In 1998, already thirty-two, Sparks surfaced with the Angels and posted a very solid 9–4 record.

It was peculiar that he got the big-league call at all, as he had an 0–8 record in AAA when the Angels called him up. Sparks said he was working his arm back into shape gradually, just throwing.

"The main thing was my arm was coming around and I was throwing well. I don't have to rely on velocity."

Ah, those famous last knuckleballer words.

Certainly, coming off his long stint in the minors, the up-and-down period with the Brewers, arm surgery and aging, too, Sparks was not highly counted on by the Angels for the '98 campaign. But they had lost three pitchers in the rotation to injury and by the end of the year, Sparks was a valued part of the rotation.

"He has been a godsend," said Angels manager Terry Collins.

When Sparks said velocity didn't matter, that was typical of a knuckleballer.

"That would defeat the purpose," he said. He scoffs at the position players who toss knucklers outside the lines and make it seem as if they know what they are doing. "It's really a much harder pitch to throw when you are on a mound. It's downhill. On flat ground they can keep their palm on the ball a bit longer. It's harder to do as a pitcher because you are on a slope."

Well aware that knuckleballers were and are an endangered species, Sparks sought help from the experts when he made his shift to the pitch, and after fellow Brewer connections Bando and Billy Castro and minor league pitching coordinator Bruce Manno suggested he try it.

"I'd gone to baseball cards to look at pictures to see how people threw it," Sparks said. "There was a lot of trial and error. Tom Candiotti was very gracious. We were in winter ball in Mexico. I had six pages worth of questions."

The fact that Sparks could even come up with six pages of questions indicated he was definitely a student of the knuckler already, if not a master of it.

"Nobody would say they're a master of that pitch," he said.

When he was still with Milwaukee, Sparks had the opportunity to sit around a bullpen shooting the breeze and picking the brain of Phil Niekro about the knuckleball. They spent two and a half hours together.

"That was one of my favorite moments," Sparks said. "Phil was just so gracious. I wrote down so many notes. He was such a wealth of information. He has been a perfect mentor to a lot of guys."

Sparks believes some pitchers have difficulty making the transition to a knuckleball pitcher because of their delivery. Useful throwing of the knuckler prohibits throwing across the body. If a pitcher can't adapt, he is not going to succeed with the knuckler.

Sparks said he thinks pitching coaches should be more proactive in teaching the knuckler rather than reactive when a pitcher is on his last chance. But he's not sure every pitching coach could handle the job because he might not know enough about the knuckler's habits.

"If you correct the wrong thing, you make things worse," Sparks said. "It's a very mechanical pitch. It's timing and tempo."

Sometimes when Sparks took the mound and began throwing the knuckler he realized fairly quickly that it could be an *uh, oh* kind of day. The knuckler was in a bad mood. Maybe it got up on the wrong side of the bed. There were only minimal adjustments to make without further jeopardizing the situation. He bore down, concentrated even more on each pitch, and occasionally things worked out with others on the field not even recognizing the pitch was not cooperating.

"I had some of my best games with bad knuckleballs," Sparks said. "You still try to change speeds. For me that was between 60 and 75 mph. I tried to change speeds every pitch."

Sparks may have been just what the Angels needed in 1998, but his control deserted him in 1999, when he finished 5–11 and he gave up too many hits (165) and walks (82).

"You have to set your ego aside and put your trust in a pitch you can't really control," Sparks said. "That's the hardest part."

That was one year the knuckleball showed him who was boss. One thing Sparks did enjoy was to have his turn in the rotation come around when his club was due to play in a domed stadium. The dome made for stable weather patterns. Not so in Comiskey Park in Chicago, where the wind often presented a bonus obstacle.

"I check the weather forecasts like a family planning a day at the beach," Sparks said.

One of the funniest things Sparks ever noted in an interview, and they were words as familiar to knuckleball pitchers as the lyrics to "Happy Birthday," was his philosophy on where the pitch might land.

"I can't say it ever goes against my expectations," he said, "because I never have any."

Sparks' time was up with the Angels after that unfortunate 1999 season. This was another insecure period in his career. Sparks became a free agent in October of 1999 and signed with the Philadelphia Phillies on February 1, 2000. The Phillies released him at the end of spring training, and three days later, he signed with the Detroit Tigers. That proved to be a good deal for everyone.

That year Sparks was pretty much a half-time pitcher for Detroit. He finished 7–5 with a 4.07 ERA while appearing in 20 games and throwing 104 innings. That represented a come-back of sorts for someone who was thirty-four and curious about where his next paycheck would come from—one hopefully stamped with the name of a big-league team.

In 2001, Sparks was at his best, going 14–9 (a .609 winning percentage) with an MLB-leading eight complete games and a 3.65 ERA. The knuckleball was definitely his friend that season. But that was a high point. After that, Sparks' career gradually slid downhill, just like that knuckleball. In 2002, he finished 8–16 and in 2003 he was released by the Tigers after going 0–6. He passed through the Oakland A's briefly and in 2004 signed with the Arizona Diamondbacks.

That's the thing about unpredictable knuckleballs and their practitioners: Even at advanced ages they might find the control of the pitch all over again for a late-career brilliant season, or control deserts them once and for all. Sparks' final year, with Arizona, fell short. He ended his pitching days with a 3–7 record and a 6.04 earned run average.

However, Sparks did not give up. He signed minor-league deals with the San Diego Padres, the A's again, and the Houston

Astros, yet did not make it back to the majors partially due to arm problems. The knuckleball that had rescued Sparks had forsaken him.

"From 2003 on, I didn't throw twenty good knuckleballs," Sparks said. "I just lost it. They were just tumbling up there. I mixed in other pitches, tried everything I could. But with the knuckleball, when you're lost, you're lost."

He was forty when he retired. That was the end of the line for Sparks on the mound, and his final overall marks were 59–76 with a 4.88 ERA.

Sparks did not ride the knuckleball to the Hall of Fame the way Phil Niekro did, but without it he would never have had a big-league career at all. And without that on his resume, it is unlikely he would have even become a Major League broadcaster.

"My arm has been in pretty good shape since I retired," Sparks said when he was forty-seven.

It is in good-enough shape to occasionally occupy the mound and throw batting practice for the Astros. Once in 2013 and once in 2014 when Houston was likely to face a knuckleball pitcher in a game, Sparks' phone rang requesting he throw a little BP to help the younger players who had never seen a knuckleball get adjusted. He did so.

"If I wasn't an employee of the Astros, I probably wouldn't do it."

Actually, he did face a similar request from the Yankees a few years ago when they were going to play against the Boston Red Sox in a playoff game with knuckleballer Tim Wakefield.

"I declined because of my friendship with Tim," Sparks said, proving that knuckleballers do stick together. "They were saying, 'Name your price.' With the Astros it was a different thing. I work for the Astros. Last year they were going up against Steven Wright of the Red Sox. This year it was R. A. Dickey with the Blue Jays. It was just so guys could see the knuckleball. I think I threw about 150 pitches. I think it is helpful to the hitters. It seemed to be early in the game [versus Wright]."

In April of 2014, the Astros anticipated a match-up with Dickey and after Sparks' batting practice session they beat the Blue Jays, 6–4. Houston manager Bo Porter said he believed Sparks earned an assist on the play.

"It's not every day that you face knuckleball pitchers," Porter said. "We are fortunate to have Steve come out and be willing to get in the cage. I think it paid dividends today."

One of the Houston hitters, Robbie Grossman, who homered in the game, agreed that it was beneficial to watch a bunch of knucklers thrown in BP in order to get used to what the pitch might do.

"I have to give credit to Sparksie on that," Grossman said. "Just seeing it, because you never see it."

Every once in a while either a young pitcher or an otherwise failing pitcher in the Astros' organization begins experimenting with the knuckleball and the club asks Sparks to take a look or help him out. So far none have made it to the majors.

"I visited for a few days," Sparks said. "I think temperament plays just as big a role as anything else. Guys that aren't as high strung and are more self-effacing tend to do better. There are so many guys throwing so hard, between 93 mph and 96 mph, and you want to take that away with the knuckleball. It's a hard pill to swallow."

The knuckleball is not far from Sparks' thoughts, even in retirement. He put on his thinking cap and tried to come up with a scientific way to make the pitch easier to catch and thus cut down on passed balls and wild pitches.

When the Blue Jays' R. A. Dickey hits the road, he packs the PROSPARKS Model catcher's mitt manufactured by Rawlings Sporting Goods from ideas presented by Sparks. It is the latest in the line of oversized mitts to aid the poor catchers who must anticipate the fluttery moves of the knuckleball twirler.

The webbing of the wide and long leather glove is quite tall and the ball can very easily fit into it and be engulfed by its size.

"I had some input into it," Sparks said. "It has some things in it to make a larger and lighter glove. The web is bigger. The ball has a tendency to scoop out on a tag play or a high pitch, or even a curve down. Catchers want to stay back as long as they can to catch a knuckler and this helps them grab it."

Compared to the good old days of the Deadball Era when players' gloves seemed to be no larger than mittens worn on a cold day, the big catcher's mitt is the Empire State Building of gloves. Catchers do need all the help they can get to field those tosses from knuckleballing teammates.

And those knuckleballers, in Sparks' mind, need to also have one very important trait to cope with the knuckleball that does so many dances, hops so much, and fools them as well as the batter.

"They should have a sense of humor."

20

KNUCKLEBALL HOPEFULS AND THE KNUCKLEBALL WORLD

THE QUESTION IS often asked: Why aren't there more knuckleball pitchers in Major League baseball? The answer is that it doesn't work for everyone. Sometimes a knuckleball hopeful comes close to saving a career because of the knuckler, but even in the limited sample of big-league knuckleballers, not everyone can pitch into their forties with the success of twenty-somethings.

Daniel Boone, born in Long Beach, California in 1954, was never a flamethrower. He stood five foot eight and he might have weighed something slightly south of 150 pounds when the majors got interested in him. Unlike the Daniel Boone who became one of the most famous Western figures of the early days of the Republic, this Daniel Boone did not have the physical tools to make a major impression. By big-league standards, he was a midget.

This Daniel Boone is related to *that* Daniel Boone, though quite distantly. The family tree indicates that the pitching Daniel

Boone is connected to the pioneer Daniel Boone's brother, Benjamin. So Daniel Boone the original would be an uncle seven generations removed.

The modern Boone may have grown up having people singing the TV show theme song to him, but wherever he went and wherever he played, the left-handed Boone also got hitters out. By 1976, after high school and his stay at Cerritos College and Cal-State Fullerton, he was drafted for a fifth time by a pro club, this time by the California Angels. The Angels liked Boone so much they drafted him three of those times, but by 1980 they had cut him. Talk about ying and yang relationships. He was next signed by the San Diego Padres, and in 1981, at the age of twenty-seven, the southpaw made his Major League debut. He was the smallest player in the majors, not correcting any writers who listed his weight as 135 or 140 pounds.

That season Boone appeared in 37 games—all in relief—and finished 1–0 with two saves and a 2.84 earned run average. He may have been small, but Boone's skills did seem to translate to the majors. Manager Frank Howard, the one-time slugger who was about twice as large as Boone, liked the way Boone pitched.

"If Danny had this much more on his fastball," Howard said, measuring a foot of distance with his hands, "he would have hitters begging for mercy."

The fun did not last very long for Boone with the Padres. While he once again finished 1–0 with one save, he played in just 10 games for San Diego and his ERA ballooned to 5.63.

Before the year was up, he was traded to the Houston Astros (for infielder Joe Pittman), for whom he toiled in 10 games with an 0–1 record. The Astros released him and he then signed with the Milwaukee Brewers, but didn't make the team and was released in 1984. So there he was, turning thirty and out of the majors with a lifetime 2–1 record.

Boone was married with kids, and unemployed. He spent the summer of 1985 pitching for the Anchorage Glacier Pilots of the Alaska Baseball League along with a bunch of college-aged players. A return to Alaska was appealing, being as his wife was from Anchorage.

No one representing a Major League city was interested in Boone. Nobody called. No one sent a telegram. He was devastated, saying some years later being released was the equivalent of being on "a great, huge ocean with a little boat sitting out there, and me sitting in the boat with miles of nothing around. Just . . . emptiness. And loneliness."

He painted a pretty bleak picture. Boone was like many hundreds, many thousands, over the years, who had a cup of coffee in professional baseball, but who fell short of fulfilling their dreams. During his early days of trying to make it in the majors and during his short stays with those Major League teams, Boone struck up conversations and friendships with Phil and Joe Niekro, separately, and quizzed them about the knuckler.

"I talked to Phil a little bit when he was with the Braves," Boone said recently.

He was a teammate of Joe Niekro's with the Astros.

"We would go out in the outfield and play catch throwing knuckleballs," Boone said. "He said, 'You should throw it in a game.' I was using it sparingly. Catchers didn't want to catch it. That was a bummer."

Boone had even attempted to throw knucklers when he was playing Little League, but then he had no control over the pitch.

Of course, he was even smaller when he was under twelve than he was at twenty-two.

"My hands were so small," Boone recalled, "it would spin and it didn't work properly. In high school I started messing with it again. I didn't even use a knuckler in the minor leagues. Coaches would say things like, 'Why would you use your number five pitch?'"

When Boone was with the Padres, the team's catcher was Terry Kennedy. One day when he entered a game in relief against the Cincinnati Reds, Boone gave up two doubles—one to future Hall of Famer Johnny Bench—who smashed the ball deep off the wall at Jack Murphy Stadium. On the mound, Boone was pondering what his next pitch should be. "I was thinking, *Oh, maybe this guy killing me is telling me what to do.*"

The next time around the order with Bench up, Boone got Kennedy to put the number five signal down for the knuckler.

"He smiled behind the mask. I threw the pitch right down the middle and I'm scared to death. He [Bench] swung and I struck him out."

However, the knuckler could not save Boone then. He hadn't evolved with it sufficiently, so he was out of the majors after 1984, though not out of baseball. He kept playing for semi-pro teams and competed in the short-lived Senior Professional Baseball Association for 35-and-overs that got its start in 1989. He excelled. Those ex-big leaguers were tortured by his knuckler.

"I was trying to get back into pro ball," Boone said. "I knew I had to come up with something better and it was the knuckler. In 1990, Birdie Tebbetts [the veteran baseball player, manager, and coach] was scouting for the Orioles."

Tebbetts was seventy-eight at the time and had been in the game forever. He liked what he saw in Boone and convinced Baltimore to sign him even though Boone was thirty-six and out of baseball almost a decade, was built more like a ninth-grader, and had zero zip on his pitches. General manager Roland Hemond took the plunge.

"Birdie kept telling me about this kid and his outstanding knuckleball," Hemond said. "Birdie kept calling him a kid. Later, I realized that Birdie's been around so long that to him a thirty-six-year-old is still a kid. That made Boone sound younger anyway."

Boone was the beneficiary of Tebbetts' sharp eye for skill and his blindness to age.

"I think they thought he was senile," Boone said. "I made the team."

Sort of.

Boone spent most of the summer at AAA Rochester—where he also kept a photo of the more famous Daniel Boone's gravesite in his locker—but was brought up in September, returning to the majors after a gap of eight years.

It did not hurt Boone's case that he pitched a no-hitter for the Red Wings, beating Syracuse 2–0 in an International League game. It was a seven-inning job because it was the second game of a doubleheader. Boone was carried off the field by teammates. One aspect of Boone's return to baseball was becoming a more religious man in-between stints. When he pitched the special game he wanted to kneel on the field and pray, giving thanks to the Lord, though he had difficulty since he was also toting the game ball.

"I tried to throw a no-hitter," Boone said. "At the beginning of the game that's not a realistic goal. I got through the fourth inning and my adrenaline started to flow. I thought it was a realistic goal. I got through the sixth inning. I said, 'Nine more outs.' Before I came out in the seventh inning, as far as pro ball is concerned, I wanted this more than anything. It was an overwhelming feeling."

That was quite an achievement. Even though his record was 0–0, Boone appeared in four games with a 2.79 earned run average.

"So I didn't get killed," he said. "I don't think [manager] Frank Robinson liked me because I didn't throw hard."

When Boone first stepped on a mound for the Orioles, almost three thousand days (2,908 to be exact) had passed between Major League appearances.

That was the end for Boone in the majors, but it was not the end of him pitching and relying on the knuckleball to keep him going wherever anyone might want a lightweight southpaw. By 1991, he was pitching for the Oklahoma City Rangers. Then in the mid-1990s he surprised long-time Alaska fans by returning to the Far North to pitch for the Fairbanks Goldpanners from 1993–96.

Almost all of the players in the Alaska Baseball League have profiles similar to Boone's when he first broke into ball in the 1980s. They were college players with pro aspirations honing their skills in quality summer play. Almost none of them had ever batted against a knuckleballer, and as Boone approached the milestone birthday—turned forty, and passed forty—he gave those nineteen-year-olds an education.

The frequency with which the slender Boone reared back and floated the knuckleballer to the plate, only to have husky hitters whiff at the air, could not be counted. Sometimes the misses were so egregious they produced laughter.

"Yeah, I chuckled sometimes," Boone said, "but I didn't want to make them feel too bad. I had no idea where the knuckler was going. All of a sudden it would drop at the last second. I didn't try to show them up."

Being twice as old as the competition, Boone did gain some incentive to bamboozle those hitters because of the names they called him like "Old Man" and "Grandpa." Maybe, he grudgingly admitted, he did want to show them up a teeny bit.

"So I didn't feel that bad."

By 1990, when he got his brief shot with the Orioles, Boone believed his knuckleball was as good as Tom Candiotti's, but that managers and coaches at the time weren't interested in giving him a chance. There is definitely some managerial prejudice against knuckleballers.

"It was a lack of understanding why I didn't get a better chance."

For how many knuckleballers may that be true? It's hard to know. Certainly, knuckleballers are at a premium. They have been during every decade, during every era. Some pitchers see Hoyt Wilhelm pitching to forty-nine and Phil Niekro right behind him and they think they have plenty of time to make an adjustment. Most wash out early because they can't get the knuckler over the plate. Only a select few throughout history even accomplish as much as Boone did with his knuckler and only the 1.1 percent or less of the rest of the best besides Wilhelm, such as Phil and Joe Niekro, Charlie Hough, Jesse Haines, and Ted Lyons, win as many as 200 games.

* * *

The odds are thousands to one against any high school baseball player reaching the majors. The odds are worse against any knuckleball pitcher making it. One who did was Charlie Haeger, if only for a short time.

Haeger, born in Livonia, Michigan in 1983, stands six foot one and his playing weight was around 210 pounds. Drafted by the Chicago White Sox in 2001, Haeger was just twenty-two in 2006 when he made his Major League debut. For a time it seemed possible that Haeger would break into Chicago's regular rotation and become the next big thing in the knuckleball world, if there is such a thing for an esoteric pitch.

That year the right-hander appeared in seven games, and went 1–1 with a 3.44 ERA. Things looked promising, but turned sour in 2007, when Haeger went 0–1 with a 7.15 ERA in eight appearances. He seemed to need more seasoning. Instead of dropping him to the minors, the White Sox put him on waivers and the San Diego Padres picked him up 2008. He was just 0–0 in four games before being given his free agency.

Haeger got a fresh chance with the Los Angeles Dodgers in 2009. That put him in proximity with veteran knuckleballer-coach Charlie Hough, who worked with Haeger in hopes of finding the magic elixir to become a big-league regular.

"He's been awesome," Haeger said. He was also thrilled to just make the Dodgers roster.

"It's hard when you're there [the majors] and you go back down," Haeger said. "Everybody experiences doubts. I think part of baseball is being able to overcome those doubts and believing in yourself. I have confidence in myself and I always had the belief I was going to get back. It was just a matter of when."

In limited action Haeger went 1–1 with a 3.32 earned run average and in 2010, after he finished 0–4 with an 8.40 ERA for LA, he was cut loose. Over the next few years Haeger tried and failed to stick with the Seattle Mariners and Boston Red Sox. He was out of the majors by twenty-six and has not bounced back again. One reason was he underwent Tommy John surgery in 2013.

Once recovered, Haeger did go 4–4 for the Red Sox' AAA Pawtucket team, and at thirty-one, is not old for a knuckleballer. Knuckleball pitchers seem to get more chances to resurface than other pitchers, probably because of the track record of many successes at advanced athletic ages.

* * *

Despite 12 wins for Pawtucket in 1999, that pattern did not quite work out for another Boston knuckleballer named Jared Fernandez. Born in Salt Lake City, Fernandez attended Fresno State and put together a 4–7 Major League record. He was big and strong at six foot two and 225 pounds, so Fernandez did not look like a man who would throw a floater. When he finished college, though, he was not drafted. His fastball was close to 90 mph, but he also mixed in a knuckler, which he soon comprehended would be his ticket to the top.

Fernandez received coaching aid from Tim Wakefield and Phil and Joe Niekro while trying to make the shift to a full-time knuckleballer. He said at first "it wasn't much fun," but that he got used to it. However, Fernandez never got over the barrier to making it in the bigs with his knuckler leading the way. He never pitched in the majors for Boston at all and his best year was a 3–3 mark and a 3.99 earned run average for Houston in 2003.

He left the Major Leagues in 2006, and in 2007, Fernandez signed a one-year contract for $200,000 to pitch in Japan for the Hiroshima Toyo Carp. That marked the end of his pitching career.

* * *

At five foot ten, right-hander Dennis Springer isn't much taller than Danny Boone, but he did weigh over 180 pounds, more common among professional athletes. Although Springer, born in Fresno, California in 1965, had a longer big-league career than Boone, Haeger, or Fernandez (spanning eight seasons), his lifetime stats were not overly impressive. He finished 24–48 with a 5.18 ERA after not breaking into the majors until he was thirty in 1995 with the Philadelphia Phillies.

Springer threw for six different teams in his eight big league seasons, with his best coming in 1999 with the Angels, when he went 9–9. When Barry Bonds hit his Major League single-season record 73rd home run in 2001, Springer was on the mound. The pitch was almost impossibly clocked at 43 miles an hour. That is nearly a surreal low speed, not even violating the speed limit in your car in some neighborhoods.

Springer previously threw faster than that—too fast in the thoughts of Phil Niekro, who slowed him down—though it's not clear if Niekro had tortoise speed in mind. Springer got knuckleball assistance from Niekro, and Charlie Hough was his advocate with the Dodgers.

As things rocked and rolled with the fickle knuckler, Springer tossed the occasional shutout. In one memorable game he out-dueled Hall of Famer Greg Maddux for a 2–0 Florida Marlins win in 1999.

"It is definitely a goofy pitch," Springer said. "You live and die with it, and hopefully you don't die too much."

The knuckler's lack of stress on the arm did permit Springer to throw 135 pitches in one game and come back two days later to throw 92. Shades of Wilbur Wood.

* * *

Throughout history the knuckleball has been a pitch of last resort for some and a pitch of experimentation for others, but it always seems to require an explanation from a pitcher about how or why he tried and incorporated it into his arsenal. Sometimes the acquisition was almost accidental.

Movement on the knuckler is what makes knuckleball pitchers winners. If the ball doesn't spin, it darts and dances. If it spins it's a fat hunk of meat waiting to be devoured by a hungry batter. The difference? Charlie Hough once said it's "about 400 feet."

Knuckleballers do indulge in self-deprecating remarks sometimes, supporting the notion that they must have a sense of humor about the pitch.

Bud Daley spent 1955 to 1964 with the Cleveland Indians, Kansas City Athletics, and New York Yankees. He developed a knuckler with the Indians when he wasn't winning and then won 16 games two years in a row for the A's. He was only a sometimes knuckler, though, and he never faired any better with the Yankees, who were a powerhouse, than he did with the lesser teams, and was out of the bigs by age thirty-one.

That was not before New York catcher Yogi Berra took some closer looks at the knuckler than he wanted to and announced that, "If everybody threw the knuckler, there wouldn't be a .200 hitter in the league." Berra was famous for saying many things, but this comment did not join the common lexicon. Of course, what he may not have realized more than fifty years ago was just how hard it is for pitchers to throw the knuckler.

Maybe Berra and other hitters would be at an unfair advantage if the knuckler was more prevalent. Bobby Murcer, another Yankee, once said of Phil Niekro, "Trying to hit him is like trying to eat Jello with chopsticks."

* * *

Over the course of time, catchers having a bad day have been charged with three passed balls in a single inning. Three of those guys were Gus Triandos, Joe Ginsberg, and Charlie Lau. One thing they all had in common on their notorious days was trying to catch Hoyt Wilhelm.

You didn't have to make frequent mistakes that showed up in the box scores to be a catcher who hated the knuckler. Butch

Wynegar, who caught Phil Niekro when he joined the Yankees late in his career, once philosophized about the pitch.

"I'm sure some hitters think the pitch was invented by the devil."

Willie Mays once said when facing Wilhelm, on the third pitch the batter should just swing and run to first. If there was no contact then it was likely the catcher missed the ball as well and the runner might be safe at first.

Part of the time J. C. Martin was catching for the White Sox, Wilhelm, Wilbur Wood, and Eddie Fisher were around throwing knuckleballs. Martin recently recounted the in-depth instructions he got from manager Eddie Stanky.

"He was giving me advice and he said, 'Catch it,'" Martin remembered. "Like I didn't know that."

The comment was definitely a little bit short on specifics since the real issue was *how*.

Once, when Bruce Benedict was catching for the Braves he was behind the plate as Atlanta faced Texas in a spring training game in Pompano Beach, Florida. On the mound for the Braves was Phil Niekro. Opposing him was Charlie Hough. That meant Benedict had to catch Niekro's knuckler and try to hit Hough's. He recalls it as being a particularly challenging day.

"I don't remember getting much leather on anything," he said, "or much wood either."

When a knuckleball documentary was filmed a couple of years ago, it made it very apparent to anyone not involved in the sport of baseball that there is a knuckleball fraternity, or sub-culture. That may have been common knowledge to insiders, but perhaps it wasn't obvious to the casual fan.

The focus of the film *Knuckleball* was Tim Wakefield, as he came to the end of his career with the Boston Red Sox, and R. A. Dickey, current big-league regular rotation knuckleballer. But interviews with many other knuckleball pitchers were woven in and demonstrated, too, the obvious camaraderie between knuckleballers of different generations. The younger guys sought out the older guys for advice, consultation, and help on an emergency basis when their balls were going flat. That also illustrated how it takes one knuckleballer to know another, otherwise the active pitchers would have sought out their own teams' pitching coaches.

Wakefield shook his head as he spoke, trying to fathom the twists and turns of his career. That's what you get when you rely on a knuckleball that moves in the same manner.

"A lot of times it has a mind of its own," Wakefield said of the knuckler. "You let it go and you see where it takes you."

Dickey was shown in his team's clubhouse—at that time the New York Mets—filing his nails. "To the masses," he said, almost sighing, "it's a circus pitch." At least a beauty salon pitch.

In the documentary, Dickey, Wakefield, Phil Niekro, and Hough gathered for a summit conference in a living room. One could image them discussing such issues as how to cure war in the Middle East. The biggies of the knuckleball world were exchanging war stories; tales from their own little wars.

"That's fun," Hough said, "really fun to strike out a batter and he has no idea why he missed it."

From a vantage point of long-ago retirement, Jim Bouton chimed in on the same theme, thinking back to the kind of power the special pitch sometimes bestows on a pitcher.

"You could humiliate the biggest, strongest guys," Bouton said. "They were at your mercy."

Phil and Joe Niekro helped Wakefield with his knuckleball when he was at a low point in his career. Hough helped Dickey when he was at a low point in his. They were passing knuckleball wisdom forward to worthy individuals who would keep the tradition of the strange pitch alive. It is important to them. They want players from a younger generation and future generations to reap the benefits.

They do not pretend that anyone who starts out fresh with the knuckler now will have an easy road. They, as well as anyone else, recognize that the path a knuckleball takes a player on is filled with potholes and offers no guarantees. Throwing the knuckler only offers the promise that a player who has lost hope can regain it. The work will be demanding and the rewards may be great, but they also may be elusive.

Meanwhile, maybe because he threw conventional pitches for a long time before switching to the knuckleball, Danny Boone said he gave up pitching for even semi-pro teams sixteen years ago.

"The last time I pitched competitively my shoulder was killing me," Boone said. "Lately, I'm watching fathers and sons play catch. But I do keep a glove and ball in my truck."

The catch would be soft toss. That sounds redundant for a guy who followed the knuckleball to the majors.

21

TIM WAKEFIELD

THE **TIM WAKEFIELD** story is similar to many of the tales that envelop knuckleball pitchers' personal histories. Without the knuckler, he never would have made it big in the majors. With the knuckler he was able to maintain a l-o-o-n-g Major League career and become one of the winningest pitchers in Boston Red Sox history. Wakefield retired in 2011, finished third all time (186) in wins for the Boston Red Sox, behind Cy Young and Roger Clemens (192).

Born in 1966 in Melbourne, Florida, Wakefield was a very good high school pitcher and attended Florida Institute of Technology, better known as Florida Tech. Wakefield was a first baseman and sometimes shortstop. He was such a good hitter that years later, in 2006, the school retired his number three uniform.

All of this other life in baseball came before he was an eighth-round draft pick of the Pittsburgh Pirates in 1988. Eighth-rounders do make it, but they do not represent heavy investments—either monetarily or philosophically—for a team.

It did not take long before Pirates experts at spring training in Bradenton informed Wakefield that the organization did not believe he had the goods to rise above AA as a position player.

What likely saved Wakefield's pro career was being spotted on the sidelines playing catch and teasing his partner with knuckleballs. Coaches saw the movement and said, "Hey, wait a minute." The team's outlook—and that of many teams—was to give an outgoing player at one position a shot at sticking as a pitcher. Gems were discovered by chance in those situations. That was what the Pirates did for Wakefield instead of shipping him home for good.

As successful Major League knuckleball pitchers often say, there is a big difference between toying with the knuckler among friends and using it as a career move. In their minds the position players who throw it on flat ground are pretenders. Wakefield had to prove he could be one of the genuine knuckleball artists. Just as being told that their fastball and curveball—which had carried them through high school, college and the big-league draft was not good enough—Wakefield could relate to other pitchers when he was told his hitting and fielding were not going to carry him.

If learning the pitch was a last desperation move for many pitchers, it was more of the same for Wakefield. It was a blow to his confidence being informed that he couldn't hit big-league stuff, and he was pretty surprised that he was being told he might have a big-league knuckleball.

Considering all of his options and still buying into the dream of playing in the majors, Wakefield converted from infielder to pitcher and began studying the knuckleball in earnest. Akin to the tale of the Niekro brothers, Wakefield was introduced to the knuckler by his father, Steve, in backyard catch games when he was about seven years old. The lob toss was just right for little kids and Wakefield's sister Kelly also participated. The funny thing was that both Wakefield and his dad agree that Tim did not like to play catch with a ball that swerved all over the place. It somehow offended him, no doubt giving him at least some kinship with catchers later in life who were paid to pluck it out of the air. But the backyard games did lay the knuckleball foundation for Wakefield, even if he never imagined that one day he would be counting on it for his livelihood.

Wakefield never forgot those early lessons and played with the pitch in his teens with friends, just to see how much he could make it break. It was more of a conversation piece than a serious tool to get batters out.

One time in college, when Florida Tech needed pitchers, Wakefield warmed up and tossed the knuckleball. Its behavior was so erratic that his catchers couldn't hold onto it and his manager didn't want him to use it. Apparently, Wakefield's latent ability was always present, even if his mind was not ready to accept the opportunity.

He made his minor-league debut as a hurler in 1989 in Class A ball. He showed promise and the next season won 15 games in AA. The knuckleball was working for him. His advancement was surprisingly swift through the Pirates' chain and in 1992, the six-foot-two, 210-pound right-hander was called up to the majors—as a pitcher.

It was a spectacular debut for Wakefield, then twenty-five. He went 8–1 with a 2.15 earned run average and made Pittsburgh fans swoon. His own head was spinning, even if the ball was not. What a change for a lifetime infielder and hitter. *The Sporting*

News named Wakefield the American League Rookie Pitcher of the Year.

When Wakefield was first notified he was going to "The Show," he was giddy if somewhat shocked.

"I freaked out," he said.

He reacted similarly when he was informed that he was going to start in his Major League debut on July 31, 1992. Nerves bugged him all day long leading up to the night game against the St. Louis Cardinals. Wakefield won the contest, 3–2.

Wakefield's knuckleball was on fire (if such a word can be applied to a slow-moving pitch), and he came out game after game and knocked off batters with aplomb, either throwing complete games or coming close. It was almost an automatic night off for the bullpen when Wakefield pitched. The Pirates manager at the time, Jim Leyland, referred to that period as "a whirlwind. I had no idea what to expect. I didn't really know who Tim Wakefield was. A lot of people didn't." Wakefield was new enough to the knuckleball that he didn't know it was supposed to come with ups and downs. (In his first seven starts, Wakefield never pitched less than six innings, and averaged over eight per start; he was 5–1 during that stretch.)

He was part of an excellent Pirates team that was on a nice run. In 1990 and 1991 the team had finished first and drawn more than two million fans both years. In 1992, his rookie year, the Pirates finished 96–66, and came in first again. He was an enormous help over the second half of the season. Capping the season for Wakefield, if not the team, was that he won two games in the National League Championship Series against the Atlanta Braves. However, the Pirates lost the playoff in seven games and did not advance to the World Series.

Unfortunately for Wakefield and the Pirates, the three-year streak of first-place finishes was about to end. Players, including Barry Bonds, one of the most feared sluggers in the game's history, left through free agency and the team finished 12 games under .500 the next year. And Wakefield was no longer a miracle man. The knuckleball went haywire and so did his performance. He finished 6–11 with a 5.61 earned run average in 1993. Everything gained was lost. He even needed minor elbow surgery.

In 1994 Wakefield, who wasn't sharp in spring training, wasn't even in the majors. He was sent to the team's AAA affiliate in Buffalo. He thought his visit near Niagara Falls would be short. Instead, he could have bathed in the Falls all summer. The trip did him little good because he finished 5–15 with a 5.84 ERA. That is not the kind of performance a Major League organization likes to see in the minors.

Wakefield learned in a hurry that the knuckler can giveth and can taketh away, and it is almost never going to be a smooth ride for long. Every single aspect of pitching with the knuckler revolves around delicate consistency and Wakefield, under pressure to produce fast, experimented with all of the pieces. None of them again added up to the whole of his rookie year.

The Pirates had been Wakefield's entire professional life. He was drafted by Pittsburgh, looked over as a position player by Pittsburgh, nurtured into a big-league pitcher by Pittsburgh, and rode the highest of highs with Pittsburgh at first. In 1995, Pittsburgh released Wakefield. The Pirates had given up on him.

It was as if Humpty Dumpty had taken a great fall and all of the king's horses and all of the king's men couldn't put his knuckleball back together again. Enter the Niekro brothers. Phil and Joe Niekro provided some emergency help and advice and treatment for Wakefield. They couldn't let a fellow knuckleballer flounder helplessly, and Wakefield had shown by his 1992 performance that he could do well with the pitch when all things were operational.

Many years later, when writing about Wakefield, Phil Niekro said, "We're a small group to begin with, so when I tell you that Tim Wakefield is one of the best knuckleballers of all time, I suppose that leaves some room for interpretation. So what I'll tell you instead is that Tim has been one of the best pitchers in the game for a long time, just so nobody gets bug-eyed from focusing on the knuckleball for too long." Niekro recalled ordering Wakefield never to lose confidence in his knuckler or he would come over and beat him up. "As knuckleballers, we really have only ourselves to rely on."

The Pirates cut Wakefield on April 20, 1995, and the Boston Red Sox signed him six days later and assigned him to AAA Pawtucket. It was the beginning of one of the great resurgences in club history. Two decades later, few remember that Wakefield was ever a member of the Pirates. He is that closely identified with the Red Sox franchise and remains wildly popular with fans.

Boston made Wakefield and he gave everything he had to them for years, establishing some estimable marks along the way. Everyone got used to the mix of good fortune and bad fortune of the knuckleball because most of the time, when it was needed most, Wakefield had the wild beast safely within his grasp. The 1995 season began with Wakefield thoroughly distressed by his employment circumstances and it concluded, as 1992 had, with him on top of the world, creating buzz every time he pitched and creating believers in the knuckler.

Wakefield was waiting for his chance at AAA. While at AAA Pawtucket, he went 2–1 with a 2.53 earned run average, showing no hints of the problems he had been saddled with in Pittsburgh. He went from being eminently hittable to almost unhittable. The Red Sox had some problems with the starting rotation because of injuries, so Wakefield got the summons to the big club earlier than he might have expected. The rest of 1995 was like a dream.

In 27 starts and 195 1/3 innings, Wakefield posted a 16–8 record with a 2.95 ERA and even finished third in the Cy Young Award voting. It was a ridiculously positive turnaround. Wakefield was almost scared to be too happy because of the extremes of ups and downs he had experienced pitching over the previous few years.

"I was in survival mode," he said. But survive, and thrive, Wakefield did.

He made big news in Boston in May 30, 1995, when the Red Sox announced plans to start him on two days' rest. Only with a knuckleballer would such a plan be viable in the modern era of the sport. Some columnists dredged up an infamous occurrence in the Red Sox past when Jim Lonborg was thrown into a 1967 World Series game on short rest and did not produce the desired result.

Lonborg was sought out to describe what pitching on two days' rest does to a man. "Knuckleball pitchers have a better shot at going on two days' rest because the nature of the pitch puts 50 percent less strain on the shoulder," said the 1967 Cy Young Award winner. "People always talk about Wilbur Wood starting both games of a doubleheader. He could do it because he was a knuckleball pitcher. A lot of other pitchers could not do that."

These days a manager would forfeit a World Series rather than shanghai a young pitcher into throwing on two days' rest. At least Lonborg knew his knuckleball history, even if he didn't throw one.

"You can pitch on two days' rest once in a while, as long as you don't do it too often," Lonborg said. Lonborg threw six innings against the Cardinals in that game and had the entire winter to recover after St. Louis won the crown.

As Wakefield's success continued, some sportswriters tried to play around and provide nicknames to him or the knuckleball world, one suggesting that the club of knuckleball pitchers be called "Phi Throwa Floata." It was humorous, but didn't stick.

"Charlie Hough once said that to be a knuckleball pitcher, you have to have the mind of a Zen Buddhist and the fingertips of a safecracker," said Wakefield, who did not confess to having either, though he didn't disagree. "I think that pretty much sums it up right there."

Although it probably still pained him to admit it, once Wakefield got rolling with the knuckler in Boston and was asked how he fell into bed with such a wild damsel, he spilled the Boston beans.

"I couldn't hit."

Wakefield was in the early stages of what has become at least two additional decades of trying to explain the knuckleball to the world at large.

"Everyone thinks there's a secret to it," Wakefield said. "And everyone tries to find out the secret, but there is no secret."

Mankind is closer to discovering what happened to Amelia Earhart than a universal theorem on how to throw the knuckleball. Probed on the ideal length of fingernails, as if that would unlock the secret, Wakefield shook his head and replied that there was no standard, only what felt right to the individual pitcher.

It was apparent that after a few seasons of good and bad allegiance to the knuckleball, Wakefield was all in. The clue was his repeating the comments of Phil and Joe Niekro that a knuckleball guy could not let frequent walks eat him up. There were going to be times when the knuckler floated more like a piece of paper in the wind than a butterfly.

"One thing they said was to be aggressive," Wakefield said. "Who cares if you walk nine or ten guys in a game?" Well, the manager for one. Or maybe the pitching coach, or perhaps teammates. "It's going to happen with the knuckleball because I don't know where it's going and neither does the hitter."

One of the coolest things any teammate ever said about Wakefield came from Mo Vaughn, the one-time Sox slugging first baseman, who got it about both the player and the pitch, summing up their relationship neatly.

"He's just like a knuckleball," Vaughn said. "He's laid back. He just floats in here. He's got that knuckleball attitude."

There may not ever have been enough knuckleball pitchers to even have a scientific sample that would generalize a thing like that. But Wakefield, who did seem to be on an even keel for his entire career (with a few exceptions), sounded like the kind of person who might throw a knuckler.

"I'm more of a down-to-earth guy that relates to the fans. I'm just a normal guy, just like everyone else."

Checking the dictionary definition of the "knuckleball," the inquisitor might not find the word "normal" in the first few sentences. He would have a better chance of finding a word like "aberration."

At one point during the '95 season Wakefield was 13–1 and Phil Niekro was fielding telephone calls to explain what magic he imparted to the previously suffering hurler. They worked together for just two weeks, Niekro said, so the main credit belonged to Wakefield, not him.

"He did it, not me," Niekro said. "We worked, but it was his show after that. And he came back from the dead."

That's it. Maybe knuckleball pitchers who revise their repertoire have more in common with zombies than other pitchers. Why not the supernatural? Wakefield was on one of the greatest hot streaks in the history of knuckleball pitchers, reaching 14–1 before the law of averages caught up to him. He helped pitch the Red Sox into first place and confused even the very best of American League hitters along the way.

"It's not like we made a lot of mistakes," said Cleveland Indians power hitter Jim Thome after a game. "It's just hard to prepare for the knuckleball. You've got to wait and get a pitch up in the zone. But his knuckleball was rising and we still couldn't hit it."

Worse for some of those teams, they barely had any idea who Wakefield *was*, since he had come over from the National League where he had only pitched for a short while. The more people talked about Wakefield's story the more amazed they were. He was a hitter ready to be thrown out of the sport; a pitcher who quickly blazed a fresh trail with a pitch practically no one uses. Then he collapsed completely and was dropped by his first team.

And there he was again, back pitching as well as anyone in the game.

"He is not only the comeback player of this year, but the comeback player of any year," said Red Sox catcher Mike Macfarlane.

One of the things Wakefield uttered when he was riding high was a cliché that pitchers mention a lot. But given where he was coming from, it seemed an appropriate comment.

"I know you're only as good as your last start."

Once Wakefield emerged from his funk and began achieving fresh standards of excellence, there was some talk about how the Pirates must have let him down or were too impatient. Pirates' officials argued back that they tried everything. Wakefield held no grudge and said Pittsburgh did all it could to regenerate him. It was Leyland who said that perhaps Wakefield needed a change of scenery. Fenway Park's scenery was looking as pretty as the finest landscape to Wakefield by then. He pretty much blamed himself for the Pittsburgh failure, partly due to pressure of his own making.

"I tried to make perfect pitches instead of just letting it go," Wakefield said of the knuckler, "letting the natural movement work for me."

Few of Wakefield's seasons with the Red Sox could match 1995, but he established himself as a reliable contributor who could pitch in the rotation, start on short notice, and throw relief when needed. Wakefield was always available to help out in whatever role the Red Sox asked of him. Some years he was an essential member of the rotation, while other times he filled in when an urgent problem arose. Wakefield was always there, always on call, and almost always came through with a big performance.

The 1996 season was shaky enough to make Wakefield worry. Although his record was 14–13, his earned run average shot up to an unacceptable 5.14. While mama did not say there would be days like this, the Niekro brothers warned him. By 1998, though, Wakefield was 17–8 again. At various times Wakefield also gained some sharp-eyed help from Charlie Hough and Tom Candiotti, other members of the knuckleball crowd always eager to assist a fellow knuckler if he seemed in need.

Macfarlane had never caught a knuckleball hurler before Wakefield came along—at first he said he was terrified to do it—but he coped and got used to the challenge. He also said Wakefield's knuckler was so good he forced batters to swing.

"The hitters can't wait him out," Macfarlane said. "I just set up in the middle of the plate and ask him to throw to the area."

Wakefield was well aware of some of his limitations and that meant the speed of the knuckler. A part of him always carried around that need-for-speed feeling that is common in the game, even if he knew deep down that wasn't him. Yes, Wakefield said when asked if it were possible that a baseball stadium reading of his knuckleball thrown in the 50-plus-mile range was accurate.

"Right now," he said in 2008, "it's pretty much in the sixties. I wish I could throw it 80 mph. If I could throw it 80, yeah, it would help. It would provide an edge. But no, I never did. It was always that maybe I got to 71 or 72 mph. That's all I got."

Usually that was enough. The Red Sox did view Wakefield as a versatile weapon, a staple of the roster, even as managers changed, players came and went, and even top management changed. He won 12 games in 1997, had that great 17–8 season in 1998, and the next year had 15 saves out of the bullpen even when he otherwise struggled. (Wakefield went 6–11 with a 5.08 ERA in 1999.)

Wakefield learned some lessons that stuck when he was praised to the sky when pitching great and denigrated when he was pitching lousy. It certainly taught him not to be complacent.

"I read so much criticism about me when I was going bad that I started believing it. I stopped reading and listening and I'm not going to start again now just because it's turned around. I can never forget where I've been and what I've been through."

Almost as distinctive about Wakefield as his prime pitch was the goatee he wore and his devotion to local charities. Wakefield gave a lot of time and effort to several groups and was recognized for it, eight times being the Red Sox team nominee for the Roberto Clemente Award. That Major League award is presented to the individual who gives the most to the community, and Wakefield received the award in 2010.

As time passed, Wakefield became the longest-serving member of the Red Sox. Especially in the age of free agency, it was rare for a player to stick around more than a half-dozen years or so. Something always came up, whether it was contract issues or varying personnel needs. But Wakefield persevered in Boston and reacted and adapted to changes, always emerging as a key player for the team.

He was 11–5 in 2002 at age thirty-five after a down year in 2001 at 9–12. Wakefield went 11–7 in 2003, 12–10 in 2004, and 16–12 in 2005. Sure there were times the knuckleball became too hittable and Wakefield was knocked around, but he always fixed things and volunteered to pitch when the team was short-handed, the bullpen was too tired, or by just taking an extra turn.

Several years into his Red Sox tenure, Wakefield was asked to pause and talk about some of his knuckleball experiences. He was asked what people don't understand about knuckleball pitchers. That could have been a book-length retort to cover all of the angles, but Wakefield kept it short and simple.

"I think the fact that I just don't throw hard," Wakefield said of his usual 62–72 mph range. "People ask, 'Why don't you throw it harder?' I can't. It doesn't make it better to throw it harder. You're relying on movement instead of speed."

One of the most telling comments—and somewhat humorous ones at the same time—suggested that Wakefield might actually be able to count on the observations of pitching coach Joe Kerrigan, a non-knuckleball expert.

"It's taken him five years to understand me," Wakefield said, "but he's gotten a grasp of what to look for if something goes wrong. My mechanics are pretty much as basic as they are for a conventional guy."

Just different is all, if anyone saw Wakefield pitch. He threw more as if he were heaving a shot put, with his wrist bent way back.

* * *

Wakefield was on the losing end of one of the most painful losses in Red Sox history, one of those seemingly jinxed failures against the overbearing New York Yankees. It was Game 7 of the American League Championship Series in 2003, and Wakefield surrendered the game-winning home run to Aaron Boone. Boone became a hero in New York for the 11th-inning blast and Wakefield was the goat.

He feared that all of his other Red Sox achievements would be overshadowed and that he would forever be vilified by the fan base. In other words, he was worried that giving up one big homer would make the locals forget about all of the good things he had done on the mound for Boston and lump him together with Bill Buckner. For years (although he now seems forgiven), Buckner was blamed in Boston for losing the 1986 World Series when he made a late-game error. He was made the butt of jokes and insults for a long time in Boston, though the passage of time and the capture of three World Series titles since then may have freed Buckner from fan vituperation for good.

"I was terrified that I would be remembered like Buckner," Wakefield said during the off-season after the 2003 loss. "I was terrified I wouldn't be able to show my face in Boston again."

Perhaps Wakefield *had* built up enough good will to avoid that fate, but he seemed to escape the worst of the vilification. Wakefield admitted he cried in the clubhouse after the deciding play. That was despite winning two other games over New York in the same series.

"I was asked to do a job and I didn't get it done. I was disappointed in myself. I felt like I let my whole team down. People said we wouldn't have gotten this far if it wasn't for me. I believed that in a sense, but I was asked to do something and I couldn't get it done."

As the start of the 2004 season approached, Wakefield had to endure revisiting the bad memory more than once with sportswriters, but he assured them he could put the experience aside and concentrate on the new season's action.

"It's not going to follow me the rest of my life. Not that I would let it, anyway. It's a new season. We move forward from here."

That next season the Red Sox staged one of baseball's greatest comebacks by overcoming the Yankees in the championship series, with Wakefield winning Game 5. They then swept the St. Louis Cardinals in the World Series, the team's first such title since 1918. Wakefield was not a pivotal factor, but he got into one game and earned a championship ring. Not every moment on the way to the crown was smooth sailing for him, though. That season Wakefield tied a Major League record he didn't want any part of by allowing six home runs in a game. The weirdest aspect of the match-up against the Detroit Tigers was that Wakefield got the victory in the 11–9 triumph.

The Red Sox won another World Series in 2007 when Wakefield was forty and after he completed the regular season with a 17–12 record. However, his back and shoulder started bothering him and much to his chagrin and sadness he was not able to take his expected spot on the Series roster.

"As a competitor I want to be out there, competing. This is the ultimate stage. This is what I've worked for from spring training through the course of the season and now I can't be available. I mean it sucks, to put it bluntly."

Ordinarily he would have been a starter, but the Red Sox swept Colorado anyway. At the time there was some talk that Wakefield might be forced to retire, but he recovered over the winter and kept going, typical knuckleballer that he was, pitching into his forties.

Wakefield won 10 games for the Sox in 2008 and partway through that season during a road trip to Chicago to play the White Sox, he discoursed on the knuckler. It was definitely a subject he could hold court about.

Then forty-one, Wakefield was mindful, but not terribly concerned, that there was once again a shortage of knuckleball pitchers on the horizon. He had spied R. A. Dickey coming along, but did not believe the pitch would disappear from the majors.

"No, there will always be somebody who comes along who throws it," Wakefield said. "Not very often. There may be a time where there might be nobody in the majors, but then you might see one or two pop up. It's very rare. I've heard that Eddie Cicotte was the first to throw it, but it is funny it's him because of his involvement in the "Black Sox" scandal. For a while it was only me and Steve Sparks in the majors and for the last three or four years I was the only one. Now R. A. Dickey is coming in."

The byplay with hitters who know him and know the knuckleball was coming their way was always a subject of interest to Wakefield.

"Sometimes they say they can't believe they missed it when they swung and sometimes I've heard them say that they couldn't believe they hit it when they hit a home run. It finds the bat somehow sometimes. Guys are not surprised by me. I've been in the big leagues so long and most of them have seen me. It is a little bit exaggerated when I say, and others say, that we don't know where the ball is going. I kind of know a little what's going on, but it does sometimes go where I don't expect it to."

In the later years of his Red Sox career, Wakefield was usually caught by Doug Mirabelli, who acquired the sobriquet of being called Wakefield's "personal catcher." It was just that Mirabelli had a gift for catching the knuckler. He didn't always love doing it, though. In the *Knuckleball* documentary, Mirabelli took note of the change in his hair color and said, "These are all Wakey's right here. All these gray hairs." He sounded a lot like J. C. Martin examining his own scalp and blaming the color on Hoyt Wilhelm, Eddie Fisher, and Wilbur Wood.

Contrary to belief, Wakefield said he did get tired from throwing the knuckler sometimes.

"Once in a while," he said. "It depends on my workload per inning, pitches per inning. It depends on that. I threw a lot of innings. That's one thing I'm very proud of doing."

One thing that Wakefield learned over the years is that the hometown Boston fans really appreciated the knuckler, though of course more so when it was working. There was just something about the slow ball twisting those muscular, athletic hitters into pretzels when they swung and missed.

"They love it," Wakefield said. "They love it. They don't take it for granted. I hear a lot of comments. When it works well, it's fun to throw. When it's not [working], it could be a quick night."

Nearing the end of his career, Wakefield could tell the difference between the younger version of himself and the older version. He admitted that his arm was not as spry as it used to be.

"Not quite," he said. "Ten years ago I could throw every day. I could start and then go in and relieve for a day or two. Not anymore. Now I need my normal four days of rest."

He could be forgiven. At the time Wakefield was forty-one, long past retirement age for most pitchers.

Wakefield outlasted more than young pitchers with the Red Sox. When he finally retired after the 2011 season at age forty-four, he had 200 wins on his resume in a 19-year career. He spent 17 of those years with the Red Sox. Wakefield was the longest-tenured pitcher in Red Sox annals and holds the club record with 3,006 innings pitched and games started with 430.

Despite being offered a minor-league contract to come to spring training at age forty-five, Wakefield thought his aching body gave him the message that it was time to go. He said he even got a Major League offer from another team. Wakefield was getting as much nationwide attention as ever because of the airing and distribution of the documentary about the knuckleball. He did not really want to retire—most players don't want to do it—but he thought it over for most of the 2011–12 winter and, as the Red Sox were beginning spring training, he announced his decision.

A retirement ceremony was conducted in Fort Myers, Florida, where the Red Sox were assembling to kick off the new season. Wakefield stood at a podium in left field. He shed a few tears as he said his good-byes and then just like those cowboys in the Westerns, Tim Wakefield walked off into the sunset, his knuckleball holstered for good.

22

R. A. DICKEY

A COUPLE OF years ago the only practicing knuckleball pitcher in the Major Leagues estimated that he and his family had moved thirty-seven times because of baseball. If ever there was an illustration of the lack of security offered to a player trying to make the grade, that number will resonate with the average American.

In other words, being a professional baseball player—especially one neither entrenched in the majors, nor comfortably on the roster of a big-league team—is not all glamour. Like many of his compatriots in the knuckleball brotherhood, Dickey came to the pitch the hard way.

He has bounced all over the map, been informed he was finished as a player, and been underestimated and almost run out of the game. But he persevered, rose up, reached heights rarely gained by knuckleballers, and after all of the hiccups and derailments, his career is still going strong with the Toronto Blue Jays.

During the 2014 season, also, Dickey was the lone Major League standard-bearer of the knuckleball, except for others' brief cameos. He was pretty much the last man standing as others got too old and retired and nobody followed through the minors in their footsteps. There were some knuckleball hopefuls attempting to make it to the top, but they were mostly on hold in the minors.

It was Dickey who was "that guy," the knuckleball man upholding the pride and lore of the quirky pitch, going solo (although help from ex-knuckleballers like Charlie Hough was only a telephone call away). Dickey is not really the lead singer in a band or the front man for a cause. He is just trying to make a living as a pitcher. For him the only way—much like Tom Candiotti, Tim Wakefield, and Hough, who wanted to either play other positions or throw pitches in a different manner—was coming to terms with the knuckleball.

The adventure continued for Dickey in 2014. Some days the knuckler was great and other days it wasn't. Some days it appeared that the Blue Jays would run away with the American League East Division title and other days they were clinging to a playoff spot. As Dickey's fortieth birthday approached at the end of October, he held on to a regular rotation slot.

In 2012, Dickey performed one of the great feats any knuckleballer has ever achieved. He won the National League Cy Young Award with a 20–6 record and a 2.73 earned run average for the New York Mets. He made the entire knuckleball clan proud.

Dickey was born in Nashville, Tennessee, grew up in Tennessee, and pitched for the University of Tennessee. His fastball peaked in the mid-90s. He was a first-round draft pick of the Texas Rangers in 1996, something he was quite excited about . . . but from that high point his career was more about lows, interspersed with the occasional good moment—for years. Dickey had been a member of Team USA and won a bronze medal at the 1996 Summer Olympics in Atlanta. He was drafted out of high school by the Detroit Tigers, but continued his education instead of turning pro right away. By '96 he was a much better pitcher with a good track record and some notoriety after being an Olympian.

In a memoir about his baseball journeys, Dickey was at first concerned that he dropped to the 18th overall pick, but was content to land with Texas.

"So how can I be unhappy?" Dickey wrote. "The Rangers hardly scouted me because they didn't think I'd still be around when they picked. Now I am in the same organization as Nolan Ryan . . ."

Dickey had insured his right arm with Lloyd's of London for $1 million when he was still playing for the Volunteers. No one ever insures their off-arm. That might be something Bill Lee would do. After the Olympics, Dickey and his agent, who negotiated an $810,000 signing bonus that pretty much blew the player's mind, flew to Arlington, Texas, to sign a contract. As a matter of routine with a first-rounder, the team set Dickey up with one of its doctors for a routine physical.

The doctor was concerned about an X-ray of Dickey's elbow and expressed concern to the team that it was oddly formed. Dickey had not had arm problems and threw in the '90s, so there was no evidence that there was any cause for concern. Still, the upshot was that the Rangers became skittish about signing him and took back the offer. It was one of those occasions when a person can hardly believe what he is being told and his stomach flip-flops.

Doctors determined that Dickey did not have an ulnar collateral ligament at his elbow in his throwing arm, and didn't trust he would fare well from the rigors of big-league pitching. After that evaluation the Rangers offered Dickey $75,000 to sign, which he took. No. 1 draft picks are normally treated like royalty and given every chance to succeed. A deal for less than 10 percent of the original offer definitely limited Texas' risk and set the Rangers up with less to lose if Dickey's arm blew out.

Years later, Dickey reflected on his emotions at the time—and the hit his bank account took—with an intriguing comparison. One minute he was a No. 1 draft pick and the next minute he was being treated like a No. 8 draft pick, or something akin to that.

"You can imagine winning the lottery and losing the ticket," Dickey said. "That led me down an interesting path."

The signing began a long battle for Dickey to reach the majors. It took five years before he even threw a pitch for Texas, making four appearances and going 0–1 in 2001, when he was already twenty-six. When he was called up to the majors, Dickey's wife Anne, his mother, and about a dozen friends and family members joined him at the park.

Dickey never threw a pitch in the majors in 2002, but in 2003, he finished 9–8 for Texas, even though his earned run average was north of five runs per game (5.09 to be exact). In 2004, Dickey went 6–7. He showed little to make the Rangers see him as an integral member of the rotation. He pitched sparingly for Texas in 2005 and 2006, and didn't even throw in the majors in 2007. Dickey was already in his thirties and his future in Major League ball looked bleak.

By then Dickey had lost velocity on his fastball. It wasn't nearly as fast anymore, not even cracking 90 mph. He developed what he called a forkball as a back-up, but whatever he called it, it had an awful lot in common with a knuckler. In fact, after some experts viewed him, the off-pitch was described as a knuckler. Only Dickey threw his knuckler harder than most other knuckleballers, hurling it to the plate mostly between 70 and 75 mph.

The conversion began with an injury early in the 2005 season. Dickey went on the disabled list because of what he described as a stabbing pain in his shoulder. That was followed by a summit meeting with manager Buck Showalter, bullpen coach Mark Connor, and pitching coach Orel Hershiser. Hershiser did most of the talking in a soothing manner, or as much of a soothing manner as possible when the team tells you everyone thinks you would be better off in AAA Oklahoma City and that it might be time to become a full-time knuckleballer.

Dickey described the circumstances as his being "a thirty-year-old journeyman whose career is hanging by a glove string." Connor later told him that the only way Dickey was going to return to the majors was as a knuckleball pitcher. His career throwing regular stuff was kaput. He was depressed, but had to admit the Rangers team bosses were right because his fastball had dropped to around 85 mph.

"It's as if I've traded in a sports car for a tricycle," Dickey wrote of changing from a 90-mph fastball pitcher to a 60-something-or-so knuckleball pitcher. "It's hard to throw the ball slow."

Just how hard it could be Dickey discovered in his first start depending on the knuckleball against the Iowa Cubs. He gave up 14 hits and 12 earned runs. He was still figuring it out when the Rangers made him a September call-up in 2005.

Early on in the conversion process, Dickey gained an audience with Charlie Hough, who had been a major addition to the Rangers staff as a knuckleballer some years earlier. Dickey not only knew his reputation, but was glad to have the advice and said it was a thrill to hang out and talk to an accomplished knuckleball pitcher. "Meeting Charlie Hough, for me, is akin to meeting Cy Young himself."

The Rangers arranged the blind date between Dickey and Hough and they immediately hit it off. Hough was quite willing to help. He also possessed a good sense of humor about the knuckler, as seems to come with the territory.

"I learned it in a day," Hough said, "and then spent twenty-five years trying to get it over the plate."

Ironically given the changing dynamics of baseball where how many pitches a starter throws is uppermost in managerial minds when it comes to strategy, Hough stressed that pitch counts are irrelevant to knuckleballers.

"Pitch counts aren't part of the equation with knuckleballers. The only reason you take one out is if you think he can't win."

Hough said he often threw 140 pitches in a game, a number that would make present-day managers gag. What Dickey needed, Hough said, as much as his own confidence and ability to accept a learning curve, is for the team and organization to support him.

"The problem with the knuckleball is that it's not a successful part-time pitch," Hough said. "The first pitch is a knuckleball and the last pitch is a knuckleball."

Dickey had to educate himself about the knuckleball, get to understand its nuances, realize it was not always going to behave the way he wanted it to and also recognize— knowledge gained over time—that not everyone liked or trusted the knuckleball.

He said he was certain that feeling stemmed from the fact that the knuckler was a slow ball.

Dickey might well be right that the knuckleball would get better public relations if it was thrown at a faster speed. It is open to ridicule when it floats into home plate at 65 mph. Fans read that on the outfield wall radar gun report and laugh. They do not cower in fear the way they might when Aroldis Chapman, the Cincinnati Reds' relief pitcher who hits 104 mph occasionally, is on the mound. The baseball person loves speed and respects speed, quantifies speed, and scouts speed.

There seems to be a general belief that if a knuckleball pitcher is hit hard, it's the fault of the pitch not doing its job. It's challenging enough for a knuckleballer to accept that sometimes the knuckler is going to be out of his control, never mind make others understand that and come to terms with it.

"You never stop working on your grip," Dickey said, and that's why he kept a ball with him at all times. When driving the car he might have a baseball in the seat next to him to grab and grip. The feel for the knuckleball is all important.

Showing just how difficult it is to shift from pitching with the know-how accumulated over time to readjusting all motion, Dickey said when he first began throwing a knuckler he managed just "two good ones" out of ten. Good ones might not mean over the plate as much as good enough to move around and handcuff a batter.

Further proof that you never know what the knuckler will do, Dickey gave up six home runs in a game to the Detroit Tigers. That tied the negative record held by Tim Wakefield and others, though unlike Wakefield Dickey did not have the extraordinary luck to win his game.

Dickey became a fixture going back and forth between Texas and Oklahoma City until in late 2006, ten years after he was drafted, the Rangers released him. He signed with the Milwaukee Brewers, didn't play in the majors in 2007, and was again granted free agency. He signed with the Minnesota Twins, but a month later was drafted from them by the Seattle Mariners. In March of 2008, before the regular season, Dickey was drafted back by the Twins. The same day he was traded back to the Mariners.

To most he was only just beginning to be identified as a knuckleball man, which was a topic when he joined Seattle.

"To take a new path in order to stay in the big leagues I've had to let go of everything that got me there," Dickey said. "I had to commit. To do that, to become somebody new, to really leave who you were behind, it's really hard. Very difficult. I still have enough of an arm to be able to get hitters out without having to throw a knuckleball to survive. But for me, the interesting thing has been to balance my pitching personality with trying to become this knuckleball pitcher."

Actually, by making such a statement that he didn't have to throw the knuckler to survive, Dickey sounded like an alcoholic in denial. If that was true at that very moment, it wasn't true for long.

"It's such a funny pitch," Dickey said. "It requires a lot of humility and a lot of hard work to get it right. And because of that it makes you really respect the pitch. And sometimes man, you'll throw one and what the ball does in the air when you throw a perfect knuckleball in a perfect condition, it's mesmerizing. And the response you get from the hitters is a lot of times comical."

Dickey went 5–8 for Seattle that season (with a 5.21 ERA). While with the Mariners Dickey tied a Major League record—one of those things that seem to happen to knuckleballers when they least expect it: he threw four wild pitches in one inning. At the time he was the fifth pitcher to reach that mark. Phil Niekro was another on the list. Coincidentally, the event occurred against the Twins. Maybe the Twins watched in horror that game thinking, *If not for fate, he could have been doing that with us.*

"It was moving violently," Dickey said of his knuckleball, as if he was reporting on a wind storm. "If I could have thrown it for strikes it would have been a real fun day. But I couldn't throw it for strikes."

After the season Dickey was granted free agency once more, and then signed with the Twins a day after Christmas. It was dizzying. Dickey actually played for the Twins during the 2009 season, going 1-1 in 35 games. At least he actually saw Minnesota that time, which he hadn't done in 2008.

* * *

Several years into knuckleball experimentation and commitment, Dickey had made the rounds of the knuckler medics—working most significantly with Hough—but also discussed the pitch with Phil Niekro and Tim Wakefield. He said he twice visited Hough in California and the other two "have both been generous with their counsel. I've been able to add to that foundation and slowly add my own personality to the pitch." That is imperative since knuckleballers are not clones.

Over the years Dickey came across other Major League players who did not have ulnar collateral ligaments. Michael Cuddyer, who led the National League in batting for the Colorado Rockies in 2013, and Carlos Gomez, thrived as outfielders without that little body piece. Scott Erickson won 142 games for six teams in the big leagues between 1990 and 2006 minus an ulnar collateral ligament.

While Dickey told sportswriters that some doctors think that ligament simply disintegrated in his body, he guesses he was born without one. Nonetheless he has been pitching for a long time without it.

After the 2009 season, Dickey became a free agent all over again. At this point in his career, if you looked up the definition of "fringe player" in the big leagues, Dickey's picture would have accompanied it. He was everywhere and nowhere all at once. He had no stability, no security. He was wanted by one team and rejected a minute later. At the very end of 2009, Dickey signed with the New York Mets, a new team rescuing him from the free agent market.

For some players the chance to become free agents is one to maximize salaries and become richer than they ever dreamed of, but for Dickey it was a matter of finding a new job and hopefully with a team that really wanted him and saw the possibilities in his knuckleball. Joining the Mets did prove to be a turning point in his career.

Dickey had been only an average pitcher, his knuckleball being a distinguishing characteristic that got him looks by several teams, but did not result in him becoming a hot property. In 2010, Dickey produced the best Major League season of his life to date with the Mets. He was thirty-five years old, so it was definitely now or never, but that season Dickey not only won 11 games while starting 27, his earned run average of 2.84 sparkled. His 174 1/3 innings pitched outdid his workload with any other team by more than 60.

It was a long time coming, but Dickey had finally arrived. He was filling the role for a big-league club which had been his long-sought goal. He was a full-time member of the Mets' starting rotation, taking the ball every fifth day and fooling batters regularly when he did.

For so many years Dickey had been signing one-year contracts and generally making around the Major League minimum.

Compared to the rest of humanity, Dickey made a lot of money with his $300,000-plus salaries and his one-year deal with Minnesota that paid $525,000. But at the end of each season, he never knew where his next paycheck was coming from or even if he still had a career. After that solid season for New York, Dickey had the luxury of asking for a two-year contract, and he got it. He also was paid $7.8 million over those two seasons. Dickey could rent a house with a longer lease; he could shelve his frequent flyer membership cards; he didn't have to worry about discounts from North American Van Lines; he could expect his kids to stay in the same school for two grades. The little things can mean a lot.

After Dickey signed the contract and embarked for spring training in Florida, he realized his status came with another perk.

"A parking spot," he said. He had one with his number on it in Port St. Lucie, Florida. "It's hard to believe that this is revving my engine the way it is, but what can I tell you? It took the better part of two decades, but I have my own big-league space."

There's nothing like making it big in New York if you are going to make it big at all. And then the genial, bearded Dickey went out and had a very mediocre 2011, going 8–13, albeit with a solid earned run average of 3.28. That was the last thing Dickey needed, as it immediately damaged his credibility. He had been a wonder, a boon to the team in 2010 and once he got his big payday he frustratingly drove off the rails.

The only thing to be done was to practice and study film. The knuckleball, old-boy network was called upon. Usually Dickey relied on Hough first. When the 2012 season began all was cured. Dickey was like a new man, or at least the knuckleball was like a new pitch. He was on fire from opening day on and by early June was standing at 10–1. One of the most pleasing victories was a complete game win over Tampa Bay on June 13, in which Dickey was untouchable, tossing a one-hitter while striking out 12 with no walks. After that game his ERA was down to 2.20. Amazingly, in his next outing, Dickey threw another one-hitter, this one over the Baltimore Orioles. He struck out 13 men that time.

Teammates creamed Dickey with a pie on the field after that second straight one-hitter. Rarely seeing such dominant pitching for long, sportswriters asked Dickey if he felt he was living in a dream. He was way too grounded for that. After all of his struggles Dickey was totally into the scene.

"I don't feel like it's a dream," he said. "But I do feel like it's fun and enjoyable. And I'm glad to be able to celebrate it in this moment."

Would that every day be that way for a pitcher, especially a knuckleballer. Dickey was out there, required to explain to sportswriters why he was so good. It was a refreshing change, instead of having to speak to reporters about why he gave up six home runs in a game.

"Imagine a vertical shoe box," said Dickey, who has more imagination than most pitchers. "Well, if I start at the top of the vertical shoe box, it may drop to the right corner or it may drop to the left corner, or it may go anywhere in-between inside that shoe box. It's still a strike. I just don't know where it's going to be a strike."

Dickey was the talk of the baseball world in 2012. He was not only the best pitcher going, but he released a revealing memoir in which he talked of being sexually abused as a child, dealing with his mother's alcoholism, his fight to keep his baseball career going, his switch to the knuckleball, and how he became a more religious man. While Dickey wrote cleverly about baseball, it was a very serious book that delved into many issues. There were many demons that Dickey conquered and he came across in the book as a nice man whom sports fans should root for as he dealt with and overcame so many struggles.

It is no picnic to become a knuckleball specialist and yet in some ways that was one of the easier challenges for Dickey to take on. Niekro was cheering Dickey from afar as he watched his games on TV in 2012, remembering the time they spent together a few years earlier. In fact, it was Niekro who called Dickey to offer help, not waiting for an emergency summons.

"Well, he's like part of the family, really," Niekro said using that metaphor for the knuckleball-throwers club. "We just talked about the mentality of it [the knuckler]. The philosophy of it. How do you stay with it?"

After the 2012 season, Dickey was basically a celebrity. It was quite a switch from bottom-of-the-roster obscurity. He won 20 games for the first time in his career. He won the Cy Young Award as the best pitcher in the NL. His book gained a lot of attention and sold a lot of copies. That was fitting because Dickey was not only a very avid reader, earlier he aspired to become an English professor. Baseball may have shoved that career option aside for good—or not. Active with charities, Dickey also climbed 19,300-foot Mount Kilimanjaro in Africa, raising $100,000.

Although Dickey had made his big splash with the Mets, the team did not feel it could afford to pay him enough after his spectacular 2012 season. There were some negotiations, but Dickey accepted a trade to the Toronto Blue Jays who rewarded him with a three-year, $37 million contract that carries through the 2015 season when he will be forty. Dickey had not pitched as well as he did at his best for New York, but still holds down a place in the Blue Jays' rotation.

For a guy who was hanging on to a Major League career by his fingernails, it is ironic that Dickey's fingernails saved him. Everyone who follows baseball knows who he is now, too. It didn't hurt that Dickey was also all over the *Knuckleball* documentary. It focused on Dickey and Wakefield as the only two knuckleball pitchers in the big leagues, following along as Wakefield wound down his career leaving Dickey as the sole knuckler at the top level of the sport.

"Tim had carried the torch for a long time," Dickey said.

Now it is Dickey who carries the torch for all knuckleballers, those that preceded him and those still to come —whoever they may be.

23

KNUCKLEBALLERS NEVER DIE

AT THE JULY 31 trading deadline of the 2014 season, the Boston Red Sox blew up their pitching staff. The 2013 World Series champions were in last place in the American League East Division and management decided the season was a hopeless case. One by one in the days approaching the deadline, and then hour by hour on the day of the deadline, the Red Sox shipped out virtually its entire starting rotation.

A byproduct of that was the need for fresh faces. Somebody had to start games. The Sox reached down to their AAA Pawtucket roster for replacements, and one of those identified for promotion was Steven Wright. The arrival of Wright in the majors on August 3 doubled the number of knuckleball pitchers in the big leagues. R. A. Dickey was no longer a lonely beacon in the night.

Wright, twenty-nine at the time, was reviving a career that had been put in jeopardy by injury. Just as so many other knuckleballers' careers are, his had been a torturous journey to the majors in the first place.

Originally from California, Wright pitched for the University of Hawaii before being drafted by the Cleveland Indians. Typical of knuckleballers who struggle he did not make his Major League debut until he was twenty-eight in 2013.

"I'm going to the big leagues!" a gleeful Wright announced on his Twitter account when he got the word Boston was bringing him up from the minors. "I'm so honored and blessed beyond belief. Very exciting time for me and my family. Thank you, Lord."

Wright had his moments during the season, finishing 2–0, but he also suffered an injury, needed surgery, and was sidelined for months until finally being activated in the minors well into the 2014 season. Back to form, Wright was 6–2 with a 2.85 earned run average, splitting his time between AA Portland and mostly AAA Pawtucket before the Red Sox fire sale created job openings.

Those knuckleball guys all seem to have nine lives . . . and they usually need them all. A few days after Wright was called up and seemed poised to get some regular starts for Boston, he was sent right back to Pawtucket. He suited up for Boston on August 3 and was sent back to Rhode Island on August 5. He did not pitch for the Red Sox over the two-day call-up.

One interested observer of these comings and goings was Wilbur Wood, who still lives in the Boston area and follows the Red Sox fortunes. He knew Wright's history, was aware of him as a knuckleballer, and was rooting for him.

"They brought him up and sent him back down," Wood said of the speed of changes in Wright's up-and-down career, agreeing the younger pitcher's stay in Boston was a blur.

For a few days Dickey had company in the knuckleball kingdom, but it was so transitory he may not even have known it.

"He's back to being lonely," Wood said of Dickey's solo knuckler act.

Wright could most likely look forward to another Boston recall before the end of the season, as long as he stayed healthy. Wood hoped it was going to happen.

"Absolutely," he said. "Sure. I'd like to see him have a lot of success."

Although it may be redundant to say so, since after all the knuckleball is the topic, but there were some strange doings surrounding the pitch in 2014. Tim Robbins, the actor who played the somewhat dense young pitcher Ebby Calvin "Nuke" LaLoosh in *Bull Durham* engaged in a joking conversation with sportscaster Dan Patrick in mid-season where he projected that the young flame thrower of years ago would have had Tommy John surgery by now and turned to a knuckleball. This was in the context of talking about the possibility of a sequel to the flick.

"I'm in my fifties," Robbins said. "I could still probably play forty-nine. That's not unheard of for a knuckleball pitcher."

Likely he was thinking of Hoyt Wilhelm and Phil Niekro.

On April 8, near the beginning of the season, one non-knuckleball pitcher decided to cross up a hitter by throwing a knuckler in a game for the first time in his career. C. J. Wilson, hurling for the Los Angeles Angels, had an 8–0 lead when Houston's Jose Guzman came to bat in the seventh inning. Wilson had tried a changeup on Guzman early in the game and gave up a double. He tried a curve on the batter and got the out, but Guzman scorched the pitch for a line drive.

Mentally running through his pitch options, the veteran southpaw opted to try something new. So Wilson tossed a knuckler to the plate. Guzman did not swing at the 80 mph pitch and took it for a ball and then made an out on a come-backer to the mound. The Angels won the game, 9–1.

"I literally threw him a knuckleball because I had no idea what to throw him here," Wilson said. "I've been working on it, but it was the only pitch (knuckler) I've never thrown in a Major League game before. I've thrown it in warm-ups a couple of times, so I was just determined at some point to filter it in there."

This did not mean that Wilson was going to switch to a knuckler full-time, though if he does some day this one at-bat will be recalled. Wilson's easy win did not presage the tough season that followed. His earned run average was sneaking up on 5.00 at one point.

So many position players are viewed with amusement by real knuckleballer throwers as they play catch on the sidelines from flat ground but never test their pitch from the mound. However, early in the season, during a 14–5 loss to the New York Yankees on April 24, Boston manager John Farrell did not want to waste any more throwers and turned to first baseman Mike Carp to hurl an inning.

On a dismal day for regular Red Sox pitchers, Carp discovered that throwing the knuckler under game circumstances is not as easy as it might seem while standing in front of the dugout. He pitched one inning and while he did not give up any hits, Carp surrendered a run because he walked five batters. Any knuckleball pitcher could sympathize with a pitching line like that.

"It was definitely a cool experience," said Carp, who had never before pitched in the majors, "but a bad situation to come into."

He did not sound like someone who was preparing to take up the knuckler to make a living with it, however. Perhaps the game could use the infusion of new knuckleball blood, though, Steven Wright notwithstanding.

Sportswriters have been speculating in their newspapers for between two and three decades about how the knuckleball is an endangered species and one day the baseball world will wake up and nobody will be left throwing it. The Niekros, Hough, Wakefield, Wood, the older guys who are still alive and owe their success to the knuckler do worry about it, but they do not necessarily think it will happen.

"It's not going to be extinct," Bouton said.

The polar bear, maybe, not the knuckleball.

Some of the knuckleball wise men work to prevent that from happening whenever they get requests to work with the next generation of butterfly tossers. Years ago Phil Niekro developed official close ties with Tim Wakefield.

"I worked with him for about three years when he was with the Red Sox and they put me on the payroll," Niekro said. That is about as formal as it gets. "I went to spring training every year and whenever he had a problem they would fly me up there and I would work with him four, five, six days."

Who says doctors don't make house calls anymore? Sometimes patients do, too. Some years ago R. A. Dickey telephoned Niekro, a cold call, asking for advice. Dickey ended up driving from Tennessee to Atlanta, bringing along a catcher, for some personal lessons.

"It got to the point where, when it was over, I felt good about what we had done and I think he felt good," Niekro said.

It is possible that there would be more knuckleball pitchers working their way through the minors to hit the majors if they were more coveted. Organizationally, big-league teams shy away from pitchers who aren't supersonic throwers. No young pitcher wants to be typecast as a slow-ball hurler.

"I've never heard of a knuckleball pitcher being drafted," Dickey said once.

Teams would likely consider that a wasted draft pick. More often clubs discover knuckleball pitchers amongst those already under contract who are falling short at a certain level in the minors. They are mostly scrap-heap guys. If an expert believes they have the potential to adapt the suggestion may be made to players like Wakefield or Dickey that they'd better be thinking more about change than more of the same.

"It's really, really hard to get a chance," Charlie Hough said. "Teams are spending a ton of money on the best arms and the best prospects. A knuckleballer usually only gets one chance. When the call comes you've got to be ready *right now*. When the manager asks who can pitch the next game, you've got to be standing right there and say, 'I can pitch and win.'"

* * *

Wilbur Wood is not as visible on the personal-lesson circuit, but he says it's not because he's not willing to help out a young pitcher, but that he is not often asked. One reason, he believes, is that he still lives in the Boston area where he grew up and Boston knuckleball talk is dominated by Wakefield, even if he is retired.

"It doesn't happen too much," Wood said, "but sometimes college kids call. My number is listed. I get a letter or a call. They want me to come by and give them some help. They think it will make a difference. A lot of college hitters have never seen anything like it. They're just fighting air when they swing. Guys today can throw about 100 mph and the batters will hit it, too. But the knuckleball guys throw 65 mph and get them out and that's because of movement. That's the name of the game."

What the older knuckleball guys are intrigued by is who will be the next big thing; who is going to come along and perpetuate knuckleball tradition. Some years ago when he was getting close to retirement, Phil Niekro expressed for the first time a little bit of worry about the future of the knuckleball.

"When I'm done, only my brother Joe and Charlie Hough will be throwing it," Niekro said in 1986. "I haven't heard of anybody throwing it in the minors. I don't want to see the knuckleball die. It's a unique pitch. If I have to open a knuckleball school, I guess I will."

It never came to that, but Dr. Phil does consult.

He has even been on-call for his nephew Lance Niekro, Joe's son. Lance, now thirty-five, and the baseball coach at Florida Southern University after serving as an assistant coach, spent parts of four seasons in the majors between 2003 and 2007 with the San Francisco Giants. A first baseman, the younger Niekro batted .246, but his career was petering out fast. He decided that if his dad and his uncle had adapted the knuckleball to their use he might be able to do so, too, and took a shot at converting to a pitcher.

"He was injury prone," Phil Niekro said. "He called me and said, 'Uncle Phil, I want to get back in the game and I'm thinking about becoming a knuckleball pitcher. Can you help me?' I said, 'Yeah, of course.' He came to me in Atlanta a few times and I went to Lakeland, Florida, where he lives, quite a few times. We worked together quite a few times and he was coming along pretty good, real good, and I talked to the Braves about maybe signing him. They said, 'We usually don't sign a twenty-six-, twenty-seven-year-old guy, but if you're going to work with him we'll take a shot at him.'" Actually Lance was older than that at the time.

Lance had batted .252 with 12 home runs and 46 RBIs in 113 games for San Francisco in 2005, his best season as a hitter. But in 2007, his final year in the majors, he got into just 11 games and hit .176.

"I always liked to hit," Lance Niekro said. "Even in high school, my dad made the decision if I was going to play at the next level it was going to be as a hitter. It was what I enjoyed better than pitching."

It was not that the younger Niekro was oblivious about the knuckleball growing up. How could he be given what his father and uncle were doing in the majors?

"I threw a knuckleball when I was in Little League, just once in a while," Lance said. "In high school I didn't throw it. When I'm throwing batting practice now and am getting loose, three or four of them are knuckleballs. I never had the ability to throw 95 mph. I firmly do believe you either have the ability to throw the knuckleball or you don't. People bite their fingernails or they don't. Pitchers either know how to throw it or physically they can't adjust. You've got to have the right manager for you who is going to be patient with you. They don't give college scholar-ships to knuckleballers."

Lance did learn many of the properties of the knuckleball from Uncle Phil. Some of the advice consisted of caveats.

"He told me you've got to suck up your ego a little bit because people are going to be yelling at you for throwing 60 mph," Lance said. "And if you throw one up there that's spinning, it's dead."

As much as Lance loved baseball, he fell into a kind of depres-sion about the sport in 2006, when his father passed away sud-denly from an aneurism.

"A large part of baseball went away for me when my dad died," Lance said. "I'd lost a passion for the game when my dad died."

Lance Niekro was jettisoned by the Giants in 2007, signed with Houston, one of his father's old teams, and was released.

"My thinking was, *I'm done*."

He returned to his home in Lakeland and went to work for a telecommunications company for six months, but missed base-ball after all.

"I had never worked behind a desk before," Lance said. He made that call to his uncle and asked for knuckleball help. He thought he would invest a year into developing the pitch and signed with Atlanta. "I jumped at it and worked at it."

Lance was held over by the Braves for extended spring training and was showing progress with the knuckler. But he was ambiv-alent about things. He was playing with eighteen-year-olds as a thirty-year-old, assigned to Class A. His wife was pregnant. His mind was on the future and getting into coaching and he was working on finishing a college degree through the University of

Phoenix, which has a very diverse curriculum, but does not offer courses in knuckleball instruction.

"I got better," Lance said of himself and the knuckler. "I had a little bit of success. But I was thinking, *What am I doing?* I thanked them [the Braves] for the opportunity and stopped. I know Phil wanted me to keep going."

He is right about that. At least Phil Niekro thought he could have kept going and maybe done some damage with the knuckler.

"He was kept at extended spring training in Florida and I thought that was good for him because he lived in Lakeland and could go home every day and eat in his own house," Phil said. "I think he had the only complete game down there. At first he didn't like the words 'extended spring training.' He said, 'What the hell's down there?' I said, 'The mound is 60 feet, 6 inches there, just as it is anyplace else. They've got prospects there. They're going to watch you.' When that was over he called me and said, 'Uncle Phil, I'm done. I'm going to give it up. I'm not going to do it.' They were going to move him to a nice level, but I never told him that. He could have had something going. I don't know how far he could have gone, but he certainly might have."

Lance Niekro became an assistant coach the NCAA Division II-power Florida Southern and was then promoted when the head coach left. He laughed when he said he did not have any knuckleball pitchers on his team, although he almost did.

"There was one kid," Lance said. "The kid couldn't quite commit to 100 percent throwing the knuckleball. The tough part about doing it in college is that if it takes you two years to perfect it, then you only have two years left."

If there is such a thing as knuckleball royalty, it would have to be people whose last name is Niekro and love polka. Lance

Niekro bowed out of the knuckleball rat race before determining if he could make the switch from big-league hitter to big-league pitcher. Others have gone from pitcher to position player, such as Smoky Joe Wood and Rick Ankiel. Would the younger Niekro been able to master the knuckler well enough to make the grade through a different door?

"Who knows?" he said. "I don't know if you can master it. I don't think they [the best knuckleballers] really master it. The good ones can't throw it over the plate eight out of ten times. But you can be successful with it."

Meanwhile, more recently Dr. Phil has been on-call for the Baltimore Orioles. The Orioles identified a couple of minor-league pitchers they thought might be able to become big-league knuckleballers with tutoring. For the last couple of seasons Niekro has worked on and off with Eddie Gamboa and Zach Clark. He also had a third player giving it a try named Stan Zackowitz.

Initially, an intermediary telephoned Niekro and asked him to look at a few knuckleball pitchers at the Braves' AAA facility near where he lives. The first player didn't impress him. Zackowitz threw a couple of pitches and Niekro said, "Whoa, that's a pretty good knuckleball." Zackowitz signed a low-level minor-league contract with Baltimore. But then along came some Baltimore minor-league coaches who told Niekro about Gamboa and Clark.

Clark and Gamboa were both fairly accomplished pitchers, but Gamboa's knuckler surprised Niekro. He thought it was very good.

"He probably wasn't going to get to the big leagues with the stuff he had, but he was a good athlete, a good pitcher," Niekro said. "Those guys, from my eyes, had a great knuckleball."

Niekro went to bat for Gamboa with Baltimore's vice president of baseball operations, Dan Duquette, and some of the team's farm officials. Gamboa had been pigeon-holed as someone with AA stuff who might make it to AAA, but wasn't going to be a Major League player. Niekro told them they were wrong and that Gamboa had the makings of a big-time knuckleballer.

Clark, now thirty-one, made it to the Orioles before the end of the 2013 season and pitched in one game for 1 2/3 innings with no decision. He began studying the knuckleball in earnest after being sent down and during the summer of 2014 was pitching for the Camden Riversharks of the Independent Atlantic League.

Gamboa was added to the Orioles' 40-man roster late in 2013. In June of 2014, while playing for AAA Norfolk, Gamboa was slapped with a 50-game suspension for violating baseball's substance abuse rules, muddying his future prospects. Gamboa was 4–6 with a 4.06 earned run average. Niekro believes that Gamboa will make the majors.

There is no question, though, that even if Clark or Gamboa do not make it to the big leagues as regulars, Phil Niekro has done his part to ensure continuity and the future of the knuckleball. There is no Knuckleball College, but private lessons are still available if the 318-game winner thinks you can be successful and he can play a part in making you into a success. The number of knuckleball pitchers—and especially achievers—remains tiny compared to the population of Major League baseball, but Niekro continues to help propagate the species.

Yet Niekro will admit, even after three-quarters of a century on earth and close to sixty-five years of experience with a knuckleball, he still can't figure out what makes it tick.

"It has something to do with physics," he said. "I remember once when I was in Florida some people from Columbia University came down and did a documentary on the knuckleball. They brought a camera that takes pictures at about 2,000 frames a second, or something like that. They used balls with seams and balls without seams. They tested wind velocity. They did every damn thing. When they were all done I read their report and I said, 'I don't understand what the hell you're talking about.'"

Niekro knows some things intuitively based on his long experience with the knuckler that scientists will probably never get. Over the years he has said the same thing to his brother Joe, to Tim Wakefield, to R. A. Dickey, and to Eddie Gamboa: If they throw the knuckleball at the same speed every time, not every one of them is going to be a good knuckler. They are going to make mistakes.

"If a batter knows the knuckler is coming, which he does almost every pitch, and I can't control it on the outsider corner, or high, like most pitchers do, I have to create some kind of thing to throw off his timing because hitting is timing. So I can throw him the same pitch at two or three different release points and two or three different speeds. Then it has become three or four or five different pitches for me."

Amazingly, remarkably, and Niekro insists it is true, he has probably thrown a knuckleball as slow as 20 mph. When informed that sounds impossible, he said, "Yes I can."

Twenty mph? Apparently a good knuckleball pitcher can really do any trick with the ball on any given day. Phil Niekro has won more games than any knuckleball pitcher in history. He pitched in the majors until he was forty-eight years old and is still throwing batting practice for a AAA baseball team at seventy-five.

A man who has been clever in print in a book and was quoted by sportswriters, a man who likes to laugh and dance the polka, Niekro did not have the hint of a smile on his face when he delivered a comment that can stand as the credo for the baseball species he represents.

"There are no age limits on knuckleball pitchers."

That is the knuckleball gospel according to Phil Niekro.

SOURCES

<u>Introduction</u>
Personal Interview, Phil Niekro, April, 2014.

<u>Chapter One</u>
Personal Interview, Phil Niekro, April, 2014.
The Sporting News, October 30, 1919, December 4, 1965.

Mark Howe: Gordie Howe's Son, A Hall of Fame Life in the Shadow of Mr. Hockey, Mark Howe and Jay Greenberg (Chicago: Triumph Books, 2012).

"Who Invented the Knuckleball?" Scott Allen, http://mental-floss.com, June 23, 2012.

Society For American Baseball Research, Eric Enders.

National Baseball Hall of Fame Research Library, undated newspaper clippings.

www.Baseball-Reference.com

Chapter Two
The Funniest Baseball Book Ever, Peter Handrings (Kansas City: Andrews McMeel Publishing LLC, 2010).

The Knucklebook, Dave Clark (Chicago: Ivan R. Dee, 2006).

"Is This the Last Dance for the Knuckleball?" *Cleveland Plain Dealer*, Bill Lubinger, July 17, 2012.

"The Knuckleball," *Newsday*, Steve Jacobson, May 6, 1984.

"The Last of the Knuckleball Brotherhood," *Inside Sports Magazine*, Charley Rosen, October 1984.

www.Baseball-Reference.com

Chapter Three
It's Anybody's Ballgame, Joe Garagiola (New York: Jove Books, 1989).

Remembrance of Swings Past, Ron Luciano and David Fisher (New York: Bantam Books, 1988).

"Batters Knuckled Under to Haines and Schultz," Neal Russo, *St. Louis Post-Dispatch*, September 6, 1964.

"Control Winning Recipe for Lyons, A.L. Pitching Star," Sid Mercer, *New York Journal-American*, (no date) 1939 (Baseball Hall of Fame library archives).

"Graham's Corner," Frank Graham, *New York Journal-American*, February (date missing), 1954. (Baseball Hall of Fame Library archives).

"On the Line: Bob Considine" (syndicated column), July 26, 1937.

"Pop Haines: Hall Induction Greatest of All My Thrills," Special to the *Dayton Daily News*, July 28, 1970.

"Pop: No Time for Slow Hurlers," Neal Russo, *St. Louis Post-Dispatch*, January 26, 1969.

"Rommel Story In *The Sporting News* Started Lyons Working On Knuckler," Ed Burns, *The Sporting News*, May 7, 1947.

"Ted Lyons Dead at 85," (No byline), *The Sporting News*, August 4, 1986.

"That Likable Lyons," Bill Bryson, *Baseball Magazine*, October 1939.

"Jesse Haines Had Another Great Year," *National League Service Bureau*, January 15, 1928.

www.Baseball-Reference.com

Chapter Four
The Ferrell Brothers Of Baseball, Dick Thompson (Jeffersonville, North Carolina: McFarland & Company, Inc. Publishers, 2005).

"Dodger Knuckleball Hurler Spurred by Stengel's Confidence," Bill McCullough, *Florida Times-Union*, March 28, 1936.

"From Woeful Wolff to Jolly Roger," J. G. Taylor Spink, *The Sporting News*, August 16, 1945.

"Knuckling Down: Brownies' Jinx of Boston," Frederick G. Lieb, Syndicated Column, September 1942.

"Leonard, Dodger Cast-Off, Becomes an Ace on Pitch that Plays Deuce with Catchers," Denman Thompson, *Washington Star*, May 26, 1938.

"Nats' Bosses Like Leonard; Hail 'Knuckle-Baller' As Star," Shirley Povich, *Washington Post*, February 28, 1938.

"Sox May Have Seen Last of Niggeling's Nothin' Ball as He Awaits Service Call, George Carens, *Boston Traveler*, July 25, 1942.

"The Last of the Knuckleball Brotherhood," Charley Rosen, *Inside Sports Magazine*, October 1984.

"This Morning," Shirley Povich, *Washington Post*, December 15, 1943.

"Too Old To Pitch? Don't Make Me Laugh!" Dutch Leonard and Stanley Frank, *Saturday Evening Post*, July 4, 1953.

"Wolff Is Tops as Work Horse," The Old Scout (aka), Herb Goren, *New York Sun*, May 1943.

"Yankees Bow 2–1, Then Win 2nd, 7–0," Jack Smith, *New York Daily News*, June 29, 1939.

(No headline). Press release American League Service Bureau, Harry P. Edwards, spring training 1942.

(No headline). Press release National League Service Bureau, Chicago Cubs, March 25, 1952

www.Baseball-Reference.com

Chapter Five
Stengel: His Life And Times, Robert W. Creamer (New York: Fireside Books, 1984).

"Bearden Hailed by Boudreau as Key Man in Cleveland's Baseball Triumph," James P. Dawson, *New York Times*, October 12, 1948.

"'Bearden's Series All the Way,' Says Boudreau as Indians Whoop It Up," Charles Heaton, *Cleveland Plain-Dealer*, October 12, 1948.

"Gene Strikes Out Science," Hal Lebovitz, *Cleveland News*, October 5, 1948.

"Indians Hero Bearden Dies," Bob Dolgan, *Cleveland Plain-Dealer*, March 20, 2004.

"Looping the Loops," J.G. Taylor Spink, *The Sporting News*, June 6, 1948.

"'Man of Guts,' Says Doc," Wallace R. Katz, *Cleveland News*, October 9, 1948.

"'No Return Trip Necessary,' Says Bearden After Taming Second Boston Club," James E. Doyle, *Cleveland Plain-Dealer*, October 9, 1948.

"Practice Makes Perfect," Herman Goldstein, *Cleveland News*, June 10, 1948.

"The Bearden Story—From Several Angles," Ed McAuley, *Cleveland News*, August 28, 1949.

"Wildness Stumps Bearden," Herman Goldstein, *Cleveland News*, August 1, 1949.

"Yanks' Manager Hails Tribe Star as 'Self-Starter,'" Hal Lebovitz, *Cleveland News*, January (day missing), 1949.

www.Baseball-Reference.com

Chapter Six
Personal interview, Eddie Fisher, July 2014.

"Knuckleball, Nerves of Steel, Put Wilhelm in Cooperstown," Stan Hochman, *Philadelphia Daily News*, January (day missing), 1985.

"The Last of the Knuckleball Brotherhood," *Inside Sports Magazine*, Charley Rosen, October 1984.

"Wilhelm Knuckler No-Hits Yanks, 1–0," Joe Trimble, *New York Daily News*, September 21, 1958.

"Wilhelm's Knuckler Best Ever," John Steadman, *Baltimore News-American*, 1961 (date missing), Baseball Hall of Fame Library Archives.

www.Baseball-Reference.com

Chapter Seven
"Bob Purkey Credits Success as Pitcher to Control, Study," Les Biederman, *Pittsburgh Press*, February 10, 1963.

"Cincinnati Ace Bob Purkey to Compile 23–5 Record, Best Among NL Moundsmen," Earl Lawson, *The Sporting News*, October 20, 1962.

"Don't Write Me Off, Bob Purkey Says," Earl Lawson, *Cincinnati Post & Times-Star*, January 1, 1964.

"Hobo Barney Tatters Yankees," Sandy Grady, *Philadelphia Bulletin*, October 8, 1964.

"Howsam Picks Purkey to Fill Out Card Hand," Neal Russo, *The Sporting News*, December 26, 1964.

"It's 42 Straight Innings Since Giants Have Scored Off Bob Purkey," Curley Grieve, *San Francisco Examiner*, July 30, 1958.

"Knuckling Barney Schultz Plays Big Role in Cardinal Comeback," (no byline) *Houston Post*, August 20, 1964.

"Mound Job Caps 20 Years' Effort," (no byline), *New York Times*, October 8, 1964.

"Pitching Student Bob Purkey Successfully 'Lectures' Giants, Earl Lawson, *Cincinnati Times-Star*, June 10, 1958.

"Purkey and Schultz, Flutterball Experts, Fortify Card Mound, Jack Herman, *The Sporting News*, April 3, 1965.

"Purkey Makes a Little Talent Go a Long Way in Sprinting to Fastest Start in Big Leagues," Cleon Walfoort, *Milwaukee Journal*, June 1, 1962.

"Purkey's at Best only on Mound," Earl Lawson, *Cincinnati Times-Star*, April 5, 1958.

"Purkey's Pinpoint Slants Spark Cincy," Earl Lawson, *The Sporting News*, June 16, 1962.

"Schultz Used Knuckleball to Earn Stint in Majors," Rich Marazzi, *Sports Collectors Digest*, April 23, 1999.

"Sport Scene," Bob Firestone, *Cincinnati Times-Star*, December 31, 1957.

"Story of Bald Card Lifesaver," Barney Kremenko, *The Sporting News*, September 30, 1964.

"Winning '61 Flat, 20 Games Purkey's Big Baseball Thrills," Les Biederman, *Pittsburgh Press*, September 20, 1962.

"Worried Purkey Contends Loss of Fastball Basis of Problem,"
Si Burick, *Dayton Daily News*, June 17, 1963.

www.Baseball-Reference.com

Chapter Eight
"At 48, Wilhelm Talks Like a Rookie," Paul Cox, *The Sporting News*, February 12, 1972.

"Ban on King-Sized Mitt Fails to Upset Hoyt," Paul Cox, *The Sporting News*, January 18, 1964.

"Best of Murray: Wilhelm's Knuckler Gives Batters Butterflies,"
Jim Murray, Los Angeles Times, October 7, 1967.

"Control of Knuckleball Made Wilhelm King of Relievers,"
Bill Gleason, *The Sporting News*, January 21, 1985.

"Down on the Farm," Norman Arey, *Atlanta Journal*, August 7, 1973.

"Hoyt Wilhelm's Philosophy: Do As I Say, Not As I Did," Bob Snyder, *Syracuse Herald-Journal*, January 30, 1977.

"Miracle of Mound – At 41, Hoyt's Deep Mystery to Batters,"
Edgar Munzel, *Chicago Tribune*, February 13, 1965.

"New Mitt Designed to Handle Knuckler," Edgar Munzel, *The Sporting News*, April 10, 1965.

"Now Hoyt Aims for 1,000 Games," Edgar Munzel, *Chicago Tribune*, August 10, 1968.

"Old Butterflies Never Die," Nick Proffitt, *Newsweek/Binghamton Press*, May 14, 1969.

"Old Man Wilhelm a Hero to Every Fan Pushing 50," Wayne Minshew, *The Sporting News*, May 16, 1970.

"Wilhelm Fires Duster at Father Time," Edgar Munzel, *The Sporting News*, March 18, 1967.

"Wilhelm First Reliever Elected to Hall of Fame," (no byline), *Associated Press*, August 25, 2002.

"Hoyt Wilhelm," Mark Liptak, *Chicago White Sox Interactive*, May, 2002.

Chapter Nine
Personal Interview, Bruce Benedict, April 2014.

Personal Interview, J. C. Martin, May 2014.

Knuckle Balls, Phil Niekro and Tom Bird (New York: Freundlich Books, 1986).

The Funniest Baseball Book Ever, Peter Handrinos (Kansas City: Andrews McMeel Publishing LLC, 2010).

"Gus Triandos, Beloved Ex-Orioles Catcher, Dies at 82," Mike Klingaman, *Baltimore Sun*, March 29, 2013.

"Pitch Is Out Of Control," Bob Ryan, *Boston Globe*, May 3, 2006.

Personal Interview, Bruce Benedict, April 2014.

Knuckleball, documentary film, 2013.

www.Baseball-Reference.com

Chapter Ten
Personal Interview Eddie Fisher, July 2014.

"Eddie Fisher Show-Stopper of ChiSox," Edgar Munzel, *The Sporting News*, July 10, 1965.

"Eddie Fisher's Knuckler Could Make Difference," Curley Grieve, *San Francisco Examiner*, June 19, 1959.

"Fireman Fisher Has Ball as Starter," Edgar Munzel, *The Sporting News*, May 5, 1973.

"Fisher Greets Sudden Success With Blushes," Curley Grieve, *San Francisco Examiner*, June 23, 1959.

"Lary Started Soaring on Butterfly Ball," Hal Middlesworth, *The Sporting News*, November 21, 1956.

"Life Begins at 30 for Fisher, White Sox Flutterball Expert," Brent Musburger, *Chicago American*, "May 15, 1965.

"'More Work,' Pleads Fisher, Angels' Fireman," John Wiebush, *The Sporting News*, May 16, 1970.

"Skinny Brown Was No Lightweight on Mound," John Steadman, *Baltimore Sun*, June 28, 1991.

www.Baseball-Reference.com

Chapter Eleven
Personal interview, Wilbur Wood, April 2014.

"Wilbur Apt Pupil of Old Prof Wilhelm," Edgar Munzel, *The Sporting News*, May 6, 1967.

"Wood, Ace ChiSox Reliever, Is Star Student of Knuckler," Jerome Holtzman, *Chicago Sun-Times*, July (date missing), 1968, Baseball Hall of Fame Library archives.

"Wood Threatening Rescuers' Record," Edgar Munzel, *The Sporting News*, September 21, 1968.

www.Baseball-Reference.com

Chapter Twelve
Personal interview, Phil Niekro, April 2014.

"Casanova Cool, Til the End," Frank Hyland, *Atlanta Journal*, August 6, 1973.

"Dad's Pitch," Phil Niekro, *Guideposts*, April 1998.

Knuckle Balls, Phil Niekro and Tom Bird (New York: Fruendlich Books, 1986).

"Niekro Knuckles Down—To Poetry," Ron Hudspeth, *Atlanta Journal*, September 21, 1971.

"Philip Niekro: The Coal Mining Father Behind Baseball's Famous Knuckleballers," Al Skinner, *Coal People Magazine*, (no date), 1980.

"Phil Niekro No-Hits S.D.," (no byline), *San Francisco Chronicle*, August 6, 1973.

"Quiet Please," Frank Hyland, *Atlanta Journal*, August 6, 1973.

www.Baseball-Reference.com

Chapter Thirteen
Personal Interview, Phil Niekro, April 2014.

The Niekro Files, Phil Niekro, Joe Niekro and Ken Picking (Chicago: Contemporary Books, 1988).

"Give Dad the Credit for Niekro Knucklers," (no byline), *Associated Press*, June 18, 1979.

"Joe Niekro, a Master of the Knuckleball, Is Dead at 61," Richard Goldstein, *New York Times*, October 29, 2006.

"Knuckling Down: Niekro at Home with 'New Pitch,'" Chuck Myers, *Houston Post*, September 5, 1976.

"Life Begins at 34 for Jolly Joe, the Astro Notable," Harry Shattuck, *The Sporting News*, July 28, 1979.

"Niekro Is Suspended for 10 Days," Murray Chass, *New York Times*, August 6, 1987.

"Niekros Keep Love of Baseball in Family," Chuck Greenwood, *Sports Collectors Digest*, August 30, 1996.

"'Wrong Niekro': Sorry, Astros!" (no byline), *Associated Press*, September 27, 1979.

Chapter Fourteen
Personal Interview, Wilbur Wood, April 2014.

"Flashes," (no byline), *The Sporting News*, August 28, 1971.

"Iron-Man Wood Has Goal—Wants to Pitch a Twin-Bill," Jerome Holtzman, August 7, 1971.

"Knuckleball Ace," Ed Rumill, *Christian Science Monitor*, September 1, 1971.

"Knuckling Down to a 20-Game Season," Arthur Daley, *New York Times*, March 28, 1972.

"Long-Ball Bats Build Contenders," Ed Rumill, *Christian Science Monitor*, May 20, 1972.

"Name's Wood, but His Arm Is Made of Rubber," Dick Young, *New York Daily News*, July 30, 1971.

"Roundup: Wood Loses," (no byline), unidentified newspaper, Baseball Hall of Fame Library archives, August 2, 1971.

"White Sox Iron Man Wood Denies 'Overwork' Charge," Edgar Munzel, August 5, 1972.

"Wilbur Wood," Peter Gammons, *Boston Globe*, June 17, 1973

"Wilbur Wood & the Art of the Knuckleball," Al Hirshberg, *Sport Magazine*, August 1972.

"Workhorse Wood—King of White Sox Hurlers," Jerome Holtzman, *The Sporting News*, October 2, 1971.

(No headline), American League Press Release, March, 1974

Chapter Fifteen
Personal Interview, Charlie Hough, May 2014.

"'Everyman' Gives Hough Every Chance," Blackie Sherrod, *Dallas Morning News*, May 19, 1989.

"Hough And His Knuckler Not Quite Down for the Count," David Casstevens, *Dallas Morning News*, March 23, 1990.

"Hough, as in Rough, All Ready for Tough Relief Chores Again," Gordon Verrell, *The Sporting News*, April 14, 1979.

"Hough Still Dreams of Starting Role as Dodger," Gordon Verrell, *The Sporting News*, January 24, 1976.

"Hough Still Tough on Batters," Steve Serby, *New York Post*, April 16, 1990.

"Hough's First Pitches, Luck Float Off in His First All-Star Appearance," Kent Baker, *Baltimore Sun*, August 16, 1986.

"Hough's Fluff Baffles Batters," Phil Elderkin, *Christian Science Monitor*, July 5, 1977.

"Hough's Knuckler Almost Hit Proof," Gordon Verrell, *The Sporting News*, May 21, 1977.

"Hough's Knuckler: Sincerest Form of Fluttery," Mike Downey, *The Sporting News* June 30, 1986.

"Hough's Magic Show Continues to Wow 'Em," (*Wire services*), *New York Daily News*, July 6, 1986.

"Knuckler Hough Could Mean Relief for Dodgers," (No byline), *Associated Press*, July 7, 1973.

"Knuckler Puffs Hough Image as Super," Gordon Verrell, *The Sporting News*, June 19, 1976.

"LA's Hough Knuckling In For Long Haul," (No byline), *United Press International*, June 19, 1977

www.Baseball-Reference.com

Chapter Sixteen
Knuckle Balls, Phil Niekro and Tom Bird (New York: Fruendlich Books, 1986).

"20th Victory Left Niekro with a Sweet-Sour Taste," Ken Picking, *The Sporting News*, October 13, 1979.

"Back to Basics," Paul Hoynes, *Cleveland Plain Dealer*, October 3, 1986.

"Braves, Turner Roll Out Carpet as Niekro's Number Is Retired," Rich Chere, *Newark Star-Ledger*, August 7, 1984.

"Dad's Pitch," Phil Niekro, "Guideposts," April 1998.

"Niekro: A Genuine Winner in a City Noted for Losers," Wayne Minshew, *The Sporting News*, October 25, 1976.

"Niekro Is Cooperstown Bound," (no byline), *Associated Press*, January 7, 1997.

"Niekro Surpasses 3,000 in Strikeouts," Craig Wolff, *New York Times*, July 6, 1984.

"Niekro to Join His Pal Havlicek as a Hall of Famer," Hal Bock, *Associated Press*, July 1997.

"Niekro Wins No. 300," Bud Shaw, *Atlanta Constitution*, October 7, 1985.

"Niekro's Story a Gripping Tale," Joel Sherman, *New York Post*, January 8, 1997.

"Phil 'Knucksie' Niekro," Kevin Huard, *Sports Collectors Digest*, February 22, 1991.

"Phil Niekro Doesn't Knuckle Under," Joe Durso, *New York Times*, May 23, 1984.

"Yankees Done Knucksie Wrong," Dick Young, *New York Post*, March 31, 1986.

www.Baseball-Reference.com

Chapter Seventeen

Personal interview, Jim Bouton, May 2014.

Ball Four, Jim Bouton (New York: Dell Books, 1970).

"Bouton Beanie Flies only on Good Pitch," Til Ferdenzi, *The Sporting News*, December 12, 1964.

"Bulldog Bouton Earns Top-Dog Rating," Til Ferdenzi, *The Sporting News*, July 20, 1963.

"Comedy Key for Bouton," Gene Duffey, *Gannett News Service,* May 25, 1976.

"From the Head of a Knuckler," Wayne Coffey, *New York Daily News*, May 21, 1995.

www.Baseball-Reference.com

Chapter Eighteen
Personal Interview, Tom Candiotti, May 2014.

"A Cameo for Candiotti," Seth Livingstone, *USA Today Baseball Weekly*, May 2, 2001.

"Beauty of His Pitch Inversely Tied to Speed," Mike Downey, *Los Angeles Times*, April 23, 1992.

"Candiotti Is Now Scioscia's Problem to Deal with," Bud Shaw, *Cleveland Plain-Dealer*, March 29, 1992.

"Candiotti's Pitchman: Niekro," David Bush, *San Francisco Chronicle*, (no date), 1987, Baseball Hall of Fame Library archives.

"Cleveland's Candiotti, Niekro Are Part of Dying Breed in Pitching," (no byline), *United Press International*, June 10, 1986.

"Hough Helped Straighten Out Candiotti," (no byline), *Associated Press*, August 5, 1987.

"Knuckling Down," Sheldon Ocker, *Akron Beacon-Journal*, May 5, 1986.

"Still Lobbing Balls for Strikes," Dennis Manoloff, *Cleveland Plain-Dealer*, July 7, 2007.

"Yanks Rally; Candiotti Loses Gem," (no byline), *Utica Observer-Dispatch*, August 4, 1990.

www.Baseball-Reference.com

Chapter Nineteen
Personal Interview, Steve Sparks, May 2014.

"A Knack for Knucklers," Frederick C. Klein, *Wall Street Journal*, March 19, 1999.

"Angels Get Sparks from Knuckleballer," Bill Koeing, *USA Today Baseball Weekly*, September 16–22, 1998.

"Astros Hold Off Blue Jays," (no byline), *Associated Press*, April 10, 2014.

"Ex-Brewer Sparks Knows Phone Book Incident Part of His Legacy," Tom Haudicourt, *Milwaukee Journal-Sentinel*, June 17, 2013.

www.Baseball-Reference.com

Chapter Twenty
Personal Interview, Bruce Benedict, April 2014.

Personal Interview, Daniel Boone, April 2014.

Personal Interview, J. C. Martin, May 2014.

"Boone No-Hits Syracuse," Patti Singer, *Rochester Democrat and Chronicle*, July 24, 1990.

"C. C. Alum Nearly Gave Up on Dream; Now He Works at Dodger Stadium," Tony Paul, *Detroit News*, April 27, 2010.

"Daniel Boone Resurrected With Orioles," (no byline), *Associated Press*, September 26, 1990.

"Danny Boone: Blazing His Way on the Comeback Trail," David Beigie, *Sports Collectors Digest*, July 13, 1990.

"How Frank Lary Learned to Pitch," Furman Bisher, *Sport Magazine*, August 1961.

"How Those Catchers Hate Wilhelm," Jim Murray, *Los Angeles Times*, September 24, 1971.

"Knuckleball" The Pitch that Neutralizes the Aging Process," Richard Hoffer, *Baseball Digest*, December 1985.

"Special Delivery," Ross Newhan and Steve Springer, *Los Angeles Times*, August 26, 1997.

"Rays' Pitcher Springs Leak Against Indians," Dave Cunningham, *Orlando Sentinel*, May 2, 1998.

"So Why Doesn't Everybody Throw the Knuckler?" Gordon Cobbledick, *Baseball Digest*, August 1959.

"The Knuckleball," Steve Jacobson, *Newsday*, May 6, 1984.

"Tiny Boone Padre Bullpen Giant," Phil Collier, *The Sporting News*, June 13, 1981.

Knuckleball, documentary film, 2013.

www.Baseball-Reference.com

Chapter Twenty-One
Personal Interview, Tim Wakefield, August 2008.

"Boston Floats to Top on Wakefield's Arm," Claire Smith, *New York Times*, August 13, 1995.

"For the Knuckleballer, the Latest Twist Is Cruelest," Bob Ryan, *Boston Globe*, October 24, 2007.

"For Wakefield, Boone's Blast a Thing of the Past," Shaun Powell, *Newsday*, February 23, 2004.

"Keeping His Grip," Gordon Edes, *Boston Globe*, January 4, 2004.

Knuckler: My Life with Baseball's Most Confounding Pitch, Tim Wakefield and Tony Massarotti (Boston: Houghton Mifflin Harcourt, 2011).

"On Good End of a Knuckle Sandwich," Ross Newhan, *Los Angeles Times*, August 23, 1995.

"Sox Knuckle Under," Steve Buckley, *Boston Herald*, May 30, 1995.

"Wakefield Throwing Hitters a Curve this Year," Seth Livingstone, *USA Today Baseball Weekly*, July 12–17, 2001.

"Wakefield's Success at the Tip of His Knuckles," Karen Guregian, *Boston Herald*, June 4, 1995.

Knuckleball, documentary film, 2013.

www.Baseball-Reference.com

Chapter Twenty-Two
"Dickey Finds Old Mentor for New Pitch," Kevin Sherrington, *Dallas Morning News*, September 14, 2005.

"Dickey Throws Second Straight One-Hitter, (no byline), *The Record* (New Jersey), June 19, 2012.

"Freak of Nature Meets Knuckler," Jim Souhan, *Minneapolis Star-Tribune*, June 27, 2009.

"New Mariner R. A. Dickey Committed to Knuckleball," Steve Kelley, *Seattle Times*, February 8, 2008.

"Otherworldly Pitch Meets Its Jedi Master," Tyler Kepner, *New York Times*, June 16, 2012.

Wherever I Wind Up, R. A. Dickey and Wayne Coffey (New York: The Penguin Group/Blue Rider Press, 2012).

"Wild, Wild Inning," (no byline), *USA Today*, August 18, 2008.

www.Baseball-Reference.com

Chapter Twenty-Three
Personal Interview, Jim Bouton, May 2014.

Personal Interview, Charlie Hough, May 2014.

Personal Interview, Wilbur Wood, April 2014 and August 2014.

Personal Interview, Lance Niekro, April 2014.

Personal Interview, Phil Niekro, April 2014.

"Family Member Niekro Aids Dickey's Reversal," Terence Moore, MLB.com, June 15, 2012.

"C. J. Wilson Wasn't Sure Which Pitch to Throw this Hitter, so He Opted for a Knuckleball," Gemma Kaneko, MLB.com, April 8, 2014.

"Hough's Knuckler: Sincerest Form of Flattery," Mike Downey, *Los Angeles Times*, June 30, 1986.

"Red Sox Bring Up Steven Wright to Replace Joel Hanrahan," Evan Drellich, MassLive.com, April 16, 2013.

"Yankees Bounce Back to Batter Red Sox in Messy Game," (no byline), Associated Press/ESPN.com, April 24, 2014.